BINGA

BINGA

THE RISE AND FALL OF CHICAGO'S FIRST BLACK BANKER

DON HAYNER

NORTHWESTERN UNIVERSITY PRESS
EVANSTON, ILLINOIS

Northwestern University Press
www.nupress.northwestern.edu

Printed in the United States of America

10 9 8 7 6 5 4 3 2 1

Library of Congress Cataloging-in-Publication Data

Names: Hayner, Don, author.
Title: Binga : the rise and fall of Chicago's first Black banker / Don Hayner.
Other titles: Second to none: Chicago stories.
Description: Evanston, Illinois : Northwestern University Press, 2019. | Series: Second
    to none: Chicago stories | Includes bibliographical references and index.
Identifiers: LCCN 2019022944 | ISBN 9780810140905 (trade paperback) | ISBN
    9780810140912 (ebook)
Subjects: LCSH: Binga, Jesse, 1865–1950. | Binga State Bank—
    History. | Bankers—Illinois—Chicago—Biography. | African American bankers—
    Illinois—Chicago—Biography. | African American banks—
    Illinois—Chicago—History—20th century. | Banks and banking—
    Illinois—Chicago—History—20th century. | Chicago (Ill.)—Race relations—
    History—20th century.
Classification: LCC HG2463.B53 H39 2019 | DDC 332.1092—dc23
LC record available at https://lccn.loc.gov/2019022944

To Dawn, for everything.

CONTENTS

1

"Do You Know Who That Is?"

TIMUEL D. BLACK JR., A REVERED CHICAGO HISTORIAN AND CIVIL RIGHTS activist, remembered seeing Jesse Binga twice.[1] The first time was in the mid-1920s, when Timuel was a little boy and his father brought him to a narrow building on Chicago's South Side in the heart of the city's crowded neighborhood known as the Black Belt. This building was where many African American fathers and mothers often brought their children; it was part of the ritual.

The gray stone building, near the corner of Thirty-Fifth and State Streets, had tall Ionic columns, large windows, and two heavy front doors of glass and wood. Little Timuel waited while his father pulled a door open, and together they walked inside.

This was a bank building, and although the city had plenty of banks, this one was unique: it was owned by an African American man, and it was the first black-owned bank in Chicago. Thousands of black men and women brought their children here, not just to see the bank but also to point out the man who owned it and to take in the lessons of his ownership.[2]

As Timuel and his father walked past the tall check writing desks with cut glass inkwells and polished brass penholders, they heard only the soft, clicking echoes of their shoe heels on the marble floor. It was the sound of wealth, a sound normally reserved for the lobbies of those massive, well-appointed banks downtown, but this was the Black Belt.

Timuel's father pulled his son to a stop when he spotted a gray-haired man in his late fifties greeting customers in front of the teller cages. The man was brown-skinned and handsome, dressed in a three-piece suit as neat as a ledger sheet. He wore a starched white shirt with a high collar and a tie pulled in a tight knot and fixed in place by a gold stickpin. His sturdy straight physique made him appear taller than his already above-average height and emphasized an already obvious point: he was the man in charge.

Timuel's dad, who had moved his family to Chicago from Alabama, where he had once witnessed a lynching in Birmingham, pointed to the man in the suit and explained that this man owned the bank and was living proof that a black man could accomplish anything.

"That," his father said, "is Jesse Binga."

Binga.

Every man, woman, and child in Chicago's Black Belt knew that name. Jesse Binga was the moneyman of the Black Belt, the king of America's black Wall Street. In the 1920s, just hearing the strange and poetic sound of his name conjured up an image as constant and permanent as the chiseled letters on the front of the bank. The Binga Bank had an unforgettable ring to it, like a cash register.

Black people—and some whites too—came from all over the city to tuck away their earnings in the safety of Binga's house of money. Their children were pulled along, with pennies rattling inside tiny tin Binga Banks. If a black man needed a loan to buy a house, he could go see Mr. Binga. If he needed a room, an apartment, a house, or some walking-around money, Mr. Binga was the man for that too.

Binga was a symbol of success in the Black Belt, someone who embodied the possibility of the American Dream. His name, or just his initial *B*, was an emblem of wealth, as much as the painted dollar signs that formed a big circle around a large advertisement on the side of his building. A swirling letter *B* was sculpted in flowers at his banquets, printed on the front of his bank's passbooks, and painted in twenty-four-karat gold on his family's china plates.

Everybody in the Black Belt knew the name "Binga," but few really knew the man. He didn't have many friends, certainly not many close friends. He mostly kept to himself in that roomy redbrick house on South Park Avenue, the one with the elevator behind the stairs, a second-floor gym, and a rotating clothes dryer the size of a small room in the basement.

"People knew his name," said Timuel D. Black Jr., "but for the most part he was a mystery."

The second time Black saw Binga was about fifteen years later. Black was then working as a clerk at Kaplan's Grocery and Liquor Store at Fifty-Ninth Street and Michigan Avenue. It was around 1940, and Black was handling sales behind the front counter one day when a slightly stooped, elderly man with short-cropped gray hair walked slowly into the store.

The man wore a business suit with a white shirt and a tie. His clothes were neat, but his suit was dated, shiny, and thinned by wear. He made his way through the aisles at a deliberate pace, carefully studying prices; his hands trembled slightly.

Up at the counter, Black was talking to a friend who saw the old man and asked, "Do you know who that is?"

Black looked down the aisle and studied the man making a path through the sawdust on the worn linoleum floor.

"That," his friend said, "is Jesse Binga."

2

The Black Sedan

SHORTLY AFTER MIDNIGHT ON JUNE 18, 1920, A BLACK SEDAN SLOWLY PULLED up in front of a two-story redbrick house in the middle of the 5900 block of South Park Avenue. A man got out, stepped off the running board and hustled to the front stairs, gingerly placed a package on the porch, and hurried back to the car.

As the sedan sped off, the package exploded in a deafening blast that sent the porch pillars spinning onto the street while shattering windows up and down the block. Neighbors, all of them white and some still in pajamas, quickly gathered in front and tiptoed through the debris to look at the damage. The portico was blown off, half of the porch floor was gone, and the remainder of the roof was left sagging. Remarkably, no one was hurt,[1] and while those who gathered were startled by the blast, they weren't surprised.

This was the fifth time in seven months that Jesse Binga's house at 5922 South Park Avenue (fig. 1) had been bombed (fig. 2). Each bombing was racially motivated. The Bingas were the first black family to move onto the block and were still the only black family, but when they settled there in 1917, nobody bothered them. In fact, neighbors were "very friendly to them, exchanging pleasant greetings whenever they came into contact with them and even unto this day Mr. and Mrs. Binga are on friendly terms with their white neighbors," according to the July 3, 1920, edition of the *Broad Ax*, one of Chicago's black newspapers.[2]

But as South Side neighborhoods increasingly turned from white to black, racial tensions grew along with threats of violence. By 1920 many whites, particularly in the neighborhoods near the Black Belt, saw Binga

Fig. 1. *Jesse Binga's house at 5922 South Park Avenue. The Bingas bought this redbrick house in 1917. (South Park Avenue was originally named Grand Boulevard, then it became South Park Avenue, then South Parkway, and today it is Dr. Martin Luther King Jr. Drive.)* PHOTOGRAPH COURTESY OF CAROLYN LOUISE DENT-JOHNSON.

Fig. 2. *Undated photo of Jesse Binga's house after a bomb exploded on the front porch, likely in the summer of 1920 or 1921—Binga's house was bombed and damaged both of those summers.* PHOTOGRAPH COURTESY OF CAROLYN LOUISE DENT-JOHNSON.

as an ominous threat to their daily lives. Binga was a fearless, freewheeling individualist out to make money without bowing to Chicago's racial boundaries and customs. To whites, he was more than just a troublemaker. He was a self-made man who listened to his own counsel as he pulled in buckets of money using his real estate firm and bank to move blacks into white neighborhoods.

Jesse Binga was in the vanguard of a growing group of individuals whom some observers called the "New Negro." By the 1920s most everyone on Chicago's South Side knew his name. In the Black Belt, he was a bright symbol of aspiration and unblinking ambition.

"The difference between savagery and civilization is thrift," one of his bank ads proclaimed. Binga advocated what he called an "economic morality."[3] That morality, as Binga preached it, meant self-sufficiency, which came from spending within your means, paying your bills on time, and working to "save, save, save," preferably in Binga's bank. It meant owning property, such as one's own house. And, perhaps its most important principle, it meant patronizing black-owned businesses.

For the first thirty years of the twentieth century, Binga was an outspoken champion of self-help in Chicago's black community. This was a time when blacks were continually under siege as the Black Belt grew and struggled to define itself. Their ambitions swelled to include jobs they never before had and homes they never before owned. And for that they were under attack. Binga preached an American gospel of hard work, self-reliance, and disciplined savings, yet he was arguably the most hated man in Chicago, at least in white Chicago.

To some whites, Binga was an American success story. To most others, he was a symbol of unwanted change as he resisted every move to control his life and business. The pressure was building for years. Every time he walked out of his house, his bank, his office, or while looking at a building to buy, everywhere Binga went, he likely had to be on guard, look over his shoulder, and size up any approaching stranger. Threatened by anonymous phone calls and unsigned letters, he had to be ever mindful of his surroundings. A trusted aide chauffeured him around town, and his wife stationed armed guards on the sidewalk, gangway, and alley around his house.[4] By 1919, Binga was a lightning rod for the worst race riot in Chicago history.

From July 1, 1917, to March 1, 1921, a black-occupied residence in Chicago was bombed every twenty-three days. There were fifty-eight bombings in that span, and while most left only property damage, two people were killed, including a six-year-old girl who was catapulted out of her bed by one blast and slammed into a ceiling.[5]

Binga's business and home were hit eight or nine times, including the bombing of his house in the late summer of 1921.[6] Other properties he leased or sold were also bombed, and Binga was routinely threatened.

Certainly many bombs were set at the properties of white and other black realtors, including the home of Chicago's first black alderman, Oscar DePriest.[7] But no one in Chicago was targeted more than Jesse Binga.

3

"In the Name of the Bingas"

ONE EARLY FEBRUARY DAY IN 1889, A NEWSPAPER REPORTER ARRIVED AT A small, two-story frame house on Indiana Avenue, in St. Paul, Minnesota. The house had a stone foundation built in such a way that it was about three feet below the sidewalk, which forced the reporter to jump down and then go up the steps leading to the front door.[1]

An old woman with "dark brilliant eyes" peering from behind gold spectacles and who wore a black dress and a knit wool cap greeted the *St. Paul Daily Globe* reporter. "She is pleasant-looking, stout and inclined to be talkative," the reporter wrote. Beneath her cap, "which comes down over her neck and ears," protruded wavy steel-gray hair. In the reporter's view, "When she smiles the wrinkles at the corners of her mouth shape themselves into deep dimples, giving her a very pleasant and good-natured appearance." Her face, the reporter said, "could not fail to strike the observer as one of considerable intelligence."

The woman led the reporter down to the basement kitchen, where they were surrounded by steaming pots, kettles, and cauldrons that bubbled and popped and fogged the windows. Glass tubing was connected to a few of the pots, along with some strange-looking paraphernalia, which the woman explained helped her make her "panacea," her miracle cure, "the greatest medicine in the world": the "Balm of Gilead, the Great Blood Purifier."

This woman was Adelphia Binga, Jesse Binga's mother (fig 3).

ABOUT A QUARTER CENTURY EARLIER, WHEN JESSE BINGA WAS BORN, THE name Binga meant something on the east side of Detroit, not far from the river near or in what is now downtown Detroit. The Bingas were used to

Fig. 3. *Adelphia Binga (born in about 1828, died 1897), mother of Jesse Binga.* PHOTOGRAPH COURTESY OF CAROLYN LOUISE DENT-JOHNSON.

people knowing their name. With ten children, a bustling barbershop, a thriving real estate business, and a reputation for making curative elixirs, they were hard to miss. The successful black family with an exotic name stood out.

The explanations for the origins of the Binga name are varied and vague.[2] A mountain peak in Mozambique, a rural commune in Mali, and a town in the Democratic Republic of the Congo all carry the name Binga. And there's a Binga village on the southeastern shore of Lake Kariba in the Republic of Zimbabwe.[3] Some relatives said the name had Middle Eastern roots; others said Binga was the name of an African chieftain.

To those who knew the Bingas in Detroit, the name meant success. It also conjured up the image of a hardworking family, albeit a somewhat eccentric one.

Jesse came from a long line of strong-willed, independent people. Bingas were known and respected for their self-reliance. Binga's family had various addresses in Detroit, many of them on or near Beaubien Street and some a mile or two from the shore of the Detroit River, just across the water from Canada, where the Binga name first took on a ring of importance. In the late 1830s one relative, Rev. Anthony Binga Sr., who escaped from his enslavement in Kentucky, founded a Baptist church in Amherstburg, Ontario, about sixteen miles south of Detroit, near the mouth of the Detroit River.[4] Amherstburg was one of the last stops for fugitive slaves on the Underground Railroad and often their first stop in Canada. Some of those who had escaped their enslavement sat in the pews of Reverend Binga's church.

"Must have been about two centuries ago that the Bingas came up from the islands to Montreal," Jesse Binga would later tell a newspaper reporter, adding some complications to the family history. "As long ago as 1780 there was a farm near Amherstburg, in the province of Ontario, in the name of Binga," he said.[5]

Jesse's father's background is something of a puzzle, although not as mysterious as that of his diligent and energetic mother. The answers to these questions of the Bingas' identity in America are both hidden and revealed in several decades of census reports and one death certificate.

William Binga gave his birthplace as Canada in the 1850 census. Since he was likely born into slavery in Kentucky, he certainly couldn't have said so in 1850 because he could have been captured as a runaway. His block's census was taken on September 21, 1850, just a few days after a tougher Fugitive Slave Act was passed by the U.S. Congress. After the Civil War, however, he reported his birthplace as Kentucky in the 1870 and 1880 censuses.[6] Later, Jesse said his dad was born in the West Indies,[7] adding a bit more confusion.

And then there's the question of race. William and his wife, Adelphia, are both listed as "black" in the 1850 census and "mulatto" in the 1880 census. Yet in the 1870 census, William is listed as "black" and Adelphia and her children are listed as "mulatto." Adelphia, whose maiden name was Powers (according to death records) or Seymour (according to her 1844 marriage record), told Jesse she was white and "descended from an Eastern socially prominent family."[8] In fact, Jesse once called himself an Irishman[9] during his days of prominence, which may have been a reference to his mother's background or just a comment made in a moment of pique. A family photo of Adelphia shows her to be a dark-haired woman with light skin. It seems she listed herself as black or mulatto for the census because interracial marriages were banned in Michigan until 1883.[10] Adelphia also once made this cryptic remark in 1889: "I was left with the Indians when

I was two weeks old, and did not find out who I was until after I had been married and had two children of my own. I wouldn't tell you who I am as I am related to some of the finest families in America, and they don't want to know where I am or anything about me."[11] When she died in Michigan in 1897, her death certificate listed her "color" as "white."[12]

Only two years before Jesse was born, Detroit had the only major race riot in the Midwest during the Civil War.[13] Thomas Faulkner, a mixed-race saloon owner, was accused of raping a nine-year-old white girl. The accusation inflamed whites and prompted a vicious attack on the city's black population. Two black people were killed, and more than thirty-five black families' homes were leveled. It was later determined that the witnesses against him lied; Faulkner was innocent and eventually pardoned in 1870 after serving seven years in prison.[14]

While Detroit was home to several black abolitionists, it was also a city where many whites looked at blacks as if they were a subspecies. Before the Civil War, stories in the *Detroit Free Press* often treated the black community in a mocking and dismissive tone. Typical of that sentiment were the words of the white alderman John Bagg, who referred to blacks as "dark bipeds—a species not equal to ourselves."[15]

Despite this backdrop, Jesse was born at a time of rising optimism and promise for blacks in Detroit and across the country.

JESSE WAS BORN ON MONDAY, APRIL 10, 1865, A TIME OF GREAT CELEBRATION in the North. It was one day after Palm Sunday when Robert E. Lee surrendered to Ulysses S. Grant in Wilmer McClean's parlor in Appomattox Court House, Virginia, which signaled the end to the bloody four-year Civil War. Although the assassination of President Abraham Lincoln just four days later quickly shifted the mood from joy to sorrow, the overall postwar period was a positive one for the Binga family.

When the war ended, more blacks began to settle in Detroit seeking jobs in the biggest city in the region. By 1870, Detroit's black population had grown by 60 percent to 2,235, although it was still less than 3 percent of the city's population.[16] To the Bingas, a family of entrepreneurs catering to the housing needs of the black community, a rise in the black population meant a rise in demand for housing. That meant higher rents and higher profits for the Bingas.

At the time of Jesse's birth, the country's laws were constantly changing to define people of mixed blood. Each state had its own formula, and Michigan's standard was the same as Mississippi's: only a person with "less than one-fourth of Negro blood" would be considered white.[17]

Jesse never viewed his race as a limitation on what he could be. He said he refused to allow discrimination to define him. Throughout his life, Binga said he never let racial hatred "destroy my soul."[18] In fact, he became a champion of his race by what he did more than what he said.

When Jesse was five years old in 1870, he lived on a mostly white block in what was then Detroit's Sixth Ward, according to the census. The neighbor on one side of the Bingas was the family of a white piano maker from Luxembourg; on the other side lived a black woman from Kentucky who worked as a "domestic servant."[19] While the "near east side," closer to where Jesse lived in 1880, had nearly 85 percent of the city's black population, his block also had a sprinkling of foreign-born whites.[20] On Jesse's block in 1880 there were immigrants from Ireland, France, Prussia, and Bohemia.[21] The Bingas' neighbors were white, black, and mulatto, and they included a shoemaker, a teamster, a cook, and two coopers. From an early age, Jesse learned how to live with people whose backgrounds were different from his own.

Jesse was reportedly the youngest surviving child of ten children.[22] Yet census, birth, and death records show nine children—five girls and four boys—possibly indicating a death that accounted for the tenth child. By 1870, only two sisters and one brother, Moses, were still living with their parents along with him; and by 1880, Jesse was the only child living with their parents.[23] Two years before that, in 1878, a story in the *Detroit Free Press* briefly mentioned a Jesse Binga in a "quarrel" with a Barney Schafer over a velocipede—a type of big-wheeled early bicycle with pedals on the front axle—in front of the *Free Press* building on a Saturday morning. During the quarrel between these two "boys," as the account described them, Schafer reportedly stabbed Binga in the arm and fled. Jesse was thirteen; his assailant's age is unknown. It seems Jesse Binga was well on his way toward a lifelong habit of standing his ground.[24]

Binga's father was a barber who owned a shop on Cadillac Square. Up to the turn of the twentieth century, many barbers were black,[25] and they made good money, held positions of respect, and were symbols of success. One of Detroit's most prominent black abolitionists was George De Baptiste, a wealthy barber and businessman who at one time was a valet to General William Henry Harrison before Harrison became president.[26] A couple of days before Jesse's fifth birthday and right after the ratification of the Fifteenth Amendment that gave black men the right to vote, De Baptiste, a self-described "capitalist," attached a celebratory sign to his building down the street from where the Bingas would later live in 1880.

It read: "NOTICE TO SHAREHOLDERS, OFFICE OF THE UNDERGROUND RAILWAY—This office is permanently closed."[27] Little Jesse Binga might have come to watch the celebration wend through the neighborhood as people carried banners promoting voting rights and raised signs painted with such slogans as "Equal privileges to all."

While many former slaves in the South were still trying to figure out how to live as free people, many free blacks in the North, including the Bingas, had been living that life for decades, and Jesse Binga was also empowered by a family culture of ambition and self-reliance.

As a little boy, Jesse would likely hang out at his father's barbershop, where he would sweep clippings, wipe scissors, run errands, and learn to cut hair. He could listen in on conversations of all who came and went. Black barbers were part of the black upper middle class in Detroit, as they were in other cities. Barbering could be a stepping-stone to much more.

IT WAS HIS MOTHER'S WORK, HOWEVER, THAT CAPTIVATED YOUNG JESSE. HE enjoyed tagging along with Adelphia as she made her rounds to the Bingas' various real estate holdings. Adelphia was a sturdy woman with her jet-black hair pulled tight into a businesslike bun. One photo of her shows she favored wearing more than a few pieces of jewelry as she posed with dangling earrings, a couple of rings, and a few gold chains hanging from a button on her dress the way a watch chain dangles from a suit vest.[28]

Adelphia was a shrewd businesswoman. Before Jesse was born, Detroit was a busy stop on the Underground Railroad because of its close proximity to Canada, where slavery had been outlawed since 1833–1834. As reverse border crossings increased after the Civil War, housing needs grew. Just as before the war, when runaway slaves needed a place to stay, after the war, black newcomers needed places to live when they found work in Detroit. Adelphia could provide them for the right price.

Jesse took it all in.

The family's holdings included "Binga Row," a one-story wood-plank tenement running along ninety-five feet of Hastings Street (fig 4). It had a long, single-slant roof that gave the appearance of a giant lean-to. It was designed to be cheap and supremely efficient, with each unit spanning little more than the width of a window and a door. Jesse saw that some of his mother's tenants took in boarders to help with the rent—something Jesse's family did and something Jesse would later do in Chicago on a much larger scale.[29] That sort of efficiency was another lesson. Jesse would later boast that in one of his own real estate projects, "I made every inch of space work for us."[30]

Fig. 4. *Jesse Binga's parents owned Binga Row, on Hastings Street and Rowena Street (now Mack Avenue) in Detroit. This photo was taken around 1890, after the Bingas' ownership.* PHOTOGRAPH COURTESY OF THE BURTON HISTORICAL COLLECTION, DETROIT PUBLIC LIBRARY.

Jesse fixed leaks, cleaned floors, collected rent, and listened to the hard-luck stories, apologies, and excuses of renters who couldn't pay on time. He marveled at his mother's skill in handling people, never evicting anybody in winter and routinely sending Jesse off to deliver food to hungry families.[31] He always said his mother was a great influence, a superb teacher with a big heart. Jesse idolized her.

Adelphia also saw profit in the waters of the Great Lakes and the sweet potato fields of the South. She bought lake whitefish from the North and sent it south for a better markup. After selling the fish in the South, her delivery people picked up sweet potatoes and brought them north through the Great Lakes to the Iron Range of northeastern Minnesota for a nice markup.[32]

Eventually, Adelphia tired of the business and sold everything, and she had an explanation for that.

"I was swindled in the deal," she told the *St. Paul Daily Globe* reporter who interviewed her in 1889. "I want no more of that. I had rather be the one to rent," she said. "It does seem so hard to take the rent from poor people when you know their children are starving. One day I collected $10 rent from a woman, when her little girl came up to me and said: 'Does Amy have bread?' 'Why, of course Amy has bread,' I replied. (Amy was my girl.) 'Well,' said the little one, 'I wish I could get a piece of Amy's bread.' 'For the love of God,' I said, 'have you no bread?' Then I went to the cupboard, and found they had absolutely nothing to eat in the house. So I said to the woman, 'Here is a dollar go and get some bread.'" As for remaining a landlord, "that was enough for me."[33]

Adelphia also told the reporter an intriguing story about her ingenuity. She said she invented a host of marvelous wonders including a life raft operated by a windmill, a device for feeding cattle on a railroad car, and a railroad tank car system for carrying live fish. And although she said she didn't patent any of them, she offered them to others who used them but never paid her. Indeed, the reason the reporter was doing the story in 1889 was because of the bubbling pots in her basement kitchen that contained her miracle balm.

Then in her sixties and living in St. Paul, Minnesota, Adelphia was making her own concoction of "Balm of Gilead," which her newspaper advertisement said could cure "liver, dyspepsia, kidneys, rheumatism, salt rheum, scrofula and all diseases of the blood, and nervousness from any cause whatever."[34]

Quite a claim.

"Patent medicine" in the form of balms, elixirs, and potions was extremely popular at the end of the nineteenth century. These "medicines" were generally not patented at all and often failed to live up to their curative billing. From the mid- to late nineteenth century, these products sold so well that by the late 1890s, almanacs were printed as a way to advertise these oils and elixirs. They had names such as August Flower and German Syrup, Seven Barks, and Burdock Blood Bitters. These homegrown cures were often advertised as coming from the natural medicine of Native Americans, with packaging depicting pastoral settings in which braves sat by campfires. The advertisements worked so well that thousands of almanacs were distributed across the country, printed at the rate of one patent medicine almanac for every two Americans.[35]

Investigative journalists, or "muckrakers," later exposed the wild curative claims for these balms and elixirs as frauds. Some of these products were dangerous, and others contained grain alcohol or opiates. Eventually the government stepped in and passed the Pure Food and Drug Act of 1906 and subsequent laws.

Adelphia's claims, however, were linked to natural cures she said she learned well after she was "left at the age of two weeks in the woods with an old Indian doctor." Adelphia said she "saw what things they used as medicine and remembered them."[36]

"Balm of Gilead" was a common name for such cures. It was originally a fragrant "cure" pulled from the resins of evergreen or poplar trees. The term, used in the King James Bible, makes reference to Gilead, a mountainous region in Palestine that was known for its spices. The term meant a substance that soothes or heals.[37]

Each jar of Adelphia's Balm of Gilead sold for $1.50. Whether helpful or not, it's clear that Adelphia Binga was a character. The world of patent medicines was a side of his mother that Jesse rarely, if ever, mentioned. He focused on her property management, not the stories of secret herbs and potions.

Education was a priority with the Bingas. Jesse had three to four years of high school and possibly some business college courses at a time when about 70 percent of blacks over the age of fourteen were illiterate.[38] Adelphia pushed her son to learn and achieve. Through her efforts, Jesse was placed in the office of Thomas Crisup, a young lawyer who in 1877 became one of the first blacks to graduate from the University of Michigan Law School.[39] For two years Jesse got a firsthand look at how the law worked in the lives of everyday people. Subpoenas, court filings, and contracts eventually seemed less mysterious. How to use the legal process to protect yourself or to gain advantage was just another lesson for Binga, another tool in the box.

Still, Jesse was a doer, a man of action, and for him, legal work probably seemed too slow and too controlled by tedious process. Jesse was a man in a hurry.

Interestingly, Jesse rarely spoke publicly of what came in the next few years of his life, the years of his first marriage and the birth of his only child, a son, Bethune. Instead, he talked of traveling thousands of miles in an ambitious journey through America's West. As Jesse would later explain, he took the Pullman job "in order to get a general idea of the conditions about the nation and also to acquaint himself with the different cities and to satisfy a desire to travel."[40] And travel he did. He would leave his wife and child for an odyssey of self-discovery before settling on Chicago as his home.

4

City of Wonder

JESSE BINGA CAME TO CHICAGO ON A TRAIN FROM THE WEST WITH A SHOE-shine kit, some well-worn luggage, and ten dollars in his pocket. He arrived on a crowded platform sometime in 1892,[1] young and ambitious, with a risky plan for his future. He was already an entrepreneur who was long accustomed to calling his own shots, and now he wanted to make his fortune in one of the fastest-growing cities in America.

At the age of twenty-seven, Binga had traveled thousands of miles, zig-zagging across midwestern prairies and western plains and up into the Rockies. Along the way, he worked as a barber and a Pullman porter, started a few businesses, and made at least one real estate investment. In his four-year trek, he logged far more miles than many nineteenth-century Americans, particularly black Americans.

Binga had a blue-collar physique with his thick, muscular carriage and calloused hands, and yet his stern, distinguished bearing gave him a patrician demeanor beyond his years. At about five feet, eleven inches, he stood a bit taller than most men of his time,[2] and his dark hazel eyes cast a confident and penetrating gaze. He had a distinctive dark mole below his right eye and another one lower in the center of his right cheek. His skin was brown, some said honey-colored, almost yellow. Years later people would argue about his color: some said he was light-skinned, others insisted he was medium-brown or even dark.[3] Few people ever agreed on the subject of Jesse Binga.

He came to Chicago to start over. Binga had tired of his travels and had already sworn off barbering.[4] Now he planned to leave his position as a Pullman porter. Both of these occupations were treasured jobs for a black man in the late 1800s, and a porter's life nourished Binga's curiosity and hunger for travel. Nonetheless, Binga had been a porter since 1887, and he was tired of the endless hours of waiting on people, catering to their whims, and answering to the snap of their fingers.

Binga was ready to strike out on his own and be his own boss, but African American entrepreneurs had some obvious disadvantages. With a legacy of slavery and daily doses of discrimination, blacks were often relegated to jobs of personal service, and some early black entrepreneurs emerged using those skills. Black entrepreneurs across the country owned farms, boardinghouses, restaurants, and stables offering horses and carriages for hire—Harry Knight, for example, reportedly operated the largest stable in Chicago in 1852.[5] And a few, like Cyprian Ricaud of Louisiana, even owned plantations and slaves.[6]

In Chicago in the mid-nineteenth century, John Jones, a tailor, was one of the most successful black entrepreneurs. He was freeborn and ambitious, having taught himself to read and write before coming to Chicago, where he opened a popular tailor shop downtown at 119 South Dearborn Street. His storefront also served as a main stop on the Underground Railroad. Jones was an outspoken advocate for abolition and civil rights. He eventually became the city and state's first black officeholder when he was elected to the Cook County Commission.[7]

But Jones was exceptional; in Chicago, as one old-timer said of those days, "our employment was chiefly barbering, cooking and waiting, while a few were hostlers at the hotels."[8] By 1885, blacks owned 111 businesses in Chicago and worked in "200 enterprises in 27 different fields."[9] With a black population of fifteen thousand by 1890 in a city of about a million people, that meant only about seven-tenths of 1 percent of blacks owned their own businesses—mostly barbershops, restaurants, and "sample rooms," which were "combined liquor stores and saloons."[10]

During the mid-nineteenth century, black business owners, such as Jones, served primarily white customers,[11] but at the turn of the twentieth century, that would begin to change dramatically—and Binga would play a major role.

When Binga arrived in Chicago, he was unique in the combination of his race, religion, and philosophy. He was a black Roman Catholic capitalist, who, as if to emphasize his individualism, would often talk about himself in the third person.

Binga also had some distinct advantages. After the Civil War, many blacks in America struggled with their new freedom as it raised issues of literacy and employment. Binga didn't. He was freeborn, apparently had a high school education, and was raised in an entrepreneurial family. His ambition was clear from the start, and he felt there were few boundaries.

Still, leaving the security of two well-paying jobs was a huge risk for any black man and particularly for Binga, given his next career choice. He decided to start on the lowest rung of the entrepreneurial ladder, where he would face intense competition and more than a modicum of danger. Binga would start over as a street peddler.

BINGA WAS NO STRANGER TO CHICAGO. HE HAD STARTED THERE AS A PORTER in 1887 and was based out of the city until 1890.[12] He knew his way around, but this was a city of wonder, changing with the speed of each locomotive arriving in this enormous, centralized railroad hub. In just the last two years since he left, Binga could see that Chicago had morphed into a city of the next century with its first electric streetcars, its first elevated train line, its rise of modern skyscrapers made of steel and glass, and its first appearance of an electric automobile in 1892.[13] He was surrounded by speed, motion, and a sense of urgency.

He was eager to give up the life of a wanderer. Traipsing through the West had been a long and unsettling journey.[14] Binga's travels were as much an expression of freedom and self-actualization as any in the late nineteenth century. They sharpened his vision and helped define his future, but not without cost. Four years earlier, in 1888, he had left a wife and child in St. Paul, Minnesota, never to return. He took off with little explanation.[15]

One of his stops was Missoula, Montana, where he visited his uncle Jordan.[16] Jordan Binga had moved there from Canada in the 1850s and built himself a budding entrepreneurial empire, which included a restaurant, a mining operation, and real estate. Jesse took careful note and moved on.[17]

Along his way to the West Coast, he bought his own barber chair in Kansas City at Ninth and Main Streets; he later cut hair in Tacoma, Washington, and once set up a shop in a waterfront squatter's tent in Seattle after the great fire of 1889.[18] The heavy rains robbed him of his health and he moved on to Oakland, California, where he finally called it quits. He was done cutting hair and sharpening razors.[19]

Around 1891, Binga went back to work as a Pullman porter, this time with the Southern Pacific Railroad, at first traveling up and down the West Coast. But the heavy snows in the Sierra Nevada could trap trains and once forced porters to trudge miles through the snow with food on their backs for women and children stranded in the passenger cars. Heavy snow and fires in some of the protective snow sheds helped convince Binga it was time to move on, again.[20]

He made his way east to Reno, Nevada, then to Ogden, Utah, on the west flank of the Rockies. He continued to work as a Pullman porter, including service on a narrow-gauge line from Ogden to Pocatello, Idaho, and to Butte, Montana. He stopped long enough to negotiate a land deal with the local tribes—likely the Shoshone and Paiute in Idaho.[21]

"He wasn't dark and he wasn't light, he was kind of yellowish," said Ripley Binga Mead Jr., whose father, Ripley Binga Mead Sr., was one of Binga's cousins, who, along with Ripley's mother, Jessie, worked for Binga. "I asked him one time about the Indians. He said the Indians used to trust him because he wasn't real dark . . . but the Indians didn't trust the white eyes."[22]

Binga invested $400 in twenty lots in Pocatello sometime after part of the Fort Hall Indian Reservation was thrown open for sale to the public. A couple of years later he sold off at a profit and moved on.[23]

When Jesse Binga finally arrived in Chicago, he was likely tired, with his clothes wrinkled from the long, smoky railroad ride. Trains from the west normally streamed into the base of the turreted towers of the Chicago and Northwestern Station at Wells and Kinzie Streets, just north of the Chicago River—where the Merchandise Mart stands today.

The platforms at the Chicago and Northwestern Station routinely bustled with the push and shove of a ragtag crowd of cowboys in broad-brimmed hats, businessmen in suits and vests, and farm folks dressed for the city—the men in new suits, the women in wide hats, long print dresses, and high-ankled shoes. Binga always projected himself as a businessman. Out in public he preferred a coat and tie. It was his uniform, always conservative, never flashy. He favored dark-colored suits: black, deep blue, or occasionally charcoal gray. He prided himself on looking sharp, and he liked how a suit defined him.

Crossing the river via the Dearborn Street bridge and walking about a half block south of the sluggish stench of the Chicago River, a traveler in 1892 would have found Lake Street, which had faded from its glory days of retail but was still jammed with carriages and pushcarts and buzzing with street hawkers and storefront vendors. One-half block east of Dearborn was what was becoming the city's most famous thoroughfare: State Street.

Looking south from the corner of State and Lake, down the full length of State Street, one could see the mighty fortresses of retail rising six or seven stories high on each side, stores such as Marshall Field's and the Fair. These were massive emporiums with thousands of workers. At street level there was an endless moat of plate-glass windows revealing huge, elegant Victorian displays with headless mannequins sporting the latest in suits, topcoats, and dresses. Chicago was helping invent the department store, and State Street's vast array of clothes, gadgets, and dry goods dazzled the eye. And then there was the fabled Palmer House, seven stories of hotel luxury with Italian marble and hundreds of spacious rooms of soft comfort. It was built by the visionary of State Street, Potter Palmer, who a few decades earlier ambitiously redirected the city's main retail strip from Lake to State. As part of his grand plan, Palmer dramatically widened State Street, even though it required shaving off twenty-seven feet of his own property.[24] This reconfiguration gave the street a majestic look with a wide expanse for traffic.

Palmer started out as a savvy retailer marketing to women by providing doting service with a generous and innovative return policy, but by the 1870s, real estate development held his focus. Palmer made State Street "that Great Street" by rebuilding much of it after the Great Chicago Fire of 1871. His earlier newly built Palmer House, a late wedding gift for his beautiful young bride, Bertha Palmer, was one of his properties destroyed by the fire. Undaunted, Palmer immediately rebuilt with a key alteration—"fireproof" rooms.[25]

Palmer was the first king of State Street, but Binga would later wear that crown on a different strip four miles south of Palmer's stretch. Binga would build a good chunk of his empire on State Street with his own skyscraper, apartment buildings, storefronts, and bank. Within twenty years of arriving in Chicago, Binga would boast that he owned more footage on State Street "than any other man in the city."[26]

FEW CHICAGOANS WOULD BOTHER TO NOTICE JESSE BINGA'S ARRIVAL. WHITES didn't pay much attention to men of color in Chicago in the 1890s, and when they did, it was often the kind no black man wanted.

Blacks were somewhat protected by law, but not by custom. That early black entrepreneur, John Jones, helped rid the state of its discriminatory so-called Black Codes, but still, it was not uncommon for a black person to be overcharged in stores, underserved in restaurants, and relegated to service jobs as waiters, butlers, or maids. Mostly, they were ignored. There weren't enough blacks in the city to be noticed much anyway, only 15,000 in a city of a million. This tiny percentage of the city's population seemed odd given the fact that a black man founded Chicago. Or as the Potawatomi used to say, "the first white man in Chicago was a Negro."[27]

Jean Baptiste Point Du Sable, like Binga, was an entrepreneur, Roman Catholic,[28] and freeborn. By 1788, Du Sable had established a trading post with a cabin, a smokehouse, and a barn along the north bank of the Chicago River several hundred yards from Lake Michigan.[29] His cabin was on what is now Michigan Avenue, next to the Tribune Tower on what is today some of the most expensive real estate in the city. Like Binga, Du Sable was a dealmaker. He traded the usual fare including flour, pork, baked bread, cotton, and even boats.[30]

Du Sable was likely born before 1746 near Kaskaskia,[31] a French settlement far southwest of Chicago along the Mississippi River. He was "a handsome Negro, well educated and settled at Eschikagou, but was much in the interest of the French," as described by a British officer at the time.[32] He married a Potawatomi woman and they had two children. Those who traded with Du Sable respected him for his honesty and integrity, traits that helped him secure close friendships with local tribes. Du Sable eventually sold his place for about $1,200 in May 1800 and moved to Missouri. He lived his final years near his children in St. Charles, where he died impoverished on August 28, 1818.[33]

After Du Sable, many blacks who came to early Chicago were mostly "fugitives and wanderers."[34] With wide access to the Great Lakes, Chicago was a popular destination for escaped slaves hoping to make it to Canada. Like Binga's hometown of Detroit, it was a well-traveled stop on the Underground Railroad.

The state of Illinois had a split personality when it came to issues of slavery and race. Some politicians in the 1820s tried to bring slavery to the state as a way to encourage southern planters to relocate. Before the Civil War, Illinois lawmakers passed the Black Code, which, among other discriminatory practices, precluded blacks from testifying in court cases and subjected them to arrest if they didn't have papers proving their freedom.[35] Later, an 1853 state law forbade blacks even to enter the state and those already in Illinois were subjected to the Illinois Black Code,[36] which was repealed in 1865.[37]

Nonetheless, Chicago had plenty of people seeking to help fugitive slaves, and it was not unusual to see abolitionists and slave catchers brawling on Chicago streets.[38] By the time of the Civil War, the Underground Railroad was operating out in the open.[39] Despite these abolitionist sentiments, many Chicago whites, including abolitionists, looked down on blacks. Those feelings hardened after the war, particularly with immigrants fearing incoming blacks would crowd them out of the job market, a fear that would last for decades even though blacks were largely excluded from the best-paying jobs.

By the time Binga came to Chicago in 1892, the Black Codes had been repealed, but the attitudes behind them lingered for decades.[40] Even though Illinois passed some of the country's most progressive antidiscrimination legislation, outlawing segregation in schools (1874) and in public accommodations (1885),[41] it didn't change behavior. While a good workable relationship existed between some blacks and whites in the city, there was an edge to it. As the number of blacks grew, that edge sharpened.

Binga's Chicago connection goes back to George Mead, a precocious fourteen-year-old from Virginia who stopped in Chicago in 1849 on his way to California's gold fields. Young George soon decided to stay in Chicago and join the small community of the city's free blacks, who first settled mostly along the Chicago River in 1840.[42] Mead eventually established what 150 years later would be one of the oldest black families in Chicago.[43]

When Mead set down roots, there were barely more than three hundred blacks living in Chicago.[44] They couldn't vote or defend themselves in court and at all times they had to carry their freedom papers. Chicago was not warm and welcoming.

Mead, however, found that Chicago suited him just fine. He was energetic and ambitious, working as a porter, a postal worker, and a waiter. By 1880, he was listed in the census as the head of a nine-member household at 216 Third Avenue (now Plymouth Court in the south Loop) right on the southern edge of downtown Chicago, just a half block over from Dearborn Street. They were part of a small cluster of black families that lived in the south part of downtown near several rail stations. Everyone in George Mead's household could read and write, and all of them were either working or in school. One of those nine children was Edwin R. Mead, who became a postal worker and in 1898 built a home on the western edge of the South Side's neighborhood of Woodlawn. Edwin moved in along with his wife, Emma, and his six-year-old son, Ripley Binga Mead. Emma was a Binga—Emma Binga Mead.[45]

WHEN BINGA SET OUT TO BE A CHICAGO STREET PEDDLER IN THE EARLY 1890s, he was greeted by a city that was a blur of motion filled with the chaos of street traffic. Streetcars rolled over iron rails, trolley bells clanged, horses clopped, and an endless crowd of people marched to work, shop, or dine. To a businessman, this was the glorious sound of commerce.

Binga would always enjoy walking the city; it was his way of finding opportunities.[46] Walking Chicago's streets could be a rattling experience. As a street peddler, he would find a noisy, smoky city, filled with the alternating stench of garbage, horse manure, and sweat. Stopping at State and Madison Streets, one of the city's busiest corners, was like standing inside a giant clattering machine. Chicago in the 1890s was not pretty, but it was mighty.

And it was dangerous.

The city had a dicey drainage system where heavy rains could mix sewage with drinking water into a toxic stew. Cholera was common, and a year before Binga arrived, typhoid fever killed some two thousand Chicagoans.[47]

The city's streets were choked with traffic, which posed a daily threat to pedestrians. Streetcars and trains ran at ground level without overpasses or tunnels and often mowed down absent-minded Chicagoans, mangling an arm or leg or crushing them to death. The city responded with booming sales of wooden legs and artificial arms.[48]

Life in Chicago was occasionally perilous and always challenging, but Binga had good reason to bet on the city. He always bet on himself as well, even though being a black peddler in a white city seemed to challenge the odds. Binga, however, surely saw that Chicago had something else going for it, something that soon would attract millions of people along with their money: the city was preparing for the great World's Columbian Exposition to begin in 1893, marking the four hundredth anniversary of Columbus coming to the New World in 1492 (never mind that the city was a year late, as long as they could sell tickets). The city prospered with the fair acting as a giant advertisement for Chicago.

Across the country, Americans were buzzing about the upcoming fair and its size, scope, and ambition as it rose like a sunrise along the city's southern shore. Many, like Binga, were pulled to Chicago hoping to make money off the crowds. Months earlier, when Jesse was shining shoes and making beds while swaying from side to side in a Pullman car, he undoubtedly heard rumors about the fair and about the cash that would flow through the "White City" (a reference to the collection of white neoclassical buildings constructed for the event). Pullman porters were close to the buzz. Every day they heard the conversations of the well-fed, wealthy, white businessmen traveling in the velvet embrace of Pullman sleeper cars. These conversations often involved two of Binga's favorites topics—money and power.

Porters were, after all, entrepreneurs at heart—hustling for tips and keeping their ears attuned to the wisdom of the wealthy. They counted on the tips—in California, they sometimes came in the form of tiny gold nuggets, and throughout his career Binga carried a watch chain made of such tiny nuggets he received while working in California.[49] Porters were paid about sixteen to thirty dollars a month at the time, and they had to pay for their own meals and two uniforms a year at eighteen dollars apiece, so tips (**T**o **I**nsure **P**romptness) were the real reason to work some thirty-seven straight hours a run and then, a few hours later, turn around and do it again. Porters traveled thousands of miles, getting only two to three hours of sleep a night and rushing or standing endlessly the rest of the time.[50] High-buff shoeshines were considered one of the best ways to earn a tip. To get those tips of pennies and nickels[51] meant discretion—no gossiping—and showing a good attitude for the customers with a snappy "Yes sir," or "That's right, boss," and "I'll get right to it, chief." Passengers often summarily summoned porters by calling out the name "George," after George Pullman.

For Jesse Binga, the porter's life was not a career; it was a business school. There were rules for everything, right down to how to make a bed, with the head always pointing toward the engine. Porters were governed by a small, brown-covered, fifty-page rule book "for sleepers and more for dining and beverage services," all of which reflected "George M. Pullman's credo that nothing be left to chance."[52] That also meant keeping porters segregated by a curtain when they ate. Porters were also selected by the hue of their skin—the Pullman company chose mostly dark-skinned men to be porters and light-skinned men to work the dining cars.[53]

The dark blue cap with the gold embroidered badge and the single-breasted blue frock coat were all part of the training. You had to look sharp. The uniform had to be spotless, the white shirts crisp and the tailoring precise—right down to the skirt of the coat extending from one-half to three-quarters the distance from hip joint to bend of knee.[54] It was a lifestyle of strict dress and comportment.

A porter walking home in his blue uniform meant something special to Chicago's small black community. They were an elite squad, a symbol of success. Pullman porters were admired, and they were listened to for their wisdom on manners and business. And when Jesse eventually did the unthinkable—leaving the ranks of the Pullman porters, albeit quickly returning to it more than he planned—he kept the habits. His new uniform was a three-piece suit.

"In those days—and yes long after—our group was mostly porters and messengers and janitors and waiters," Jesse said later. "I thought that was the great weakness of our group—the individual so seldom striking out for himself."[55] Binga could handle the work of a porter, but he wanted a bigger payoff. He headed to Chicago to find it.

5

World's Fair

THE WORLD'S COLUMBIAN EXPOSITION OF 1893 SPREAD ACROSS MORE THAN six hundred acres on the South Side lakefront, lined with gleaming white neoclassical buildings reflecting into glittering canals and lagoons. It would attract some 27 million people—21.5 million paid—equal to nearly half the population of the United States at that time; or, looked at in a way that Jesse Binga would appreciate, as much as $11 million up front, at fifty cents a ticket just to walk through the front gate. Binga was always good with numbers.[1]

When Jesse arrived in Chicago, the dazzling White City of this world's fair was still being built along Chicago's lakeshore some fifty blocks south of downtown. Rows of massive, but temporary, white plaster buildings with Greek columns and ancient-looking sculptures were built amid a stunning mosaic of landscaped gardens and artificially created canals and lagoons. A wide midway stretching east to west would soon be populated by hoochie-coochie dancers, makeshift tribal villages, colorful booths offering food, games, and amusements, and one massive feature not to be missed: the first Ferris wheel, a steel circle 264 feet high that rotated 2,160 passengers in containers the size of boxcars and took nine minutes to complete one revolution.[2]

The fair was a showcase for electricity as lightbulbs glittered like diamonds to illuminate the White City while casting thousands of reflections off its lagoons. When President Grover Cleveland opened the fair with the push of a button, it turned on 100,000 electric lights powered by Westinghouse's innovative alternating current (AC), which contrasted with the direct current (DC) in predominant use at that time. The feat was not lost on a thirty-three-year-old newcomer, a white Englishman named Samuel Insull, who arrived in 1892 to become president of Chicago Edison Company and who eventually became an enormously wealthy utility mogul.[3] It seemed impossible then, when Jesse Binga was a peddler and a shoeshine man, that in years to come Insull would become Binga's dinner companion and an important business ally.

For young men on the make, Chicago was a siren call, and for fairgoer L. Frank Baum, the White City of the fair became the inspiration for the Emerald City of his fanciful 1900 novel *The Wonderful Wizard of Oz*.[4]

JESSE BINGA WAS, OF COURSE, NATURALLY DRAWN TO THE GROUNDS OF THE world's fair, which offered dazzling displays, presentations of the newest inventions, and shows featuring music and entertainment from around the world. The Haitian Pavilion, a magnet for black visitors to the fair, including Binga,[5] was also a good place to hustle shoeshines, network, or listen to ragtime pianist Scott Joplin and other black musicians who played at the fair.

It seems likely that Binga would also have come to the fair on August 25, 1893, which had been designated "Colored American Day." This was a Binga kind of event, one he wouldn't have wanted to miss. He wanted to stay current, be in the know, and so that day's speech by Frederick Douglass—the former slave turned abolitionist, author, diplomat, and orator—was likely a must-see for a young black man on the move. At seventy-five years old, Douglass was an aging but still formidable intellectual who stood as a living argument for the talent and potential of his race, but he had deep concerns about this day, this event, and this place.[6]

Colored American Day came on a bright, sunny summer day—and here was the most famous black man in the United States taking the stage at a world's fair that he and other black leaders of varying philosophies had attacked for its failure to show blacks as useful contributors to post–Civil War America. Theirs was part of a larger debate they were forced to confront about the future of black America. How should blacks integrate into American society? Would segregation disappear through the hard work and achievement of blacks? To men like Douglass, the issue was inherently insulting when basic civil rights for whites in the country were considered God-given, self-evident, and at the core of the country's belief system.[7]

When Colored American Day had been suggested to appease protests, some black leaders rejected the idea. A separate day was not only humiliating, they said, it also legitimized their separateness and marginalized their race.[8] Others, including Douglass, argued that the day provided a forum that allowed blacks to describe their situation, dispel stereotypes, and highlight their progress since the Civil War. But Douglass, like others, was conflicted.[9]

Before it opened, Douglass had railed against the fair. He and fellow activist Ida B. Wells published a pamphlet that described the unfairness of the "White City," called that because of its many whitewashed neoclassical buildings yet probably perceived by blacks as underscoring their marginalization. About twenty thousand copies of the pamphlet, titled *The Reason Why the Colored American Is Not in the World's Columbian Exposition*, were distributed at three cents a copy—the price of postage.[10]

The pamphlet laid out a case for the progress of blacks in America and showed how that story was excluded from the world's fair. It also detailed the remaining hardships of blacks in in the United States. Wells was a crusading journalist who worked to expose the persistent problem of lynchings of blacks at the end of the century—161 in 1892, the year before the fair.[11] She documented some of the mob lynchings in the pamphlet while concluding that "the lynchings are conducted in much the same way they were by the Ku Klux Klans when Negroes were mobbed for attempting to vote."[12]

Educator Irvine Garland Penn wrote in the pamphlet of the progress of blacks while pointing to their collective wealth of $300 million and promoting their ingenuity by citing examples of patents held by blacks ranging from a "Locomotive Smoke-stack" to a "Folding Chair."[13]

Lawyer Ferdinand L. Barnett, who two years later would marry Wells, listed the many failings of the world's fair in his essay "The Reason Why" that concluded the pamphlet. "The colored people were untiring in their demands for some responsible work," he said, yet the various state boards "gave good ground for the belief that colored people were not wanted in any responsible connection with the Exposition work."[14]

As part of his introduction for the pamphlet, Douglass wrote about how blacks were being mistreated in America and at the fair, and he took a swipe at how the fair's village of the Dahomey portrayed blacks. The village became one of the must-see exhibits on the popular midway— today roughly occupied by the Midway Plaisance—fifty-nine blocks south of downtown running a mile east to west along the southern part of the University of Chicago. There, in 1893, next to the Austrian exhibit, was a thatched village meant to be from sub-Saharan Africa. It contained one hundred Fon men, women, and children, all of them subjects of the King of Abomey, also known as Dahomey. The Fon were dark-skinned and scantily clad, and they fascinated the crowds. Several times each afternoon the Fon pounded out hypnotic rhythms on animal skin drums, banged gongs, shook rattles, and jangled stones in a bag made of animal skin. Some newspaper reporters praised their skills and artistry; others mocked them as ugly and barbaric. Douglass said their presence at the fair was "as if to shame the Negro, the Dahomians are also here to exhibit the Negro as a repulsive savage."[15]

Ultimately, Douglass, who was also Haiti's representative to the fair because he was once a U.S. diplomat there, decided to speak on Colored American Day to spread a message that he believed remained unheard. Crusading journalist Ida B. Wells, however, refused to attend, and fair organizers outraged more than a few African Americans when they set up free watermelon stands, thinking that would attract blacks to Colored American Day.[16]

There were many theories on how black leaders could handle the problems they saw with Chicago's world's fair—and, for that matter, with America. Black leadership was worried about the place of blacks in America, and the World's Columbian Exposition of 1893 sharpened that debate, which would continue for decades. Deep fear for their future was the only uniting theme. Three years after the fair, the U.S. Supreme Court would try to settle part of the debate with a doctrine of "separate but equal" in its *Plessy v. Ferguson* decision. That ruling held that laws mandating segregation in public places, such as bathrooms and railcars, were legal if the facilities were comparable, or equal. It would take more than half a century for the Supreme Court to overturn the *Plessy* decision and declare that "separate" was inherently unequal, in its 1954 ruling in *Brown v. Board of Education.*[17]

Admission to the world's fair was open to "colored" men and women, but there weren't any black commissioners appointed to the fair, although one was later added as an alternate.[18] Historian, author, and black studies scholar Christopher Reed said there were few jobs for blacks in building the fair since most of the trades such as "designing, glaziering, surveying, painting, sculpting or molding" excluded blacks. Only a handful of black men were lucky enough to work as carpenters at $3.25 per day, and at least one black man worked as a plasterer at $4.50.[19]

During the fair, blacks largely had to settle for the lower-paying jobs such as washroom attendant or janitor. Still, the fair had an all-black uniformed staff of 140 janitors, and there was a group of both black and white college students who made good money—up to forty dollars a week—as "chair boys," rolling customers in wheeled chairs through miles of fair grounds.[20] But these numbers were a small percentage of the more than

40,000 workers employed to build and staff the fair.[21] On the other hand, the number of blacks living in Chicago at the time was minuscule as well.

African American leaders argued for a greater black presence in the fair's exhibits, but with differing theories, according to historian Robert W. Rydell. Some argued for adding separate "colored" exhibits to highlight the progress of blacks since the abolition of slavery; others argued for integrating a black presence into already existing exhibits so as not to segregate blacks. Blacks should be judged on their merits in an integrated world, they reasoned.[22]

Black women also tried various ways to get greater representation in the fair, but the all-white board of the Lady Managers, led by Bertha Palmer (wife of Potter Palmer, the wealthy retailer, realtor, hotelier and visionary of State Street), delayed and effectively stood in the way of any meaningful participation.[23]

Some blacks, following Wells's lead, boycotted Colored American Day and the fair itself; others encouraged attendance that day in order to show a strong black presence. Of the 1,000 to 2,500 visitors who came for Douglass's speech, about two-thirds were black.[24] Douglass spoke at Festival Hall, a white building fronted by massive columns that made it look like a Greek temple. The hall, used for organ recitals and choral performances, overlooked a lagoon about two blocks south of the Fine Arts Building, which still exists today as Chicago's Museum of Science and Industry. The applause began before Douglass made it to the front of the stage. As he walked forward, the ovation grew louder.[25]

As Douglass began, a white heckler interrupted with hoots and catcalls as he chided Douglass about the "Negro problem."

Douglass veered off his prepared remarks and bore in. "Men talk of the Negro problem. There is no Negro problem," he said. "The problem is whether the American people have honesty enough, loyalty enough, honor enough, patriotism enough to live up to their own Constitution."[26]

His speech proved masterful. After Wells read about it, she was so moved that she asked Douglass to forgive her actions and her absence.[27]

Standing in the crowd that day was nine-year-old Ulysses Grant Dailey, who would one day become a prominent doctor in the Black Belt and an investor in Jesse Binga's bank as well as Binga's personal physician. Dailey's mother brought him to hear Douglass and to inspire him to dream big for his own future.[28]

Also sitting in the crowd was a dark-skinned young man from Georgia, the son of two former slaves. Robert Sengstacke Abbott was attending the fair as part of the popular Hampton Quartet singing group. A little over a decade later, Abbott would found the *Chicago Defender*, one of the most important black newspapers in the country. His newspaper would make him a millionaire, one of the wealthiest black men in Chicago, and a champion of his race. It also positioned him as a key figure in increasing the city's black population by encouraging blacks from the South to move to Chicago. Like Dailey, Abbott would also become Binga's friend and later invest in Binga's bank.[29]

At the time, Binga, then twenty-eight years old, and Abbott, twenty-two, were both trying to find their way in a rapidly changing American landscape. In a couple years they would meet each other and begin a valuable friendship, one that would help make them both rich.

ANYWHERE BINGA LOOKED AROUND CHICAGO AT THE TIME OF THE FAIR, HE saw the bright, bold signs of commerce. There were signs for restaurants, candy stores, saloons, saddle shops, bakeries, and dry goods stores. There were signs hung in windows, set out on curbs, painted on buildings, and hung over sidewalks. The signs came in myriad colors, hues, and black-and-white, all of them hawking wares in an assortment of languages—English, German, Italian, Polish, Swedish, and Chinese. When the architect Frank Lloyd Wright came to Chicago for the first time a few years before Binga arrived in the early 1890s, he called these big painted signs a "demoralization of the eye." Names, Wright said, obliterated everything. "Names and what they would do for you or with you or to you for your money."[30]

Binga saw only one problem with this dazzling array of large painted names: they didn't include his.

6

"Jesse C. Binga"

IMAGINE TRYING TO PICK THE PERFECT SPOT FOR A STREET PEDDLER IN CHI-
cago in 1893. Where would it be?

There were plenty of sites to choose from: downtown, by the river, or
in front of a broad array of office buildings and warehouses around the
city. A peddler could sell to the mass of exiting workers near the stockyard
gates, at the entrance of Peabody Coal, or by the sprawling steel mills
along the lake, which would eventually be known as South Works.

To be a peddler, all you needed were a desirable product, ten dollars
for a city license, and a certain degree of hustle. To be a successful peddler required a good deal more.

The life of a peddler was often the first and only choice of a man on
the move. It was the entry level for would-be entrepreneurs and a breed-
ing ground for businessmen and politicians. Future Chicago Mayor
Anton Cermak began his career selling kindling wood from a pushcart.
The notoriously corrupt Michael "Hinky Dink" Kenna, alderman of Chicago's wild Levee district, once hawked newspapers on street corners.
His fellow—equally corrupt—alderman of the Levee, "Bathhouse John"
Coughlin, also began as a street peddler.[1] Successful peddlers needed to
be both people smart and street savvy.

Competition was fierce. Chicago had an army of as many as thirty
thousand peddlers (estimates on the number are difficult because many
peddlers didn't bother to buy a license) scattered across city streets and
perched on corners in the mid-1890s, always with an eye out for a better location.[2] Jesse Binga believed he could find the perfect spot and
then outwork and outsmart his competition. As he once said, "Jesse

Binga knows what he's doing and he's doing it like Jesse Binga wants it done."[3]

Every neighborhood had a wide array of street vendors; each competing to work a special corner or a certain strip. But if you weren't Polish, German, or Irish, or whatever ethnic group ruled the neighborhood or the trade, you might have to put up with an occasional beating or a tossed cart. There were sporadic threats from teenage street toughs who took delight in pummeling a peddler for his goods or seizing his daily take, particularly if he was the wrong nationality or the wrong color or in the wrong part of town. It was more complicated for a black street peddler, so for Jesse Binga, a neutral location near or close to downtown might work best.

How about a spot in front of City Hall? There were always aldermen hurrying by and city workers coming and going, but there were also plenty of peddlers stationed around the hall and in front of many other key downtown locations. These sites had guaranteed traffic, but they also had battalions of entrenched peddlers, each keyed to the rhythm of a location and fixed to the habits of customers needing a 10:00 A.M. apple or a 3:00 P.M. piece of pie wrapped in paper.

Construction sites were another possibility, such as the site of the glassy white Reliance building rising at Washington and State Streets—the first skyscraper with large plate glass windows. A stream of workers there could get pretty hungry during the day, and they were well employed with ready cash.

For Jesse Binga, the safest bet might be a black neighborhood, but in a city of a million people, there were only some fifteen thousand blacks scattered in small enclaves, a building here or a building there.[4] And all city neighborhoods had established peddlers keyed to main streets and crowded corners, including mixed-race neighborhoods.

A peddler wanted downtown traffic but didn't want to be too close to South Water Market or Haymarket since those were wholesale markets for grocers and restaurants. South Water Street, just south of the Chicago River and north of City Hall, had "miles of bananas, oranges, apples and other colorful fruit," along with meat from the stockyards and fish brought in by boats from the Great Lakes.[5] The Haymarket on West Randolph Street attracted a steady stream of fresh produce brought in every night by local truck farmers.[6] But peddlers who picked up their daily fare or snapped up remainders of overly ripe or damaged produce in these markets would certainly sell anything they could on their way back to their spots in the city. So rule that out.

No, a peddler's site had to have some permanence while avoiding the more intense competition of street vendors who had months or years on the same corner with the earned trust and habits of regular customers. A new peddler needed a fresh site, someplace safe and reliable, with a steady flow of people who had hunger in their bellies and a couple coins in their pockets.

Jesse Binga figured he found just the right spot: the corner of Twelfth Street and Michigan Avenue.[7]

STANDING THIRTEEN STORIES HIGH WITH A COMMANDING FOUR-SIDED CLOCK tower, the massive Romanesque Illinois Central Station was built of granite and brick by railroad architect Bradford L. Gilbert. It was said to be "the largest train shed in the world."[8] Built at what is now Roosevelt Road and Michigan Avenue, it was designed to handle huge crowds expected for the World's Columbian Exposition of 1893.

When Jesse Binga set up his stand in front of Central Station, the smell of fresh mortar and construction dust was still in the air. While Binga certainly wasn't the only peddler at the station, his competitors were now just like him, plying their wares at a new location at an equal starting point. After that, it was just a question of hustle and guile. The station, which was near the south end of what is today Grant Park, opened on April 17, 1893, a couple of weeks before the world's fair began.

Some of the most profitable peddlers were organ grinders. They reportedly made eight to ten dollars a day, compared with the low-end peddlers who netted only a few dollars a week. But to earn that kind of cash, an organ grinder needed a barker's gab, enough money to buy a mechanical street organ, and some theatrical flair, which usually required a monkey, a parrot, or some dancing family members. None of that was Binga's style, and there were already four hundred organ grinders performing on Chicago streets.[9]

Well before he chose his site, Binga had ruled out door-to-door household jobs such as knife sharpening or junk collecting. Even though Binga had considerable fix-it skills, those services were already sewn up: German immigrants were skilled at making household repairs, and Jewish peddlers were adept at collecting and selling recycled clothes, rags, and junk.[10]

So what did Binga choose to sell?

Binga chose something more in his wheelhouse, something that catered to what he knew very well: railroad travel.

Train passengers—coming or going—were often hungry and in a hurry. So, despite the possible competition of Italians and Greeks, who were experts in street produce sales, Binga chose to sell fruit. This offering would be perfect for the weary passengers arriving after a long trip or for outbound travelers preparing for a lengthy day on the rails. And if things got slow, Binga could always offer shoeshines to newcomers hoping to make a good impression.

The corner at Twelfth and Michigan was as much of a sure thing as one could get. It was guaranteed to be jammed with high-volume train traffic until the world's fair ended, and since this was an intercity hub, there also would be plenty of traffic after the fair—in fact, there should be plenty of action for decades. Plus, it was a fresh site: no established peddlers, no regulars. Binga knew he would be starting with a clean slate and could go head-to-head with any seasoned peddlers, and Binga believed he could easily handle that. He began with a pushcart.[11]

It all worked well, at least in the beginning. Binga, who was always a disciplined saver, eventually earned enough money to expand his operation to a horse-drawn wagon. And for the first time, Binga had his name publicly displayed in big broad painted letters, on the side of his wagon: JESSE C. BINGA.

The horse and wagon allowed Binga to easily pick up his daily supplies, and gave him the flexibility to sell on neighborhood streets. And if he couldn't sell everything, he routinely dropped off leftover fruit or vegetables at the two-year-old Provident Hospital and Training School for Nurses, the first black-owned and -operated hospital in the country.[12] Years later, Binga would be an important benefactor of Provident.[13]

Only months after Binga set up his cart, a young Provident doctor made surgical history. Founded by noted black surgeon, Dr. Daniel Hale Williams, Provident Hospital was a place where black Chicagoans could feel safe and well taken care of as patients or as doctors. Williams, who in 1913 would become the first black member of the American College of Surgeons, earned international fame on a July night in 1893 when he stitched up a ragged cut in the lining of the heart of James Cornish,[14] who had been stabbed in a tavern brawl. With that delicate procedure, Williams became the first physician to perform successful open-heart surgery on a human being.[15] Cornish went on to live another fifty years.[16]

Provident, located in a converted three-story brick house at Twenty-Ninth and Dearborn Streets, was close to Binga's room at 3202 State Street, where he lived in 1894—the first year he appears in the Chicago City Directory, listed simply as "peddler."

Before that year, however, Binga was living by his wits, shining shoes when he could, perhaps occasionally staying with relatives or finding cheap places to stay while he saved for bigger things. But eventually his savings faded along with his prospects.

The first warning came on May 3, two days after the World's Columbian Exposition of 1893 opened. The stock market plunged—the deepest dive since 1884—and hysteria set in. A robust economic boom had led to excess and wild speculation.[17] The market crashed in June, and eventually more than 550 banks failed nationally, 15,000 businesses were shuttered, and in the next year about 125 railroad companies went into receivership.[18] Mills and factories slowed or shut down, jobs dried up, and confidence vanished. No city was harder hit than Chicago, "where the boom period of the World's Fair had attracted a large number of workers, who now were left by the prostration of the city's industries without employment or the prospect of any."[19]

The Panic of 1893, as it became known, shadowed the city and the nation for four years as it became the worst depression in U.S. history up to then. It was a bad time to own a business or to be connected to the railroads, and Binga was doing both.

Despite a sagging economy, the crowds still came to the world's fair in 1893 and Binga was seemingly thriving, until the depression took deep root more than a year later and in May 1894 when about five thousand factory workers walked off the job at Pullman's Palace Car Company in Pullman's "model" industrial town just south of Chicago.[20]

George Pullman, Binga's longtime employer, had cut his employees' hours and wages, yet he didn't cut the rent he charged in company-owned housing. Workers were fed up. Eventually the strike spread through the American Railway Union, and about 125,000 employees walked out across the country and more than twenty railroads were shut down.[21] Since union members had to be "born of white parents," blacks gladly crossed picket lines as strikebreakers.[22] Pullman porters didn't join in the strike, even though Pullman banned porters and all but a few blacks from living or working in his model town. In what would become a common American theme, blacks felt squeezed and excluded from jobs and housing as racial tensions and a bad economy continued to rise. For the budding young entrepreneur Binga, the following years were a test of endurance.

Binga worked as a peddler in 1894, but as the economy stumbled and railroad traffic slowed, he struggled with street sales. Occasionally he found himself without a place to stay and little money to pay for lodging. He was forced to sleep where he could, sometimes on top of a pool table.[23]

Tens of thousands of workers lost their jobs; unemployment ran higher than 20 percent in manufacturing centers including Chicago.[24] Sleeping homeless men were spread like carpets across sidewalks, and cops routinely found babies abandoned on church steps. The streets became more dangerous, particularly for a peddler with produce on his cart and coins jangling in his pocket.

Adding to this woe, the world's fair ended on an ominous note. On October 28, 1893, the night before the fair closed, there was a knock on the front door of the South Side mansion of Carter Harrison, the wildly popular mayor of Chicago. When the maid opened the door, she let in an unemployed newspaper distributor named Patrick Eugene Prendergast, an Irish immigrant and onetime supporter of Harrison. Strangers at the door were nothing new to the mayor's household; after all, Harrison was known as "the common man's mayor" and touted his welcoming open-door policy.[25] Unfortunately, too much so: Prendergast drew a .38-caliber revolver and shot Harrison three times at point-blank range.

The deranged Prendergast was angry about being turned down for a city job—not just any city job, but that of corporation counsel, for which Prendergast had absolutely no qualifications. The day after the fair closed, Harrison was buried. And so ended Chicago's first world's fair, with a funeral.[26]

After the fair closed, Binga managed, but barely. A successful peddler needed to be up before sunrise to face a life that was routine and tedious. In winter, tenants in Binga's area often woke up shivering in darkness. By dawn, the little heat they were able to get had long faded from any dimly lit rentals, and on some days the air was tainted by stench from the often clogged or broken toilets typical of the housing in his area. Sometimes renters had to tramp through garbage and the frozen muck of a back-yard to a cold, stained, and stink-ridden outhouse. When Binga lived on Thirty-Fourth Street in 1894, only one of four families in neighborhoods like his had access to an indoor bathroom, and those without one had to use "privy vaults," which might be outside or under porches caked in frozen waste.[27]

Summers weren't much better. The heat and humidity of July or August in Chicago could shrivel and spoil a peddler's produce, necessitating constant repositioning of the pushcart or wagon into shade.

Binga's story in the 1890s is vague and sometimes puzzling, but there is evidence that he hustled and struggled, working on and off as a Pullman porter and a peddler. As early as 1893, he "went into the real estate business helping to locate colored people in homes, at that time there being a great influx of colored people to Chicago." By 1894, he may have even had a real estate office at 3331 South State Street.[28]

Binga managed to keep his wagon rolling in those early years, and he added coal to his product line, which helped him snag winter sales. Still, it was likely a meager existence even if he allowed another man to work the wagon (when Binga took a break or worked elsewhere), as was often done. Eventually Binga was forced to give up working as a full-time street peddler (although he might have done it part-time between stints as a Pullman porter). He worked as a porter in 1893 while also likely working as a peddler for the fair crowds. He was apparently a full-time peddler in 1894 but then worked as a Pullman porter off and on from 1895 to 1899.[29]

By 1897, near the end of the depression, Binga was living at 3738 Armour Avenue (what is now Federal Street), a half block west of State Street. He was working as a Pullman porter and living on a block filled with about two hundred people[30] distributed among shabby rooms and small, drafty apartments.

City blocks were beginning to be sorted by race. Binga's building had only black tenants, but most other residents of his block were white. The racial composition in all but one building was either all white or all black, and the sole racially mixed one, at 3722 Armour Avenue, was just barely so: all black except for Delie Ricks, a white woman from Ireland, who lived there with her husband, J. B. Ricks, a black waiter from Tennessee. In Jesse Binga's building, his neighbors were from Kentucky, Virginia, and Louisiana. They included a bellboy, a butler, a caterer, a dressmaker, and a railroad cook. His white neighbors down the block were immigrants from Ireland, Denmark, England, and Germany with jobs including machinist, bricklayer, railroad brakeman, carpenter, and the relatively new position of telephone operator.[31]

Nonetheless, in the early 1890s, black–white segregation was not yet the rigid unwritten rule of the city. "As late as 1898, only slightly more than one-fourth of Chicago's black residents lived in precincts in which blacks constituted a majority of the population," according to historian and author James R. Grossman, and "more than 30 percent inhabited precincts at least 95 percent white."[32] As on Binga's street, black families could be found living on the same block as whites and in some cases in the same building or on the same floor. At the time—and for some years to come— Italians were more segregated than blacks.[33] That would soon change.

As it turned out, 1894 was the only year Jesse Binga was listed as a peddler. He likely lived a transient life; there are no city listings for him in 1895 or 1896. The next time Binga shows up in the city directory is 1897, when he's listed as a "porter" living at the Armour Avenue address. Jesse Binga would not appear again in the city directory until 1902.

ON FRIDAY, JULY 9, 1897, A ROMAN CATHOLIC PRIEST IN A FADED BLACK CAS-sock swayed and weaved in a slow zigzag pattern around Thirty-Sixth Street and Ellis Avenue before he stumbled and collapsed. Several people rushed to his side, and a passing police patrol stopped and took him to Mercy Hospital. Chicago was baking in a two-week heat wave, and Friday's temperature had hit 105 degrees Fahrenheit.[34] The priest was one of many to drop in the heat. The city had already seen deaths "from all diseases" spike to more than 600, with Tuesday, July 6, recording a one-day high of 125 deaths.[35]

The priest, Father Augustine Tolton, was on his way home to his rectory behind St. Monica Church, which was about two blocks from Jesse Binga's rented room. While there were dozens of Catholic churches in Chicago, none were like St. Monica, named for the mother of Saint Augustine of Hippo in north Africa. Still under construction, St. Monica Church was designed by a black architect, built by black workmen, and supervised by black contractors. St. Monica Parish was the first and only black parish in Chicago.[36] And "Father Gus," as he was affectionately known, was the first black priest in the United States.[37]

If Jesse Binga hadn't met Father Gus, he certainly had heard of him and his groundbreaking legacy. St. Monica was Binga's church, although it's unclear exactly when Jesse became a parishioner. Binga was something of a rarity in Chicago in the 1890s, a black man who was also Catholic. Less than 4 percent of Chicago's tiny black population was Catholic.[38] In fact, some of the St. Monica parishioners were actually Protestant, and some were even white. It is unclear how or why Binga became Catholic, but the closest description of the origins of his faith comes in a 1981 family history by Anthony J. Binga Sr.: "Having embraced Catholicism around 1885, Binga remained devote [sic] and generous to his church. . . . It is also revealed that the Catholic Church remained loyal to him until he died."[39]

Slavery played a strange and melancholy role in the roots of black Catholics in America. The first black Catholic community was composed of slaves and free blacks in St. Augustine, Florida, in the late sixteenth century.[40] Jesuits owned slaves in Maryland in the early nineteenth century, and the Vincentians owned slaves in Missouri.[41] Catholic slaveholders routinely baptized their slaves to promote their faith. Augustine Tolton, for example, was born a slave in Missouri and baptized Catholic by his owner. When little Gus was seven years old, his mother grabbed him, his brother, and a sister and escaped to Illinois.

Evidence of Binga's faith can be seen in his almost daily relationship with the church for more than half a century. By 1912, he was financial secretary for the St. Monica Catholic Order of Foresters,[42] and he regularly contributed money and time to the three Chicago parishes where he worshipped for decades.

Binga had long and close working relationships with the white Sisters of the Blessed Sacrament who came in 1912 to teach the children of St. Monica Church. One of them, Sister M. Berenice, was close to Katharine Drexel, who founded the Sisters of the Blessed Sacrament for Indians and Colored People in 1891 (and would be canonized by Pope John Paul II in 2000). Drexel organized what is now known simply as the Sisters of the Blessed Sacrament as "a religious community of women to live among people of color, Native Americans and African Americans, and teach their children."[43] Katharine's father was a wealthy Philadelphia banker—a street on the South Side of Chicago is named Drexel because her family owned property there and donated the land to be used as a city thoroughfare. When her father died, Katharine used her $20 million inheritance[44] to fund the Sisters of the Blessed Sacrament and help parishes like those of Father Gus. Mother Katharine, who became a supporter of Binga, accompanied the six Blessed Sacrament sisters to St. Monica in August 1912 to start their work in Chicago.[45]

Some of the Sisters of the Blessed Sacrament who came to the city had high school diplomas; none had attended college. Mother Katharine trained them to teach. Many of these sisters were working-class Irish women from the East Coast whose families were worried how they would be received in Chicago.[46] These sisters were some of just a handful of white women who lived in the Black Belt, and Binga was a key to their welcoming reception.

"People were very friendly and very generous to us—both white and colored," Sister Berenice later said. "I must mention especially Mr. Jesse Binga, who was exceptionally kind to us."[47] The sisters never forgot that kindness.

These devoted sisters were also part of a strange and often uncomfortable relationship between Chicago's Irish and black populations. The Irish, who as immigrants were often castigated as brawlers and drunks by Chicago's newspapers, often clashed with black Chicagoans, whom they frequently saw as beneath them and as rivals for their jobs. There were many turf wars between Irish "clubs" and residents of the Black Belt. Yet there were many instances where the Irish were generous and helpful, particularly when it came to Catholic charity. White women from the Holy Family Parish gave $500 to St. Monica Church, and in 1888, Annie O'Neil—whose husband, Patrick, was a wealthy liquor and wine dealer—donated the phenomenal sum of $10,000, which was eventually used in part to buy the land for the church.[48] Binga, too, would eventually have close ties with Irish politicians and priests, and later, when he needed it most, Binga would be helped by an Irish businessman he had never met.

Similar to Binga as Chicago's first black banker, Tolton was the city's and nation's first black priest, with all that entails. Binga suffered bombings, threats, and vilification. Tolton suffered poverty, slights, and isolation.

The city's first black parish began in 1882 but didn't get its own church until construction of St. Monica began. The church was located in an impoverished area near a vice district at the corner of Thirty-Sixth and Dearborn Streets—today just a couple of blocks east of the Dan Ryan Expressway and the ballpark of the Chicago White Sox. When Jesse Binga was a street vendor in 1893, St. Monica was only one story high, with wide front steps, an unfinished steeple, and a flat roof because there wasn't enough money to finish building the first floor. The church was never completed.[49]

Communion was offered on a plain, barren altar, and parishioners sat on a makeshift variety of chairs, stools, and wooden boxes. Father Tolton celebrated Mass wearing a black cassock sometimes belted with a red sash, indicating he was trained in Rome. He was tall, thin, and extremely dark-skinned, which prompted taunts of "black boy" from mulatto classmates in his younger years and rejections by U.S. seminaries when he tried to become a priest later. Father Tolton was said to sing like a songbird and give beautiful, eloquent homilies.[50]

His congregation was relentlessly poor, and Father Gus reflected that poverty. The rectory behind the church was spare and largely empty, with only a few basic pieces of furniture. The dining area had a table, some chairs, and a kerosene lamp, according to a letter from a visiting monsignor.[51]

As the first black priest in the United States, Father Gus was something of a celebrity and was often asked to travel to give speeches and sermons. But in a letter to Mother Katharine, Tolton wrote of being worn down by the constant unwanted side of his celebrity: "The South is looking on with an angry eye; the North in many places is criticising every act, just as it is watching every move I make."[52]

On July 10, 1897, a *Chicago Daily News* headline proclaimed, "Sun God Is Still Pitiless." The heat wave's one hundred-plus-degree temperatures were roasting the city. A subhead added, "Many Additional Deaths Follow a Night and Morning of Almost Unendurable Heat." Father Tolton, only forty-three years old, was one of the victims. He died of heat stroke and uremia, although some observers might have thought it was overwork or a nervous breakdown.[53]

7

"A Man of Low and Vicious Habits"

AS JESSE BINGA WAS FINDING HIS ENTREPRENEURIAL WAY ON THE STREETS OF
Chicago, his personal life was unraveling, largely without him. His mother
died in Michigan in 1897 after being involved in a highly publicized family drama. A few years later, a part of his past that he had put behind him
resurfaced.

On a warm, late September day in 1901, Frances Binga, then in
her midthirties, entered the Cook County building in the center of
a city block bounded by Washington, Randolph, Clark, and LaSalle
Streets. This building, with its thirty-five-foot-tall Corinthian columns of granite, was built after the Great Chicago Fire of 1871 leveled
the old courthouse, and it was constructed on the same block where
Chicago's City Hall / County Building stands today. In 1901 this building was already in trouble. It, like its adjoining City Hall building, was
poorly constructed on a faulty foundation amid cries of corruption and
insider deals, most of which were true. Its rooms were poorly ventilated
and its hallways dark and gloomy. In several years it would be declared
unsafe and torn down.[1] It was into this building that Frances came to get
divorced.

Jesse Binga had married Frances Scott on April 14, 1885,[2] four days
after his twentieth birthday. She was eighteen. He had met her in Dresden, Ontario, which was also the same town that was home to Josiah
Henson, an author and abolitionist believed to be the model for the fic-
tional fugitive slave George Harris in Harriet Beecher Stowe's *Uncle Tom's
Cabin*. Dresden is considered one of the last stops of the Underground
Railroad. Sometime after their meeting—it's unclear how long—Binga

wrote Frances a letter asking her to marry him.[3] She later kept his letters tucked away in a trunk.

Binga's young wife was an attractive woman with broad cheekbones and a delicate smile. Frances was the daughter of Josiah Scott, shown in a family photo with a handlebar mustache and straight, businesslike posture.[4] Josiah was a plasterer and carpenter in Canada.[5]

When Jesse and Frances got married, Frances was already pregnant. Their son, Bethune, was born on July 16, 1885,[6] in the Binga Flats where the young couple lived.[7]

An article in *The Crisis* written later by a top Binga aide says Jesse Binga left Detroit for travels to the West in 1885,[8] and Binga later said the same thing in sworn testimony,[9] but the full story is a bit more complicated.

Jesse, who was working as a barber, and Frances lived in Detroit before moving to St. Paul, Minnesota. His mother and father, William and Adelphia, would later follow. William Binga was then in his seventies, and barbering wasn't what it was years back. By the 1890s white immigrants had flooded the ranks of barbers, and discrimination against black barbers intensified. In 1870 more than half of Detroit's barbers were black, but by 1890 that number had dropped to 24 percent.[10] The money didn't flow as fast, and barbering was becoming less of a sure thing. Still, William would stick with his razor and scissors when he got to St. Paul.

Unlike Detroit, the various Binga addresses in St. Paul were outside the small but concentrated black areas of the city. While there is not much to go on for Jesse Binga's years in St. Paul, there are some hints.

"Jesse G. Binga" is listed as a "col'd [colored] barber" living at 501 Bradley in the St. Paul city directory for 1887–1888.[11] But he also worked as a Pullman porter based out of Chicago in 1887.[12] He does not appear in the St. Paul directories after 1888. His father, also listed as a colored barber, is shown living at 878 Park Avenue in the city directory for 1889–1890 and at 266 State for 1890–1891. William died in August 1890.

A year later, Binga's mother, "Adelpa," is listed as a widow living at 266 State and working as a "medicine mnfr." (medicine manufacturer) in the 1892–1893 city directory. The Indiana Avenue home mentioned in the *St. Paul Daily Globe* story recounted in chapter 3 may have belonged to a relative. Her next appearance, in the 1893 directory, as "Mrs. Adelpha Binga," lists her as having "moved to Detroit, Mich." She is never referred to as "colored."

Adding to the mystique of Adelphia is a set of newspaper stories that explains why she moved back to Michigan. Apparently while still in St.

Paul, Adelphia "entered a railroad office to make inquiries about her son, who was running between St. Paul and Butte, Mont. There she met a man of her acquaintance and the conversation drifted to her brother's imprisonment,"[13] according to a July 23, 1896, story in the *Detroit Free Press*.

A brother is a twist to the Adelphia story with little more to explain it than the newspaper story, about John H. Thomas. Thomas was serving a life sentence for the April 28, 1875, murder of his wife, Elizabeth Thomas, and his stepdaughter Hattie Fisher in Detroit. Adelphia apparently thought Thomas had died, and after hearing he was still alive, she immediately went to Jackson, Michigan, where Thomas was imprisoned, to work on a pardon for the eighty-one-year-old man.

"Mrs. Binga who herself is quite old, but as active and vigorous of mind as many women thirty years younger, resolved to devote the remainder of her days to the relief of her brother—to securing his pardon or to witness his death, or to die herself. With that object in view she took up her residence in Jackson," the July 23 newspaper story reported.[14]

Thomas, described as a "quadroon,"[15] had insisted he was innocent and said he had an alibi that was never allowed in court. Thomas said he worked at William Binga's barbershop on Cadillac Square the day of the murder and had lunch and a drink with a man named White. He twice went home—the scene of the murder—and said he found the doors locked and thought his wife had left on errands. On the second try, he broke in and found "the horribly mutilated bodies of his wife and step-daughter on their beds."[16]

Thomas said if he could have called White, William Binga, and other witnesses to the stand, he would have been cleared. Those other witnesses, according to the *Detroit Free Press* account, would have said Thomas was drunk the night before the murder and was put in a lounge above the barbershop with the door locked and was found there the next day at 5:00 A.M. still "very stupid from the drink."[17]

But a string of witnesses speaking against Thomas in a July 24, 1896, *Detroit Free Press* story said Adelphia "is actuated by motives no reasonable person would for a moment countenance."[18] Those witnesses said Thomas was quarrelsome, "with a vicious temper," and he "unmercifully whipped" his wife and made advances on his stepdaughter. They also said that if Thomas were pardoned, he would seek vengeance and kill them for their testimony against him. One of the witnesses even said she unwittingly loaned Thomas the ax "that did the bloody deed."[19]

Thomas lost his bid for a pardon. Adelphia died on December 23, 1897, in Saginaw, Michigan.

Thomas's murder trial was front-page news in May 1875, when Jesse was ten years old. The family had to have been mortified by the intensity of the proceedings. Mobs gathered outside the courthouse and near the jail, and "a crowd of perhaps 400 colored persons, a large majority of whom were women," called for the lynching of Thomas.[20] Thomas was defiant upon his conviction and said he would outlive some of the witnesses against him and "dance on some of their graves yet."[21]

The murder scandal, however, didn't prompt the Binga family to leave Detroit. That didn't happen for twelve more years, when there were other reasons to move.

By 1887, William Binga was seventy-four years old, and standing all day had to be increasingly taxing. While barbering had been one of the surer paths to wealth in the African American community, by the end of the nineteenth century it had grown more complicated, particularly in Detroit.

Cutting hair was a personal service, requiring personal contact, touching. In the years after the Civil War, whites increasingly didn't want a shave from a black man or with a razor that had been used on a black man's chin. By the late 1880s white immigrants were setting up shop, and the racial line in barbering grew more extreme. "White Only" barbershops edged out longtime black barbershops,[22] and William Binga's business had to have suffered.

Adelphia told a more breathless story. She said the Bingas left town because "the doctors were going to have me run out of Detroit." In the February 10, 1889, interview with a *St. Paul Daily Globe* reporter, she explained, "Yes, they were afraid of me. I cured people when they utterly failed. . . . No disease is so insidious, no malady so remote, that it can not be reached by this panacea"[23]—namely, her Balm of Gilead.

If that led the Bingas to leave Detroit, Jesse's exit from St. Paul is still puzzling. One of Jesse's sisters lived in St. Paul, and then his parents. Why Jesse left his wife, his parents, and his family remains unexplained, except by Frances.

Her side of the story was set out in court papers when she filed for divorce in Chicago on June 5, 1901. She claimed in that filing that Jesse Binga "willfully deserted and absented himself" from her in November 1888 even though she "always conducted herself toward her said husband as a true, kind and indulgent wife." And, she continued, "Jesse C. Binga is a man of low and vicious habits, and a person wholly unfit to be entrusted with the care, custody and education of children"[24]—specifically, their son, Bethune.

Despite being raised in a close family and seemingly earning a decent income, something wasn't right with his marriage in St. Paul, and one day, Jesse decided to go.

The divorce proceedings were ex parte and pleaded with perhaps inflated language to ensure victory, although the phrase "low and vicious habits" was common in pleadings of the time. Frances told her side of the story when she testified, according to court documents, on September 21, 1901 (which may have been a misprint since that date was a Saturday). Frances testified before Chancery Judge Richard S. Tuthill, who in 1899 became a part of Chicago history when he became the first juvenile court judge in Cook County and the nation.[25] Frances Binga's attorney S. H. Trude conducted the direct examination.[26] It was short and to the point, resulting in just a few pages of court transcript.

Q: How long did you live with the defendant in St. Paul, Minnesota?
A: About two years.
Q: What happened then?
A: Then he went and left me.
Q: Did he leave you or did you leave him?
A: No sir, he went to Montana.

Frances said she received no support from her husband, and she learned that her marriage was over in a blunt letter from him.

Q: What did he say in that letter about coming back?
A: He said he never would come back again to me, that he never intended to live with me again.

Frances went on to testify that Jesse Binga was a barber when they got married and now he was a porter living in Boston—although there are no Pullman records indicating that. She said she didn't see Jesse for almost all of the nine years she lived in Chicago and didn't see him for the two years before that when she still lived in St. Paul. She also testified that her son, Bethune, was living in Canada under the care of her mother. Frances was "working in service," according to Alice Brackin, another witness. Brackin owned the house where Frances often stayed.

As for Frances's last contact with Jesse:

A: Oh, I haven't seen him for a year or more now.
Q: How did you come to see him then?

A: Just happened to pass him on the street.
Q: Did he speak to you?
A: No sir.

Frances was given custody of Bethune, who was then living in Canada with his grandparents, when the divorce was finalized on September 26, 1901. Twenty-five days after the divorce decree, Frances married J. Oscar Davis and continued to live in Chicago.[27]

Two things were clear about the breakup: it was bitter, and Frances and Jesse had each moved on, Frances to a new marriage and a new life, and Jesse to yet another career change—one that would stick. Jesse's new calling was in the business of real estate, and his choices and actions would soon help shape the South Side of Chicago for decades to come.

CHAPTER 7

8

Vernon Avenue

ON AUGUST 19, 1900, A FRONT-PAGE HEADLINE OF THE CHICAGO *Daily Inter Ocean* called it a story of "Woe on Vernon Avenue." Described as a possible "nervous prostration epidemic,"[1] it took place less than a mile from Jesse Binga's rented room, and while he wasn't directly connected to it, stories like this would define Binga and his career for the next two decades. This was one of the first Chicago stories about "blockbusting." Ultimately, it was a story about blame, and Binga would be blamed more than any other person for later causing "problems" similar to what happened on Vernon Avenue.

And, in years to come, he would one day live on the same block involved in that late summer story.

It began when a "colored man" went knocking door-to-door on the "select" and "exclusive" all-white block of 3300 Vernon Avenue, about five blocks east of Binga's place. The man rang several doorbells, introduced himself as the agent for the owner of 3342 Vernon, and offered to sell the home for $8,000. The house had been vacant for more than a year, and the price wasn't out of line for a home on this street lined with shade trees, nicely trimmed lawns, and houses occupied by judges, a doctor, and some well-to-do businessmen. But there were no takers.

A couple of days later that same agent drove up in a horse-drawn, four-wheeled, enclosed carriage with four "colored persons" sitting inside. He rang the doorbells of the next-door neighbors of 3342 Vernon and asked if anyone had the keys to the building. Then he fished around in the pockets of his plaid trousers and said he had the key after all. He then let himself and his companions into the solid, pressed stone building with two stories and a basement.

Shortly after that the agent led a group of potential "colored" renters up and down the street as if they were in a parade.[2] He had them make a showy walk with arms swinging wildly and exaggerated motions, periodically stopping to stare into the homes' windows as white residents stared out from behind lace curtains.

Eventually rooms were cut up to make more apartments, paper hangers came in, repairs were made, a back stairway was built, and furniture was moved in, including red plush lounges, carpets with bright pink roses, and iron bedsteads.[3] Then several black families moved in, some spending their days camped in chairs on the front porch. What seemed to rile neighbors the most was the black man in the basement who every day would clank out of his apartment wearing a sandwich board with bright red letters that read, "SAVE YOUR CASH BY WEARING BLANK'S NEVER-RIP PANTS."

The neighbors were horrified.

"How will it look when we have afternoon teas for that sandwich man to appear with his dreadful sign?" a young woman told a reporter from the *Inter Ocean*, who identified her as a "debutante of last season."[4]

Chicago would come to call this "blockbusting"—or, more to the point, "panic peddling"—a play on the fears of whites so real estate agents could get white people to sell at a low price and then a profit could be made later by charging a higher selling price or a higher rental to blacks.

The white residents of Vernon Avenue did not move off the block right away, but eventually they would. Blockbusting was a new thing for Chicago as it developed over a couple of years when the black population grew beyond the limits of what came to be known as the "Black Belt." As more blacks came up from the South, many whites and established blacks viewed these new arrivals as low-class, uneducated, and rude. Certainly, many native-born whites discriminated against some white European immigrants as well, attacking them for also being uneducated, rude, and in many cases unable to speak English. But there was a qualitative difference in the discrimination of blacks.

Many native-born Chicagoans, and white immigrants too, saw these black newcomers, and blacks in general, as the lowest class, the bottom rung. Some white immigrants moving into apartments and houses of the South Side were convinced that black neighbors were a clear sign of blight and depreciation and would cause home values to plummet. And many just flat out didn't like black people. It didn't matter if they were rich or educated. The lesson on the South Side was that even a new black neighbor with money and education could cause a panic—as Jesse Binga (and his wealthy black friends) would eventually see when whites on his block soon fled. In Chicago, it seemed, all ethnic groups could work hard, make money, and move up—all except African Americans.

The language of neighborhoods facing racial change quickly became the language of war. It was called a "colored invasion" in the *Inter Ocean* story about Vernon Avenue. The language characterized racial change in home ownership in terms of battles and survival. How long until a block would "fall?" How long could a block "hold out"? When would the whole neighborhood be "lost"?[5] Chicago was beginning to see a new set of rules, racial rules of the South Side. By 1900 a thin line of land had formed the rough outline of a segregated black neighborhood that would come to be called the Black Belt. Early on, it roughly ran from Twenty-Second Street south to Thirty-First Street along State Street[6] and was only a few blocks wide, from Wentworth to Wabash Avenues. Slowly it would lengthen and expand, and eventually resistance to this expansion would turn bloody.

On the edges of this segregated and isolated enclave, the borders were constantly tested. When blacks moved in, whites moved out. In some cases panic peddlers would come in to start the "panic," then real estate agents would buy low from whites and rent high to blacks. The new tenants would bring in more newly arrived family members from the South to help pay the rent, which caused more wear and tear on the property that was often already decades old. Often the landlords would not spend money to repair the apartments, and some of the new tenants were unfamiliar with some of the conveniences in the North and didn't know how to use them or fix them. This was supply and demand served Chicago style, with a dash of hysteria and a healthy dose of profit.

Jesse Binga understood this as well as anyone. While he wouldn't use the tactics of Vernon Avenue,[7] he would soon profit from the fear—all it took was one black family to move in and whites began to worry they would lose the biggest investment of their lives and it was time to get out while prices were holding. For Binga, and other real estate agents, black and white, there was a profit to be made from racial enmity. Selling prices plummeted with panic and fear, and purchase prices soared with the demand from blacks, who couldn't freely move about the larger marketplace. Binga pocketed plenty from the rising rents and house prices. Yet he was also expanding the housing inventory for blacks. Binga was ambitious, and he exploited the conditions he found and which he soon would help create.

Eventually the block of Thirty-Third Street and Vernon Avenue "fell," but not to cut-up and crowded apartments, although that would come too. By 1908, the stretch of Vernon Avenue from Thirty-Third to Thirty-Sixth Streets was considered one of the most beautiful of streets where "Negroes" owned homes.[8]

The street was fifty feet wide, nicely paved, and lined with well-built houses. Black businessmen and professionals now owned these homes. The houses on this tree-lined street with manicured lawns went for $3,500 to $14,000.[9]

One of the first men of wealth to buy a house on the 3300 block of Vernon Avenue was one of the city's biggest policy kings. In 1901 John "Mushmouth" Johnson bought 3324 Vernon Avenue, just a couple doors down from the subdivided house with the sandwich board man.[10]

In a few more years, Jesse Binga would live on that same block, on the same side of the street, a couple of doors down from the same house that caused a panic on Vernon Avenue.

WHILE CHICAGO'S BLACK POPULATION HAD GROWN TO 30,000 BY 1900, IT was still just a tiny dot in a city of 1.7 million. Nonetheless, it had doubled in the last decade, and it would continue to grow by 50 to 100 percent in each of the next three decades.[11] Binga didn't need a census to know this: he saw it on the streets, and he saw it was increasingly difficult to find rooms to rent. Like his mother thirty years earlier in Detroit, Jesse saw opportunity and decided to open a real estate business.

It was 1901 when Binga, who had been in and out of the city for a couple of years working for Pullman, finally decided he could make a permanent go of it in Chicago, about nine years after he had first arrived with a plan to be a street peddler. His foray into real estate began, probably as early as 1893 or 1894, when he rented out some bed space in his own rented room. It produced steady money. Years later he bought a house at 365 Thirty-Fourth Street, which he used to rent rooms to black boarders coming up from the South looking for jobs in the stockyards and other Chicago industries on the South Side.[12] He rented to single men by the week, which was how they were paid at their jobs.[13] Landlords showed up on payday to collect.

"I did considerable work with the Stockyards people," Binga later said, "in furnishing help and housing them when the colored people come up from the South, with Armour, and in fact, all of the people over there, the people came here from the South and worked in the Stockyards during the summer months and they would go back, and I had pretty much all of that business from them."[14]

As his business increased, Binga eventually needed an office to keep his books straight and his operation running smoothly. Since he was plowing money back into new leases to turn into rentals for himself, he didn't have a lot of ready cash. Nonetheless, in 1902, he saw a vacant office in a building close to where he lived on Thirty-Fourth Street and pounced on it, even though he had only a few bucks in his pocket.[15] He put together $5.00 for a down payment, half the monthly rent. He bought a desk for $1.50 and hauled in a couple of rickety chairs and a table. For heat, he had an old stove that rested on two legs and a brick.[16]

He didn't, however, have enough cash for an essential part of his enterprise: business cards. He needed cards to hand out to newcomers arriving in the Black Belt. Knowing he couldn't pay in full, he talked a printer into giving him twenty-five proofs as samples before he signed an order for one thousand cards. Binga strategically handed out those samples to generate some deals until he earned enough money to pay for the order.[17]

By 1902, the city directory had a new name in its listings: J. C. Binga & Co., 3331 State.

Every morning Jesse Binga got up early to walk the neighborhood, looking at buildings like a farmer sizing up crops for harvest. Each vacant apartment building and empty house represented a place to grow some money.

"He was hard working and he was thrifty," said Ripley Binga Mead Jr., Binga's first cousin once removed. "My mother used to say he'd walk down the street every morning looking for buildings to lease."[18]

Binga would rent a two-flat or a three-flat, fix it up, and sublet it with a boost in rent. He gladly paid the cost of repairs and decorating with his own grit and sweat.

"That was the point," Binga explained to a *Chicago Tribune* reporter years later. "I could do the repair work myself. I could do everything from digging a posthole to topping a chimney. I knew. Many a night I've worked all night on boilers and plumbing, and wiping joints and mending stairs, and hanging paper. I knew materials and I knew when work was right."[19]

Binga gobbled up apartment buildings and rooms whenever he could. If he couldn't rent it, he'd buy it. And if he couldn't rent or buy, he'd watch and wait until he could. Eventually, white landlords hired Binga to handle their building rentals for black tenants because Binga was efficient and, as Ripley's father, who worked for Binga, once said, the white landlords "were afraid of colored people."[20]

The rent money started as a trickle of singles and fives and soon became a river of tens and twenties. Binga sat in his office and inked in the numbers with care and precision.

Binga seemed to do it all: repairman, sales agent, bookkeeper. "He has been the man that never sleeps when business is at hand or can be got by going after it," said the *Chicago Defender* in a 1910 story that included a photo of a distinguished and handsome Binga with a thick mustache and perfect posture.[21]

As the number of Binga's tenants grew, he inevitably was approached for short-term loans for emergencies or sometimes just to make the rent or a trip south. It could all be done if some security was provided and the interest paid on time. Soon a full loan business emerged.[22] Binga became a kind of street banker, accepting rings, necklaces, watches, and any other personal property as collateral.[23] Eventually property mortgages filled that role.

AS HE EXPANDED HIS REAL ESTATE HOLDINGS, BINGA COULDN'T HELP BUT notice how being a black man in a predominantly white city created unexpected forms of opportunity. The lessons of Vernon Avenue played out for Binga in the Bates Building.

On May 21, 1905, Binga leased the Bates apartment building at 3635 and 3637 State Street and promptly relocated his real estate office there. He became the first black tenant. Interestingly, a black man previously owned the building, but he never lived in it. After Binga moved in, white tenants moved out over the next couple of years. Binga then moved black tenants in, raising the rent in the process.[24]

After the building "changed," as the shift from white to black occupancy was called, whites soon moved out of the apartments next door, and within a few years whites had vacated all the buildings within a radius of three to four blocks of the Bates building. The neighborhood indeed had "changed," and more often than not, the new rent collector was Jesse Binga.

While Binga wasn't using the wild street tactics of some of his white competitors—tactics similar to what happened on Vernon Avenue in 1900—he was taking advantage of the rent hikes that went with block-busting. Rent hikes for black tenants could be as high as 40 to 50 percent more than the previous white tenants had paid. Binga figured he put in long hours of work, he took the risks, and he made the sacrifices, so that justified charging any rents the market would bear.[25] Jesse Binga was a steely-eyed realist and a proudly unapologetic capitalist. And he wasn't alone.

One house painter and decorator, a black man with blue eyes, sandy hair, and a light complexion, was doing the same. Oscar DePriest leased and bought apartment buildings, fixed them up, jacked up the rent, and leased them out. DePriest became a trusted business associate of Binga's, and he eventually became the city's first black alderman and the country's first black congressman elected since Reconstruction.[26]

As another fellow black real estate agent, William D. Neighbors, said at the time, "If the Colored real estate dealers did not charge the rent required by the owner, there would be found plenty of white agents who would."[27]

"I started with Jesse Binga in about 1907," said Ripley Mead Sr., who worked for Binga up through the 1920s. "I was collecting rent. Of course you can't say this now, but he was one of the original blockbusters."[28]

Not exactly.

Blockbusting to whites meant something very different from what it meant to blacks. As one official of the Chicago Commission on Human Relations later said, selling a home to an African American family in an all-white neighborhood did not automatically make it blockbusting.[29] Blockbusting included panic-peddling acts designed to convince whites that if blacks moved into their neighborhood, on their block, or next door, properties would deteriorate and values would plummet.

It would take more than half a century before the Fair Housing Act of 1968 and other open occupancy laws addressed discrimination in housing sales. Those laws largely dealt with prohibiting people from refusing to sell or rent to people if they were black or in another protected class. And it prohibited charging blacks much more than whites for the same property.[30] Still, before and after those laws, some real estate agents sent out mass mailings alerting white homeowners that blacks had recently bought on their block and more were coming, so now was the time to sell—at reduced prices—before home values really dropped. Then those properties were resold to blacks at inflated prices. Ominous, sometimes anonymous, phone calls were also used, and sometimes blacks were hired to merely walk or drive through white neighborhoods. There were stories in the 1970s that blacks were hired to walk around in all-white neighborhoods with blasting boom boxes, or that real estate agents at Christmastime left ornaments on doorknobs with attached notes that warned it was time to get out, before it's too late.

Binga used none of those tactics. He simply moved black families in, and then whites moved out. This could hardly be called blockbusting, let alone panic peddling. He surely knew that white flight would often be the result, but if whites moved out, that was their business. Binga did, however, spike rents and push sale prices higher, in much the same way that many other real estate agents did.[31] For Binga, this was efficient business; it was the law of supply and demand; it was how you got ahead in America, it was the capitalist way. And despite being hemmed in by the borders of the Black Belt and surrounded by political maneuvers to stop them, blacks were showing signs of entrepreneurial might. They were cutting into the market previously controlled by whites.

A PERSISTENT AND OMINOUS THREAT HOVERED OVER MANY OF BINGA'S REAL estate deals. As more blacks moved into rooms and apartments or found jobs in or close to white neighborhoods, there was a growing white backlash. When blacks crossed picket lines in the stockyards strike of 1904 and the Teamsters' strike of 1905, beatings, knifings and shootings followed.

One Saturday in May 1905, whites attacked several black men who worked at Peabody Coal Company. The black men were knocked down, beaten, and kicked in the face.[32] One of the black men pulled a gun and shot an attacker who later died at a nearby hospital, where "he passed into the next world with all his imperfections resting on his head," the *Broad Ax* said. The next day "colored people were assaulted, spat on, dragged from street cars and beat into insensibility," yet police did little to stop it, the *Broad Ax* reported.[33]

White men used a rope to create a boundary line at Twenty-Seventh Street and Wentworth Avenue and attached signs painted with thick black letters proclaiming, "Negroes Not Allowed to Cross this Dead Line."[34] Wentworth Avenue became another unofficial borderline dividing blacks and whites, and many more such color lines followed.

At first it was about jobs. But housing soon became a larger flashpoint, and a more personal one.

Tensions continued to rise as whites living near the Black Belt accused blacks of wrecking neighborhood housing and black leadership responded. A November 23, 1907, article in the *Broad Ax* said, "It is the duty of Afro-American real estate agents, as well as it is the duty of the preachers to admonish the Colored people that they must keep their property up in first-class shape." And if they do, the reporter contended, "The whites will not then be in a position to set up the hue and cry, that wherever Colored people from the highest to the lowest live, they destroy the value of property."[35] But as time would show, no matter how wealthy or accomplished a black family would be, many whites began to panic at the sight of any blacks moving onto their block.

As a real estate broker and financier, Jesse Binga was at the center of the storm.

"First on the list of Afro-American real estate agents in this city is Jesse Binga, 3637 State Street,"[36] the *Broad Ax* article said. Blacks and whites both saw Binga as an agent of change.

By 1907, nearly a dozen black agents were in real estate that only years before was controlled completely by whites. In 1910, black real estate agents handled less than 5 percent of black business, but seven years later, blacks controlled 25 percent of that market.[37] Still, this was limited to just black business, not the broader city market.

Binga was among the biggest, if not the biggest, of the city's black real estate agents. He controlled three-flats, six-flats, houses, and a five-story building with twenty-four units. He had "four assistants, a lady stenographer and bookkeeper and he handles much property for some of the leading white citizens in Chicago," according to a November 23, 1907, article in the *Broad Ax*.[38]

AT ABOUT THIS TIME, BINGA SENT OUT AN INTRIGUING MESSAGE TO ANYONE who was asking: Jesse Binga was his own man. The name Binga stood by itself. He was once listed with a business associate named James Nelson in 1903, but that was over. Now he didn't want anyone thinking he got any help from anybody—whites, blacks, or otherwise. "Mr. Binga," as everyone now called him, had the following announcement printed in the *Broad Ax* on January 11, 1908: "In order to disabuse, the minds of those who may think otherwise, it may be proper to state that Jesse Binga, 3637 State Street, has no partners in any manner, shape or form associated with him in the real estate business, and that he is conducting the business on his own individual responsibility."[39]

Binga was considered aloof and arrogant. His talk was bold and self-assured, and he could stare a man down with silence. This attitude created enemies. He was demanding, and everyone knew that you don't talk foolishness with him. He didn't loan money for foolishness. He didn't have patience for people who squandered their paychecks at billiard parlors or at late-night clubs. "Save, save, save," he'd say.[40]

Binga could also come off as pompous and condescending.

"He had a peculiar manner of making those who entered into business dealings antagonistic to him before the deal was closed," Lucius C. Harper wrote in the *Chicago Defender* years later. "He seemed to get a great deal of joy out of this. He said to me on one occasion when I was present during such a transaction with a customer who had demonstrated a fit of anger over a loan: 'He'll pay me back; I made him fight for the money!' Then he laughed with joy and remarked rather boastfully: 'You know

Fig. 5. *Jesse Binga leased and later owned a stretch of 504 feet along State Street that became known as the "Binga Block" (4712–4752 State Street), with twenty-one stores and fifty-four flats* (upper right photo). *Jesse Binga appears in the lower left photo, standing to the right of Margaret Murray Washington (aka Mrs. Booker T. Washington); this photograph was taken when Mrs. Washington visited the Associated Business Club of Chicago in July 1924.* "THE BINGA BLOCK; A VISIT OF MRS. BOOKER T. WASHINGTON TO THE ASSOCIATED BUSINESS CLUB OF CHICAGO, JULY 10TH, 1924." SCHOMBURG CENTER FOR RESEARCH IN BLACK CULTURE, JEAN BLACKWELL HUTSON RESEARCH AND REFERENCE DIVISION, NEW YORK PUBLIC LIBRARY. FROM THE NEW YORK PUBLIC LIBRARY DIGITAL COLLECTIONS: HTTP://DIGITALCOLLECTIONS.NYPL.ORG/ITEMS/510D47DE-518F-A3D9 -E040-E00A18064A99.

Jesse Binga knows how to deal with Negroes.' He always spoke of himself in the third person. He seemed to have taken special delight in pronouncing his own name."[41]

Binga was business. He thought well of himself, but "Mr. Binga" was a button-down type. He didn't swear and didn't smoke except for an occasional Cuban cigar. And he rarely, if ever, drank alcohol.[42]

Everybody knew his word was solid, and "whenever he is presented with a bill he will write you a check on the First National Bank so quick that it will make your head swim," the 1907 *Broad Ax* article reported.[43]

BY 1910, BINGA WAS MAKING BIGGER DEALS, OFTEN WITH WEALTHY WHITE businessmen, such as Henry Botsford, president of the Chicago Packing Company. He made a $240,000 deal with Botsford for a thirty-year lease of 4712–4752 State Street with its twenty-one stores and fifty-four flats. The land ran for 504 feet along State Street and was 100 feet in depth.[44]

At the time of the deal, occupancy on the State Street block was all white, but as "a considerable part of the city has gone over to the occupancy of Colored people, and is destined to eventually go to that use, the completion of the occupancy of the flats may change," Binga told the *Broad Ax* in 1910.[45] For years to come, this row of buildings would now be called simply the "Binga Block" (fig 5).

Jesse Binga was expanding the Black Belt in a straight line moving block by block southward, but he was finding it much tougher to expand beyond a couple of blocks eastward or westward. His name was now becoming symbolic of racial progress and even more so of racial change.

In the Black Belt, everybody grew to trust anything connected to the name "Binga"; it became synonymous with reliability and racial uplift. And since one of Jesse Binga's favorite mantras was "Save, save, save," where better to do so than in a place called the Binga Bank? That would come next.

9

The Binga Bank

BY 1909, JESSE BINGA CONTROLLED ENOUGH HOUSING FOR A SMALL CITY. More than two thousand people had Binga for a landlord.[1] And he wasn't done. As more blacks came to Chicago, more business came to Binga.

He now had valuable and strategic friendships with Julius Taylor, editor and publisher of the *Broad Ax*, and Robert Abbott, editor and publisher of the *Chicago Defender*. These two black newspaper editors would provide a megaphone for Binga's success.

Taylor, eccentric and outspoken, was born into slavery in Virginia in 1853 and started his paper, oddly enough, in Salt Lake City, Utah, before moving to Chicago in 1899.[2] Abbott, an ambitious and racially sensitive newspaperman, was born to former slaves on St. Simons Island in Georgia in 1870.[3] Abbott founded the *Chicago Defender* in 1905, and it became the most widely circulated black newspaper in the country. Both of these papers gave Binga plenty of coverage as a steady stream of black migrants from the South came to the city. These newspapers virtually endorsed Binga's real estate business. While Binga also placed some of his real estate ads in the *Chicago Tribune* and the *Inter Ocean*, he used the *Broad Ax* and the *Defender* far more.

Almost every day there was an advertisement in the *Broad Ax* for Jesse Binga Real Estate and Loans: "Leases negotiated, exchanges made, property managed." His offerings included brick and frame two-flats, freestanding single-family homes, and rooming houses. Three properties in the 3700 block of LaSalle Street were offered in August 1908. Or for $9,000 a buyer could have two nine-room stone-front residences at 3444–3445 Wabash Avenue—yet deals could be made: "will sell separate. Make terms," the ad read.[4]

Jesse Binga was always willing to deal. And if his name wasn't in an ad, there was enthusiastic newspaper coverage of him traveling with Margaret Murray Washington (or, as the newspapers of the time called her, Mrs. Booker T. Washington) to speak to the boys and girls at the Amanda Smith Home in south suburban Harvey or glowing reports of how he leased a whole block of stores and buildings for housing at Forty-Seventh and State Streets.[5]

Jesse Binga was now an unavoidable presence in the Black Belt. He was a man to see for an apartment, house, or storefront. He was a man who could be trusted. Some people thought he had a cold, businesslike manner, but he was known to keep his word. It was only natural that his next step was to become a banker. He opened the Binga Bank in 1908.

IT WASN'T DIFFICULT TO OPEN A PRIVATE BANK IN 1908. THERE WERE HUNdreds of them in Illinois.

"You see, in those days if you wanted to open a bank, you just put (a) bank (sign) in the front window and you were a bank," said Binga relative Ripley Binga Mead Jr., whose mother and father worked for Binga for several decades.[6]

Private banks offered an unregulated banking operation with little capitalization. In 1909, the average capitalization for private banks in midwestern states was about $11,000.[7] Brokers like Binga used them as an extension of their other businesses—in Binga's case, his real estate business. By 1909 there were at least 420 private banks in Illinois,[8] but the state counts weren't very reliable since many of the banks operated in their own unregulated world. They weren't required to give annual or monthly reports or to be examined by the state.[9] (The state legislature wouldn't regulate these private banks until 1917, when state law would require private banks to either get a state or national charter by 1921 or be dissolved.[10]) With this kind of loose operation, Binga got into some bad habits that would haunt him years later. But for the time, it was perfect.

Binga had long eyed a vacant lot at the southeast corner of Thirty-Sixth Place and State Street as an ideal spot for his bank, taking the same strategic care with which he had scouted out Twelfth Street and Michigan Avenue for his street peddler's cart back in 1892. He convinced the lot's owner to erect a three-story building to Binga's specifications by promising to make a long-term lease.[11] This new building had teller cages and safety deposit vaults, and in 1908 it became the Binga Bank, the first black-owned bank in Chicago. It was also conveniently next door to his business offices in the Bates apartment building at 3637 South State Street.

Fig. 6. *The first Binga Bank (*lower building at left*) stood at the corner of Thirty-Sixth Place and State Street. Opened in 1908, it stood next to the taller Bates apartment building (right), at 3635 and 3637 State Street, an early Binga management deal (1905) that held his business offices and was painted with advertising for the adjacent bank.* BROAD AX, DECEMBER 25, 1909.

Binga's name was everywhere (see fig. 6). It was big and bold on the front and side windows of his new building, and along the top were three big painted words: "JESSE BINGA BANKER." Next door, above the roofline of his bank and on the brick exterior of the taller neighboring Bates Building, there was an enormous painted circle some thirty feet in diameter rimmed with dollar signs. In the center of the circle were the words "BEGIN WITH ONE DOLLAR." To the right of the circle, in white letters ten feet tall, were the words "JESSE BINGA BANKER." And lest anyone forget, above his bank name was a slightly smaller painted sign: "JESSE BINGA—REAL ESTATE—RENTING."[12] Later the circle on the Bates Building would contain a ten-foot-tall letter *B*, identical to the one on the front of the bank's passbooks.[13]

Binga put his name on everything he owned. He was proud of it. As the *Chicago Defender* editor and columnist Lucius C. Harper said years later, Binga "seemed to have taken special delight in pronouncing his own name."[14]

Binga was now offering something never before seen in the Black Belt—a black-owned neighborhood bank.

THE FIRST U.S. BANK DESIGNED FOR AFRICAN AMERICAN DEPOSITORS WAS RUN by white men, and not well. The Freedman's Bank, formed with the trusted signature of Abraham Lincoln in 1865, grew out of a need to help black soldiers in the Union Army place their salary in a secure place, while "safeguarding the interests of the nation's 'wards.' "[15] Eventually it included nonmilitary free blacks as depositors "to instill in the minds of the untutored Africans lessons of sobriety, wisdom and economy, and to show how to rise in the world," said Frederick Douglass. "The history of civilization shows that no people can rise to a high degree of mental or moral excellence without wealth."[16]

The Freedman's Bank was supposed to be a kind of petri dish for entrepreneurs, but as deposits grew, so did the reckless misconduct and self-dealing of its white managers. By 1873 there was a run on the bank, and by 1874 it had failed.[17]

Twenty-eight black-owned and -run U.S. banks were formed from 1899 to 1905, usually growing out of the expansion of black "fraternal insurance and burial societies that took place in the first twenty years of the post-Civil War period."[18]

Abram L. Harris, a grandson of slaves who became a nationally recognized economist, explained that the growth of these societies aimed toward achieving the "ideal of 'respectable' American citizenship that began to dominate Negro life after the Civil War."[19] It was a push toward independence and self-reliance. That, in turn, implied that property and wealth could bring freedom.

Fraternal burial societies and churches were behind the organization of most of these early "Negro banks."[20] In some ways, burial societies were the first black banks in the United States.

Before the Civil War, many enslaved people feared dying unremembered in unmarked graves. When an enslaved person died, a piece of his or her clothing, such as a sock or a hat, was often tacked to the door of the family quarters as a memorial.[21] To ensure proper burials, "pennies were laid aside in a sort of burial society, whose records were kept by a slave 'treasurer,'" according to mid-twentieth-century black journalist and author Roi Ottley. If enslaved people couldn't control their everyday lives, at least they could manage some control in death. As a consequence, well after emancipation, blacks often carried some form of burial insurance because, as one undertaker said, "they don't want to be thrown away."[22]

The first bank founded and run by blacks was the Savings Bank of the Grand Fountain United Order of True Reformers in Richmond, Virginia.[23] It was founded in March 1888 by William Washington Browne, a minister who had been enslaved and then later served as a Union soldier. The Capital Savings Bank of Washington, D.C., opened later that year.

In 1903, Maggie L. Walker, the top officer in the Independent Order of St. Luke, a benevolent burial society, became the first American woman to found a bank when she opened St. Luke's Penny Savings Bank.[24] Walker, the daughter of an African American laundress and an Irish American journalist who were not legally allowed to marry because of racial differences, was a lifelong champion of equal rights and would go on to lead the order for another thirty years until her death.[25] St. Luke's Penny Savings Bank had a church connection, with ministers sitting on the board. Similarly, the Alabama Penny Savings Bank (established in 1890) and the Nickel Savings Bank of Richmond, Virginia (opened in 1896) had both been founded by preachers.[26]

Binga's bank was different: he was Roman Catholic, and he started his bank as a private business entrepreneur rather than part of a benevolent society. In fact, he had a difficult time in his bank's early years getting the deposits of the "colored churches," according to the *Chicago Defender*.[27]

WITH HIS BANK IN PLACE IN 1908, JESSE BINGA MOVED HIS ENTIRE OPERATION into the new building. On the outside, Binga's bank looked more like a storefront than a house of finance. Yet on the inside, it was so much more. He offered a one-stop shop for finding a place to live, a way to pay for it, and a safe place to deposit savings and earn interest. Binga also offered fire insurance.

Here, Black Belt residents could open a savings account with as little as one dollar. A checking account required a minimum deposit of one hundred dollars, however. Savings accounts earned 3 percent per annum semiannually, payable on the first days of January and July. And if you needed something secretly and safely tucked away, fireproof safety deposit boxes were offered for three dollars a year.[28]

Like Frederick Douglass before him, Jesse Binga believed that wealth was the real key to personal freedom in America. He saw property owner-ship as a critical foundation of that wealth. For Binga, capitalism was the engine of success, and personal ambition was its steam.

Binga preached a self-help philosophy, and he argued that a black-owned and black-run business should always be in the mix. In a 1911 *Chicago Defender* advertisement, Binga challenged readers to consider a choice: make deposits in (white) downtown banks or with him. He asked, "Would you not give a part of your patronage to a man of your own race?"[29]

This was a golden rule of capitalism in the Black Belt: shop at black-owned businesses, patronize a black-run bank, bring your business to your neighborhood. Binga was at the front of that push, with many black business owners behind him.

Abbott's *Chicago Defender* made it clear that when it came to business, race should be a major consideration. Even while praising the opening of a new bank, Lincoln State Savings Bank, in the Black Belt, the subhead on the *Defender* article also made it clear who owned it—or rather, who didn't: "Not a Colored Institution." The article went on to say, "There is only one colored bank in Chicago, that of Mr. Jesse Binga."[30]

Business for Binga was good. Before the leases on the bank and the Bates Building expired, Binga bought both buildings outright.[31] The House of Binga was rising.

10

Dream Book

ONE OF JESSE BINGA'S FAVORITE SAYINGS WAS "SAVE, SAVE, SAVE," AND ANOTHER was "give, give, give."[1] Binga was hardworking and deeply religious; he followed his own advice, gave generously to charities, and rarely, if ever, drank. But he was a man of contradiction. He always warned against the sporting life, gambling, and the evils of the red-light district,[2] yet he was no stranger to them.

It was not unusual for Binga to spend a night at the fabled Pekin Theatre, with its smoky saloon and raucous gambling operation run by his friend Robert T. Motts.[3] Several gambling bosses were in his social and business circles, and his bank was deeply connected to that world. But he would soon have an even closer tie to the spoils of policy, booze, and underworld misadventure. It started with Chicago's biggest turn-of-the-century "policy king."

It's unclear what, if any, personal relationship Jesse Binga had with John V. "Mushmouth" Johnson, but it's undeniable that Mushmouth had a profound effect on Binga's life. Binga's ties to Mushmouth arose through a series of events that involved a scandal over the skin color of Mushmouth's beautiful cousin Cecelia, Mushmouth's death, and an inheritance of more than $200,000.

JOHN V. JOHNSON WAS A TURN-OF-THE-CENTURY SUCCESS STORY WRITTEN IN Chicago's underworld. He was a pioneer of "policy," an enormously popular betting game that survived in various forms in Chicago for close to a century before it transmogrified into what is now the Illinois State Lottery.

The origins of policy are murky. It has been given Chinese, Spanish, and Cuban roots, and some accounts say it dates back to sixteenth-century Italy. It was played for decades across the United States, from Harlem to Chicago, and it's been said that Phineas Taylor Barnum, of Barnum and Bailey Circus fame, once ran a policy wheel.[4]

The game's simplicity was part of its appeal. Policy, which got its name as a kind of low-end insurance policy, was basically just a lottery. The most popular bet was to pick three numbers called a "gig." A customer picked the three numbers and hoped they would be drawn from a rotating "wheel" or barrel that contained seventy-eight small rubber capsules, each marked with a number from 1 to 78. A blindfolded "policy writer" pulled twelve capsules from the wheel for what was called a "leg." To win, all three of the bettor's numbers had to be included in one leg. The odds against the bettor were 346 to 1. Variations of the game could make the odds soar, sometimes as high as 1,000 to 1 or worse.[5]

Betting was influenced by folklore and superstition. As the business evolved, policy writers would eventually sell tickets using a "Dream Book," a small booklet that translated a customer's dreams into numbers. It's unclear what mysterious alchemy went into the author's interpretations, but the Dream Book was a great marketing tool. Customers who were willing to bet amounts ranging from pennies to dollars would simply tell the policy writer of their previous night's dreams, and the policy writer would pull out the Dream Book to find the corresponding gig. For example, if a customer dreamed of a white policeman the night before, that customer was given the numbers 28-35-67. If the dream included a coffin, then the Dream Book said it was a sign that the customer would soon be married and own a house, and so the gig should be 9-49-50.[6] And on it went.

The Dream Book was filled with gigs matched to dreams of death, birth, marriage, and work. It was part of a small industry surrounding the policy racket. A player could buy a Dream Book, lucky number candles, or jinx-removing incense. Bets were made at South Side policy stations found in basements, barbershops, beauty parlors, restaurants, and grocery stores. Hundreds of people earned their living in the business—"walking writers," the salesmen, could earn up to 25 percent on all bets they placed for customers.[7] Typically, there were three daily drawings: morning, afternoon, and midnight. The "book" was the drawing for one of those sessions. The books had names, including "Wall Street," "Rio Grande," "Red Devil," "Green Dragon," and "Black Gold." Policy kings acted like underground banks, using some of their street cash to invest in legitimate businesses.[8]

For a policy customer, the odds were tough and the payoff rare. It was a five-cent daydream that provided a glimmer of hope and a moment of entertainment. A nickel bet payoff could mean five dollars, a dime could get you ten bucks.

Mushmouth liked the house odds. For the owner of a wheel, it was close to a sure thing.

BORN IN ST. LOUIS IN 1854, JOHN V. JOHNSON CAME TO CHICAGO WITH HIS parents when he was three years old,[9] which was shortly after the city got its first gas streetlights and telegraph wires.[10] In the 1870s, he worked as a waiter at the Palmer House, and in the 1880s, he was a porter in a white gambling house. He was smart and ambitious and soon rose to be a floor man and then partner.[11]

In 1892, around the time Jesse Binga arrived in Chicago, the city directory listed Johnson as a bartender; in 1893 Johnson was listed as a saloon owner at 464 State Street, which was part of a vice strip of bordellos and bars known as "Whisky Row" or "Satan's Mile." Johnson's Emporium Saloon, known as "464," was the center of his lucrative operation.[12] And he wasn't shy: painted on his front windows in foot-high letters were the name "John Johnson" and the number "464."[13]

Armed with what he learned in the gambling house, Johnson added his own take. For games in his saloon, the house never played. Instead, he pulled a small take from each hand of cards and each craps game. Johnson's rule was simple and safe: "Any two men with money and a gambling disposition can fight it out at 464 and there'll be a gamekeeper on the spot to collect the rake-off." [14]

In the late 1890s, Johnson partnered with a white man named Patsy King and an Asian man called King Foo, who ran a gambling operation in the nearby small Chinese settlement on Clark Street between Van Buren and Harrison Streets a few blocks west of Johnson's saloon. The three of them shared the proceeds of a lucrative wheel in Chicago's notorious First Ward.[15]

Johnson, who was short, heavy, and built like a bowling ball (fig. 7), had little formal education, but he became so successful that downstate lawmakers soon tried to stop him. While considered by some people to be loud and uncouth, Johnson was a clear-eyed businessman who knew how to hang on to nickels and dimes wagered by the factory workers, railroad employees, porters, and waiters who patronized his saloon. He favored suits from Marshall Field's and gorgeous billiard tables outfitted with ivory balls.[16] The roots of his nickname "Mushmouth" are elusive; some accounts said it came from his creative and prolific profanity.[17]

Fig 7. *Policy king John V. "Mushmouth" Johnson (1854–1907).*

Mushmouth's customers were black, white, and Chinese, and his political connections were such that he once sold "protection" to more than "twenty Chinatown opium dens and gambling [operations] where Fan Tan and Bung Loo card games were played."[18]

Policy in Chicago had begun in about 1885 when a black man named Samuel "Policy Sam" Young ran a wheel near State and Madison Streets. He became known as the father of policy. Unlike Mushmouth, Sam gambled his money away.[19] Mushmouth never gambled and never drank. He was careful, shrewd, and cagey.

As Mushmouth told losers, "A man that gambles had better be without money anyway. I may put it to some good use. You wouldn't know how."[20]

Mushmouth outdistanced his competition, and an anti-policy law targeting him was passed in 1905.[21] That didn't stop him.

"I am fifty-three years of age and have lived in Chicago for fifty years," he said in 1907. "I guess I know the city pretty well and it knows me."[22]

MUSHMOUTH AND POLICY SAM WERE AT THE BEGINNING OF A SORT OF BLACK Belt mythology. As the mid-twentieth-century sociologists and authors St. Clair Drake and Horace Cayton wrote in *Black Metropolis: A Study of Negro Life in a Northern City*, "All the Negroes involved in the game became legendary figures who 'never let a man starve,' who were 'honest,' 'big hearted,' 'kind' gamblers."[23] In fact, Mushmouth and Sam were both big donors to charities ranging from homes for the elderly to fraternal lodges. They would often also make loans, but there was an unmistakable dangerous side—Mushmouth was once linked to the shooting of a man who testified against him.[24]

Politics and racial animosity funneled gambling, prostitution, and crime into or near the Black Belt from its beginning. Policy kings were the early capitalists of the Black Belt, self-made moneymen. Since discriminatory politics and exclusion from housing and jobs forced many blacks to live in the more available housing in or near the vice district, it was natural for entrepreneurial men like Johnson to find opportunity there.

Chicago reformers periodically sought to clean up the open vice that earlier thrived in the legendary Levee district, centered roughly between Eighteenth Street south to Twenty-Second Street from Wabash Avenue west to Clark Street just a couple blocks north of the nascent Black Belt. Eventually the sporting life merged into the city's evolving black community because it didn't draw as much white political pressure: politicians from white neighborhoods didn't seem to care as long as it wasn't in their neighborhoods. Because of the sheer proximity and the perpetual need for jobs, many blacks worked in taverns and brothels a few blocks from their homes. Sometimes, these seemed to be the only jobs available.

Early vice districts formed just south of the Loop, where Johnson's saloon flourished, before the turn of the twentieth century. These districts had such names as Whiskey Row, Little Cheyenne, and Satan's Mile, where Johnson did business. The Levee contained the Everleigh Club, 2131–2133 South Dearborn Street, the city's most legendary brothel, run by Ada and Minna Everleigh, two white entrepreneurial sisters from Omaha.[25] The area was run by two white, supremely corrupt First Ward aldermen: Michael "Hinky Dink" Kenna and "Bathhouse John" Coughlin.[26] Payoffs from brothels and gambling joints caused plenty of cops and aldermen to look the other way.

Reformers eventually pressured the city council to clean up red-light districts across the city, and in 1908 the council set up the Committee of Fifteen to help get it done. Landlords were pressured, undercover investigators were hired, and restrictive policies were enacted.[27] With a public fed up with sporting houses and the sporting life, the Levee was effectively closed down by 1912.[28] By 1917, Chicago reformers believed that prostitution had been "wiped out."[29] Actually, it just relocated.

Prostitution migrated south, so much so that in the early 1910s, there were only 10 vice establishments on the North Side and 38 on the West Side, yet there were 119 in the Black Belt, according to findings of the Committee of Fifteen.[30] By 1916, there were about 50 houses of prostitution on or near State Street alone, from Twenty-Seventh to Thirty-Ninth Streets.[31]

By the 1920s, the white hostesses of the Everleigh Club were replaced primarily by African American women.[32] By 1930, while black women "represented 3.5 percent of the population . . . they accounted for 69 percent of the total number of convicted prostitutes."[33]

Johnson himself didn't gamble, but he bet on sure things, such as both sides of an election. In mayoral races, Mushmouth would give $10,000 to Democrats and $10,000 to Republicans. He was always covered.[34] Johnson also made sure the palms of his First Ward aldermen, tiny "Hinky Dink" and his taller partner, "Bathhouse John"—poet and wearer of loud, yellow plaid suits—were greased with green. Mushmouth routinely cajoled his customers to vote for the strange pair.[35]

His extensive political connections paid off. He was never in serious trouble and was indicted only once: for running a gambling house.

Mushmouth also invested wisely. He bought a home at Fifty-Eighth Street and Wabash Avenue in a fashionable white neighborhood. He owned a three-story brick building near his State Street saloon, a couple frame and brick homes, apartment buildings, a few vacant lots, and a house on Vernon Avenue.[36]

Not everyone viewed men like Johnson as benevolent, "big hearted" moneymen. When Johnson nominated Colonel John R. Marshall (who later became a Binga Bank director) for county commissioner in 1902, the *Broad Ax*, run by Jesse Binga's friend Julius Taylor, attacked the colonel, saying that he "spends much of his time in the company of Mush-mouth, which proves that the majority of the Republican Afro-Americans are willing to permit gamblers and owners of gambling houses to select their leaders for them."[37]

Many of the "old settlers," aristocrats of the Black Belt, rejected sporting men like Johnson. Even when Mushmouth was giving to charity, he had to do it through his mother or his sister.[38]

SOME FRIENDS THOUGHT MUSHMOUTH'S LIFE BEGAN TO UNRAVEL WHEN reporters started snooping around his cousin Cecelia. Mushmouth was like a father to Cecelia, and he, along with his sister Eudora, doted on her.

She was born Cecelia Morrison in St. Louis, Missouri, in March 1885. Cecelia's father, Joseph Morrison, died six months before Cecelia was born, and the family was left impoverished. When Cecelia was a toddler, Eudora Johnson came to St. Louis and took little Cecelia back to Chicago to become part of the Johnson family. Eudora and Mushmouth lived with their mother, Ellen Johnson, the sister of Cecelia's father. Cecelia, known as "Cissy," soon came to refer to Eudora and Mushmouth as her sister and brother and eventually changed her last name to Johnson.[39]

Despite living on an "all-white" block, the Johnsons had no problems with neighbors, and her cousin Fenton Johnson recounted that Cecelia "played and visited" with the white children on her block and in her neighborhood. All along, it was more than obvious that the Johnsons were a black family.

Still, Fenton Johnson said few people probably knew that the pretty, light-skinned Cecelia was black, though she never tried to hide her race. She was popular in high school, cast in school plays, and a member of various clubs. Her popularity followed her to college, where she was elected president of Englewood House, an organization of girls who, like Cecelia, were alumnae of Englewood High School. Her good looks and kind demeanor were obviously attractive, and once she was asked to a dance by the white captain of the football team—she declined.

When Cecelia graduated from the University of Chicago in 1906 with honors in history, she was awarded a scholarship toward a master's degree. In the spring of 1907, she returned to campus.

Her troubles began when she invited a white college friend to her home at 5830 Wabash Avenue, not far from the University of Chicago. It was actually the home of Mushmouth Johnson, who was not her brother, as was widely reported, or her father. The home was a two-story brick building on the tree-lined avenue, and the Johnsons were the only black family on the block. It was a big, spacious house, and one of Cecelia's classmates described it as "magnificently furnished."

The friend walked through Cissy's house and happened upon a "collection of Negro photographs and the unmasking followed," according to the front-page story of the July 22, 1907, *Chicago Record-Herald*.[40]

As her cousin and fellow student at the University of Chicago, poet Fenton Johnson, later wrote, "Cecelia herself never referred to race. Nobody asked her what her race was and she had no occasion to broadcast the news."[41]

Yet suddenly her quiet student life at the University of Chicago was transformed into loud, scandalous news. Reporters weren't interested in Cecelia because of her good grades or her popularity on campus. No, it was her smooth, pale, "peaches and cream" complexion and her relationship to John "Mushmouth" Johnson that drew their attention.[42]

Cecelia, they claimed, used her complexion to be someone she was not: white. The reporters posed the question: How could she be white, living as a relative in the house of a notorious black policy king? Some wrote that she was Mushmouth's sister. Others suggested a closer relationship. Readers couldn't get enough.

The story of Cecelia Johnson "passing" for white soon spread to Philadelphia, New York, and then Europe. The stories had headlines like the subhead to the *Chicago Record-Herald*'s story: "Backed by Gambler, Brother's Coin, Smart Girl, Near White, Deceives University."[43]

Stories about "passing" were nothing new to the black community. From New Orleans to Nashville, there were plenty of stories of "octoroons" (people with one-eighth black ancestry), "mulattoes" (people of mixed race, often one black and one white parent), and light-skinned blacks "passing" as whites to escape the hardships or just the plain hassle of being black in America. To whites, "passing" was seen as a fraudulent masquerade. To some blacks, it could mean betrayal or shame.[44] Others understood it as a means of survival in a society that placed a higher value on whiter skin, from hiring practices to restaurant service. Newspaper stories and ads celebrated white beauty and culture while bombarding readers with denigrating caricatures of blacks, including mocking portrayals of black skin, hair, and lips. Even in black newspapers, advertisers pushed the "need" for blacks to lighten their skin or straighten their hair.

Sometimes "passing" happened accidentally; it could start as a way to get a job and turn into a lifestyle. Debates over skin color, tone, and hue were common in Chicago's Black Belt. Some light-skinned blacks "passed" to further their education or enhance employment. Sometimes light-skinned sons or daughters said good-bye to their mothers and fathers, never to be seen again.

Skin color was a part of the pecking order of black society. Light-skinned blacks in the early twentieth century even tended to be viewed as the more educated, aristocratic crowd.

Jesse Binga knew the distinctions as well as anyone. He hired two light-skinned black sisters from Ohio to work in his real estate office in 1907, and then they later became part of his bank staff. Jessie and Anna Cole could both "pass" for white. In fact, before joining Binga, Jessie Cole "passed" while working downtown as a typist for Dunn and Bradstreet. Most of Binga's employees were college educated and light-skinned. Some Binga critics said he preferred light-skinned employees, but Ripley Binga Mead Jr., the grandson of Binga's cousin and the son of Jessie Cole Mead, said Binga's bank employees were hired because of their education, not the shade of their skin.[45]

Black Belt newspapers advertised ointments that would bleach skin and tonics that would straighten hair. "Why Be Dark and Swarthy?" asked a 1911 advertisement for face bleach sold for a dollar a bottle at Rankin & White Drugs at Thirty-Sixth and State Streets,[46] down the block from the Binga Bank. For some African Americans, light skin, straight hair, and sharp features were an obsession.

Robert Abbott, one of Binga's closest friends and a future investor, was himself dark-skinned and, according to his biographer Roi Ottley, Abbott grew to hate the color black. He didn't wear black clothes and was rarely seen in public with a dark-skinned woman, "yet he was fiercely loyal to any man who was black as distinct from those who were brown or fair of complexion."[47] Abbott's feelings had a painful history. When he was in college at his beloved Hampton Institute, where Booker T. Washington was educated, Abbott was invited to the house of a light-skinned college classmate. The invitation was actually part of a cruel prank. When he arrived at the classmate's home, according to Ottley, the door opened and the classmate said, "Set outside, 'cause you're too black to come in here."[48] Abbott was humiliated. Similarly, he once called on a young woman and, as he waited at the door, he overheard the woman tell her mother that Abbott was too dark to date her.

Binga's own life was marked by constant grinding questions on the gradations of skin color. As described in earlier chapters, in the 1870 and 1880 census reports he was listed as "mulatto," yet in 1920, he was listed as "black." The birth certificate of Binga's son, Bethune, listed his race as "mulatto."

Few, if any, people in the Black Belt encouraged "passing." But most understood it. If, say, they ran into a friend working at a downtown department store, they would avoid openly recognizing their friend. To do so might cost the worker his or her job. When some black women working downtown "passed" under the mistaken belief they were Jewish, it required them to miss work on Jewish holidays.[49] Some blacks who "passed" were absorbed into a white world and disappeared like mist in the wind.

In the same year of the Cecelia Johnson story, 1907, the widow of a Chicago millionaire had to fight for her inheritance after claims were made that she concealed "the presence of Negro blood in her veins."[50] A custody battle that same year was complicated for a light-skinned doctor when his wife, also light-skinned, chose to live as a black woman and accused her husband of masquerading as a white man.[51] A short time after that, an elderly black woman claimed an inheritance from the estate of a wealthy owner of a midwestern publishing firm who had been "passing" as white for thirty years.[52]

CECELIA JOHNSON, HOWEVER, MADE NO SUCH EFFORTS TO "PASS." IN FACT, not only was the accusation humiliating for Cecelia, it was also dead wrong. While "passing" was reluctantly understood in the Black Belt, it could also cost a person her friends and reputation. The social pressure was tougher on a woman.

At the University of Chicago, after the story about Cecelia broke, three-fourths of the young women in Englewood House withdrew and organized a new sorority. Cissy was not asked to join, but some of the coeds of Englewood House stood by Cecelia and refused to leave.[53] And while the story had traction for a few weeks, the university immediately pointed out that Cecelia never tried to hide who she was. In a follow-up story published in the *Chicago Record-Herald* shortly after the first story, the university's dean of women said that Cecelia Johnson never tried to conceal the fact that she had "colored blood."[54]

The story that she hid her race was eventually retracted, but it was too late. Cecelia shut herself in at home, embarrassed and humiliated. As the story spread, so did her notoriety. The mailman had to carry a special pouch bulging with letters including offers of "spectacular jobs" and marriage proposals from admiring white men.[55]

MUSHMOUTH JOHNSON, HOWEVER, MAY HAVE PAID THE ULTIMATE PRICE FOR the scandal.

The tough, hardheaded businessman and policy king was under siege. He tried to shield Cissy. He felt he had brought all this on her. He talked to reporters to get his version of the story into newspapers, doing whatever he could to clear her name. After three such stories ran in the African American *Philadelphia Tribune* in late summer of 1907, he bought a thousand copies at five cents each and had them sent to a list of people so he could "off-set and correct certain impressions concerning his relatives and friends."[56]

The last interview Mushmouth ever gave was with Hearst reporters in New York City. It was about Cecelia.[57]

Shortly after that, Mushmouth "breathed his last" on September 12, 1907, at 7:00 A.M. He died in the company of "one of his best lady friends," a Miss West, in the fashionable St. George Hotel in Brooklyn. He had traveled to see her from Atlantic City, where he had been staying while trying to recover from illness.[58]

As Fenton Johnson wrote, "it is said the incident (involving Cecelia) troubled him exceedingly, probably hastening his death."[59]

Even the *Broad Ax*, which was once critical of Mushmouth, gave some backhanded praise while perhaps suggesting another cause of death. The obituary for John Johnson in the September 21, 1907, issue of the *Broad Ax* explained that his attempt to regain his health in Atlantic City was a "no go, for the greatest of all Negro gambling kings in Chicago could not or he would not control himself or remain quiet for a short length of time, and having a weak heart he brought on his own death."[60]

His death certificate said he died of "Pneumonia, Pulmonary Adema" and "Mitral Valvular disease."[61] He likely died gasping for air as his heart gave out.

Services were held at Institutional African Methodist Episcopal Church, 3825 South Dearborn Street, a church which had once been firebombed after an anti-policy sermon by its Rev. Reverdy Cassius Ransom.[62] The pews and corridors were filled, and Dearborn Street was crowded for several blocks in each direction.[63]

Fifteen carriages were hired for his funeral procession, including two filled with flowers. John V. "Mushmouth" Johnson was buried wearing a $25 black broadcloth suit and laid to rest in a casket with extra plating that cost $277.[64]

IT WOULD TAKE A FEW YEARS FOR JOHN JOHNSON'S ESTATE TO BE SETTLED. Some of the bills included purchases of jewelry, watches, rings, diamonds, musical instruments, ties, suspenders, ivory billiard balls, a pair of black Russian shoes, and a couple of revolvers. Mushmouth left about $11,000 in cash, eight pieces of real estate, a handful of notes owed to him from various people, and three warehouse receipts for five barrels of Anderson Club Whiskey.[65]

Estimates of his estate were around $250,000. A good part of it, roughly $150,000 or more, went to Johnson's sister Eudora, who ultimately ended up controlling almost all of the estate. A final accounting was filed in Cook County Probate Court on January 2, 1912.[66]

A little more than a month later, Eudora, now a wealthy woman, was married for the first and only time. Her new husband was Jesse Binga.[67]

11

Pink

JESSE BINGA AND EUDORA JOHNSON WERE MARRIED ON TUESDAY EVENING, February 20, 1912, in a twelve-room house on Vernon Avenue on Chicago's South Side. Pink was the color of the day. Pink carnations were set out in the second-floor bedrooms, in the first-floor library, and in the billiard parlor in the basement. There were pink decorations in the dining room, and there was a pink dress in the wedding party.[1] The only thing more plentiful than the pink was the gossip.

As soon as the wedding was announced, the rumors began—Jesse Binga was marrying Eudora Johnson for her money. The fortune left by her late brother, John V. "Mushmouth" Johnson, was all Binga really wanted, they whispered. Jesse was good-looking, while Eudora was big-boned and plain, they murmured. Like other gossip in the Black Belt, it also included inescapable comparisons of skin color. Why else would Jesse, who was brown-skinned, marry Eudora, who was much darker? Gerri Major, a society columnist, newspaper writer, and editor who married Binga's cousin Binga Dismond, wrote this stark assessment: "Miss Eudora Johnson was not a young woman at the time of her marriage to Mr. Binga. She looked like a caricature of a 'big, fat, black mammy,' but she was the first black person I ever knew to stay at the Plaza in New York. . . . Mr. Binga was a distinguished looking gentlemen. I would not say that he married Miss Dora for her money, but $200,000 in those days was an awful lot of money. Mr. Binga could probably have chosen anyone he wanted."[2]

Binga himself confirmed that Eudora was worth about $200,000 when he married her, but he was quick to add that he was worth "half a million" at the time.[3] He also consistently stressed that Eudora and his mother were the two most important people to his success, and not because of Eudora's wealth.

The wedding house at 3324 Vernon Avenue was part of Eudora's inheritance from Mushmouth, who bought it in 1901 when the block was nearly all white. The Bingas would now live in Mushmouth's house. Eudora, along with her widowed sister, Louise Ray, inherited Mushmouth's saloon at 464 State Street and two other buildings on that block; the house where their cousin Cecelia Johnson lived at 5830 Wabash Avenue; some vacant lots at Seventy-Fifth and State Streets; a three-story brick building at 3734 State Street; and a two-story frame building at 5622 Dearborn Street. Interestingly, each of those properties had been quitclaimed from Eudora to Mushmouth a year before his death, suggesting that perhaps Eudora was holding title in her name to keep it insulated from the illicit activities of her brother. Eudora, a graduate of a Chicago business college, certainly knew something about real estate, and the property she inherited was free and clear, with plenty of paying tenants.[4]

Despite the rumors, Jesse Binga clearly was doing fine without Eudora Johnson's money and property. After all, he had a booming real estate business in which he owned, leased, and managed dozens of properties and controlled buildings with hundreds of tenants—and he operated his own bank.

Some of the Black Belt elite saw Eudora's money as tainted. Mushmouth had been reviled by some people because he was one of the "shadies"—a man whose business was illegal and unrespectable.[5] Binga didn't care. Binga was a rising star of the Black Belt. He believed in a life of self-determination, and he never apologized for marrying the sister of a policy king—and he did his own share of business with the sporting crowd. As for gossip, Binga, who was a man comfortable in his own skin, didn't pay it any mind. As a businessman, he worked in all levels of society: black, white, shady, or respectable.

Some sixty wedding guests strolled through the Vernon Avenue home on that chilly February night in 1912, but distinctions of class and race were not left at the door.

"The 12 rooms in their more than spacious mansion, which far surpasses the homes of the vast majority of the wealthiest Afro-Americans in any section of the United States, and it will more than favorably compare with the fine homes of many of the wealthy whites in this city," according to the Broad Ax coverage that ran in the February 24, 1912, edition of the paper.[6]

Binga's wedding wasn't a segregated affair, as was duly noted. Among the guests were Mr. and Mrs. Frank Collins. Collins was the assistant secretary of the Union Trust Company, Tribune building, and "he represented the white bankers at the wedding," according to the *Broad Ax*. And there was George H. Roth, who was in the "merchant tailoring business and a member of the opposite race."[7]

Press coverage of such events typically spoke of style and wealth. The bride wore a gown of "Marie Antoinette gold brocade silk, cut low, and with a bodice of heavy embroidered silver leaves. The train was five yards long, trimmed effectively with silver leaves," according to the *Chicago Defender*'s story bearing the headline "The Binga-Johnson Wedding the Most Brilliant Ever Held in Chicago."[8] And all elements of the dress were imported from Paris.

Eudora's closeness to family was reflected in her bridal party. Her matron of honor was her sister, Louise Ray, who wore a gown of silver gray satin and gray chiffon embroidered in "silver and electric blue palettes."[9] Eudora's bridesmaid was her cousin Cecelia Johnson, who wore a gown of "pink crepe demeteor draped with pink chiffon"; her crystal bodice edged with crystal fringe was held up with pink and green rosebuds.[10] Three months after the Binga wedding, Cecelia would marry Dr. Theodore R. Mozee, a handsome, young, light-skinned black dentist who was once described as being "intensely loyal to his race."[11] Eudora doted on Cecelia and often had the young couple over for dinner or took them out. Cecelia still lived in Mushmouth's old house on Wabash—now owned by Eudora. It was the same house where she lived as a student at the University of Chicago. She lived there with a maid from Louisiana, likely supplied by Eudora, who treated Cecelia like a little sister.

On Binga's side, his cousin Emma and her husband, Edwin Mead, were part of the wedding party. Binga's best man was Vance Anderson, who in 1914 would receive a patent for a safety streetcar fender that could scoop up objects without injuring anyone,[12] and his groomsman was Pedro T. Tinsley, a musician and a baritone who was once a member of the Apollo Musical Club of Chicago, which performed on Chicago Day at the world's fair in 1893.[13] Tinsley was related by marriage to Eudora.[14]

There were, however, a few odd details about the Binga wedding.

Jesse, who courted Eudora for several years, was a leader, a reliable donor, and a constant volunteer at St. Monica and later St. Elizabeth and St. Anselm churches. Even though he was Roman Catholic, a priest didn't perform the marriage ceremony, and he wasn't married in a church. Rev. E. T. Martin,[15] pastor of Bethesda Baptist Church,[16] performed the ceremony at the Johnson house with the assistance of Jesse's cousin Rev. Anthony Binga of Richmond, Virginia. Eudora had been a member of

Bethesda Baptist since she was twelve years old,[17] and Binga couldn't be married in a Catholic church because he was divorced (although some relatives later said they believed Binga had had his first marriage annulled by the Roman Catholic Church, but no evidence of that claim could be found).

Another odd though small detail came in their listed ages on the marriage license. Both were recorded as being thirty-one years old, even though Eudora was actually forty-one and Jesse was forty-six.

Missing from the wedding celebration was Binga's only child: his son, Bethune. Their relationship was cordial but distant. It's unclear whether Bethune was invited, but he didn't attend. Bethune, by then in his late twenties, was married and working as a carpenter in Canada,[18] and it was a long trip to Chicago.

What is clear is that the wedding was a grand society event. Classical music floated over the crowd as "Ferullo's band and Tomaso's Orchestra" played from behind tall palms in the library as guests admired "the hand-painted walls" and, of course, the pink flowers.[19]

The wedding cake had two raised letters of icing: "J. B."[20] These either stood for his own initials or for Johnson and Binga.

Wedding gifts included a linen table cover, hand-embroidered hand-kerchiefs, a hand-painted vase and water tray, silver napkin rings, a cut-glass berry bowl, and a silver bread tray. Cecelia gave an imported pearl-and-lace fan; *Broad Ax* editor Julius Taylor gave a leather-bound book of Walter Scott's poems; and a gift of "drawn work" came from the Sisters of Good Shepherd, again showing Binga's close ties to the Roman Catholic Church.[21] (The Sisters of Good Shepherd, who first came to Chicago in 1859, were devoted to the care of the city's poor and homeless women and children.)

Despite the Bingas' wealth and status, the gossip continued for years to come, particularly when it later involved a pretty manicurist who sat by the front window of a storefront barbershop at 206 East Thirty-Sixth Street, just a couple of blocks from the Binga Bank. The manicurist in the window was the ambitious Bessie Coleman, who in 1915, at the age of twenty-three, had moved to Chicago from a small town in Texas with dreams of becoming a pilot. She was rumored to be Jesse Binga's mistress.[22]

While their true relationship is difficult to know, it's clear that Binga and *Chicago Defender* editor Robert Abbott helped Coleman's dream come true. She couldn't convince anyone in the United States to teach her to fly, so with Abbott's and Binga's encouragement and financial backing,

Coleman traveled to Paris in 1920, where she eventually became the first black woman to earn a pilot's license. She became a media sensation and a barnstorming stunt flier until she was killed in 1926, when she was thrown from a rear cockpit of a plane flown by another pilot. Hurled out of her seat when the plane went into a tailspin and "flipped upside-down" at five hundred feet over Jacksonville, Florida, she fell somersaulting "end over end until she hit the ground."[23]

Despite any rumors, Dora (as her family called Eudora) remained by Jesse's side as a devoted wife, able financial partner, and confidante as the Bingas increasingly lived a life of self-imposed isolation. Newspaper columnist Gerri Major "got to know Miss Dora. I knew what a sweet, delightful woman she was," she recalled. "The Bingas very seldom went out socially, as (Dora) explained, and they were not the entertaining kind. Although they had a large Christmas party every year, it was like a public relations soiree, meant to pay obligations. They probably could have gone wherever they wanted, but whether they stayed [in] to avoid the opportunity for snubs, I don't know. They never had any children, and somehow I felt it was very sad that they were so alone."[24]

WHILE THE BINGAS' WEDDING WAS A "SOCIETY EVENT," MAJORS SAID, "YOU could tell from the people who were not there, just how society it was . . . Miss Dora did not belong to black society, and that was that."[25]

The Bingas' social life was public and elegant, but it was also limited. There was an occasional outing to the opera, they held holiday parties for children at church, and Mr. and Mrs. Binga were cheered as being among the first of their set to own automobiles of "note and speed," Jesse in his "high geared car" and Dora in her "handsome electric coupe."[26] In fact, Jesse and some friends planned to motor to the Indianapolis 500 (at that time the fifth annual running) in May 1915, according to the *Chicago Defender*.[27] Still, the Bingas hosted only one major society party a year, although it was a big one: the Christmas Twilight Party, which represented the most coveted invitation in the Black Belt.

In photos taken throughout his career, Jesse often looked as though he was alone in a crowd. While he didn't hesitate to express his opinion and push his advantage, he seemed to be an outlier, a loner. His parents were long dead, his son's family was distant, and his inner circle was made up of a few relatives in Chicago—a sister, the Meads, and Dora's family, including her sister Louise and cousin Cecelia. Out-of-town visitors were usually family members from Detroit or Virginia or business connections. Abbott, Taylor, and Dr. Ulysses Grant Dailey, who were probably as close to

Binga as anyone, were more business associates than close friends. Editors Abbott and Taylor provided public relations through their newspapers and received Binga's advertising dollars. Dailey was his physician and later, along with Abbott, invested in Binga's bank and became a director.

Although men like Binga often have been able to overcome a limited education on their way to success, Binga's three to four years of high school didn't help party conversation or remove any rungs on the social ladder. The new emerging elite had college and graduate degrees. Binga did not.

Binga "was obviously not highly educated, but he knew figures and knew what he wanted to do," said lawyer and civil rights activist Truman K. Gibson Jr. Gibson's father, an insurance executive, knew Binga, and Gibson himself met Binga in 1930 when Gibson was a student at the University of Chicago doing research work for Harold Gosnell, a professor of political science. While Binga rarely turned down a request for donations to the numerous civic activities of the Black Belt, he "was not at all active in the community," said Gibson, "only (if) situations forced him to be."[28]

Binga's religion could also be problematic. He was Catholic when almost all of the power and influence of the Black Belt was Protestant. And the congregants of the many Protestant churches were deeply suspicious of Polish, Irish, and other white Catholic immigrants who were sometimes behind the violence toward blacks in surrounding neighborhoods. Binga, however, had a way of turning disadvantage to advantage. He could call on his white Catholic connections for help, since many of the white local politicians, ward heelers, and cops in his world were Catholic. This group included Third Ward alderman Thomas D. Nash, a powerful Irish politician and later a lawyer for Al Capone, who along with Binga was a member of St. Elizabeth parish in the 1920s. And, while most blacks were die-hard members of the Republican Party, "the party of Lincoln," Binga nourished friendships with Democrats, such as Nash, whom he met through his Catholic contacts.

Eudora's background represented another social obstacle since her money was tied to the world of gamblers, drinkers, and sporting people. Despite her extensive charitable work, particularly with elderly residents of the Black Belt, Eudora and her mother had lived on the fringe of the aristocratic society of the so-called old settlers—the black elite who had been in the city for years; they never seemed fully accepted.

Eudora was by all accounts smart, sweet, kind, and generous. She was also shrewd. Although she was the youngest of Mushmouth's siblings, she received the lion's share of his estate and made good money in her later real estate dealings. Dora was an able, strong, and determined woman, and Jesse often spoke of her wisdom, enduring strength, and devotion.

Wealth has a way of easing some of the sting of social snubs, and the Bingas were a power couple with cash, real estate, and connections.

The guests at his wedding, however, reflected some belonging to an elite Black Belt society that was both old and new. The wedding list included eminent doctors, lawyers, newspaper editors, and businessmen. There were a few old settlers, but there were plenty of the wealthy new-comers, such as Abbott.

Some guests had roots in slavery, including Colonel John R. Marshall, who attended with his wife and gave a bronze tray to the newlyweds. Marshall was born into slavery in Alexandria, Virginia, and became the first black colonel in the U.S. Army as commander of the heralded all-black Eighth Illinois Volunteer Regiment, which fought in the Spanish-American War.[29]

And some guests represented the world of the arts, such as Vivian Harsh, who in 1924 would become Chicago's first black librarian. As director of the George Cleveland Hall branch, she would compile a "Special Negro Collection," which today is part of the Chicago Public Library's Vivian G. Harsh Research Collection of Afro-American History and Literature.[30]

Yet Binga's wedding was mostly about power. While the wedding party included an inner circle of family and a few friends, most of the other guests were more business associates than friends.

THE LIST OF THOSE AT THE WEDDING REFLECTED THE WEALTH, GROWING influence, and diverse views of a new black elite. It wasn't just the old aristocrats of the Black Belt who now had money and status; there were various other well-heeled groups too.

Jesse and Eudora Binga were two of many new people coming into the mix of the black power elite. The wealthy in the Black Belt represented an intellectual diversity in this increasingly cloistered population. Even though they didn't have to deal with the usual questions of survival—money, finding a decent place to live and getting ahead—one problem unified them: how to survive in a racially hostile city and country.

Chicago's Black Belt was awash in a stew of theories on how to do just that. There were segregationists, integrationists, separatists, communists, and black nationalists, united only in their quest for the rights and free-doms the rest of the country enjoyed.

Some theories veered toward a more radical view, such as the Back to Africa movement headed by Jamaican-born New York-based Marcus

Garvey, which advocated a return of African Americans to Africa. More extreme were the actions of the self-styled "Abyssinians," who in 1920 burned two American flags on Thirty-Fifth Street before shooting a black policeman and several other people.[31] These approaches didn't interest Binga's crowd. In fact, Binga's friend and ally Abbott would become a pronounced enemy of Garvey and his views. Abbott used his paper to campaign against Garvey, and Garvey ended up suing him for libel.[32]

The Black Belt was filled with various philosophies of getting ahead and working around the racial complications of American society. Many of those at the wedding were outspoken activists. Some, such as Abbott, believed aggressive tactics were the way to secure civil rights and that it was insulting to believe that blacks had to earn rights that were already freely given to all other Americans.

Well before the establishment of the National Association for the Advancement of Colored People (NAACP) in 1909, some Chicago business leaders had aligned themselves with the former slave-turned-educator Booker T. Washington. Others embraced the more confrontational tactics of people such as the brilliant, Harvard-educated W. E. B. Du Bois, a leader of the Niagara movement and later editor of the NAACP magazine *The Crisis*, which championed civil rights activism and tenacious opposition to segregation.

Binga drew from a blend of these philosophies while adding ingredients of his own. On Binga's wedding day he received a congratulatory telegram from Washington, who sent regrets he couldn't attend because of bad health and the press of business. Years earlier, Washington had introduced Binga to a packed hall of the Negro National Business Men's League in Louisville, where Washington called him the most successful Afro-American real estate broker and banker in the country.[33] Conversely, Du Bois, who was often harshly critical of Washington, praised Binga as a bold individualist who bowed to no one. Du Bois visited Binga in Chicago and admired his daring and independence, saying that Binga "was outspoken; he was self-assertive; he could not be bluffed or frightened . . . he did not bend his neck nor kow-tow when he spoke to white men or about them; he represented the self-assertive Negro, and was even at times rough and dictatorial."[34]

This new power elite of the Black Belt was engraved all over Binga's wedding list, and they had plenty of internal fights of their own.

Robert Abbott was on track to become one of the most successful black businessmen in America as founder of the *Chicago Defender*, which would soon become the most influential black newspaper in the country.

Abbott's experiences shortly after he arrived in Chicago said a great deal about society life among the city's older black elite. Abbott tried to join the choir of Grace Presbyterian Church, a congregation of old settlers who tended to be light-skinned. Even though Abbott once toured as a talented tenor in the Hampton Quartet and sang at the World's Columbian Exposition in 1893, he was rejected from the church choir because he was part of those "uncultured elements" from the South, and because he was too dark-skinned.[35]

By 1912, Abbott was on his way up. He was a friend of Binga, and his sports reporter Julius N. Avendorph was often the master of ceremony for high-society parties, including Binga's wedding. The snobbish Avendorph, who became the *Defender*'s first society editor, was a Fisk University graduate and a man about town. He not only worked for the Pullman Company and was a reporter for Abbott, but he was also president of the Columbia Club baseball team. And as a clerk at the Cook County Courthouse, he was "the first colored man to be appointed to an official position in the courthouse of Chicago."[36] He was a must-invite guest for those in the know.

Abbott was a fiery outspoken champion of his race, using his paper to attack discrimination, condemn lynchings, and address racial wrongs. While Avendorph was an ambassador for the wealthy, and at heart an exclusionary elitist who once said, "Society must stand for something and its cardinal principle ought to be class distinction,"[37] Abbott spoke up for the rich and poor of his race, no matter whom it might affect, even if it was Jesse Binga.

In 1913, Abbot blasted Binga's cherished St. Monica Church, claiming it had a "Jim Crow" school and demanding its closure. He said the church's Catholic school segregated blacks and whites. "God pity the simpleminded mother and father who would drag their children down so low as to send them to a Jim Crow school in the heart of this great city," Abbott's *Defender* said.[38] Despite the attack on his church, Binga remained friends with Abbott.

Two other guests, Mr. and Mrs. S. Laing Williams, were an example of the blending of the philosophies of Washington and Du Bois and others. They favored a bolder approach. S. Laing Williams, a lawyer and founder of the Prudence Crandall Club, a literary society of socially prominent blacks, was part of the old elite, yet he found himself drawn to the dynamic world of Binga. Williams was a friend of Booker T. Washington, and he was once Washington's "closest aide in Chicago," but he also became active in civil rights issues and eventually became vice president of the

Chicago branch of the NAACP.[39] And, as historian Allan Spear points out, Williams's wife, Fannie Barrier Williams, originally of Brockport, New York, had urged a white audience at the World's Columbian Exposition of 1893 to remember that slavery was responsible for "every moral imperfection that mars the character of the colored American," and that it was ridiculous to deny equal opportunity to blacks in that doing so attempts "to repress the yearnings of common humanity."[40]

And then there was Julius T. Taylor, editor of the *Broad Ax*. Taylor's opinions were usually unfiltered and blunt, which could make for uncomfortable social moments, including at Binga's wedding. He had once said that Colonel Marshall, a light-skinned fellow wedding guest, "never claims he is a Negro unless he is looking for an (political) office, or wants to be at the head of some big doings among the Afro-Americans."[41]

Taylor also had years earlier called Booker T. Washington "the greatest white man's Nigger in the world."[42] Then two years before Binga's wedding, Taylor seemingly changed his view toward Washington and started printing news releases from Tuskegee Institute, Washington's college base. He explained that his change of heart came because Washington had moderated his views and was devoting himself more to educational concerns.[43] But less than two weeks after Binga's wedding, the *Broad Ax* ran a front-page story headed "Booker T. Washington Bitterly Denounced as a Traitor to His Race" and urged new leadership "of the Race." His sense of outrage against Washington came over complacency about lynchings. At a gathering in Philadelphia, reported the *Broad Ax*, the first speaker said, "If Doctor Washington urges us to be still when men of our race are put to death without trial, when they are burned to death within sight of courts of justice, when they are disfranchised wholesale when our women are forced into Jim Crow cars which are worse than hog pens, he is a traitor to his race and to American citizenship."[44]

Of sixty-four known lynchings in the United States in 1912, sixty-two of them were lynchings of blacks, according to—interestingly enough—the archives of the Tuskegee Institute.[45] Tuskegee had been compiling those statistics since 1892; the NAACP started keeping those statistics in 1912. Ida B. Wells, a journalist and activist and later an ally of sorts to Binga, cast a constant spotlight on the lynching problem. She later joined Binga in fighting white real estate agents trying to halt black home rentals and purchases.

Years later some black activists would see communism as a path to equality. But that world ran counter to Binga's goals and aspirations. Binga was not a communist, a separatist, or an accommodationist. He was first and foremost a capitalist.

Binga spoke against segregation, but he also saw strength and advantage in the Black Belt. Here was a concentrated economic power. A black businessperson could be shut out of the white financial world, but not in the Black Belt. Binga would be a key part of establishing a full, separate city of blacks on Chicago's South Side while using his powers to expand and break its borders.

Like the larger city of Chicago, this city within a city would have the same main strip. The Black Belt was becoming the country's capital of black capitalism, and, like downtown Chicago, State Street was its main thoroughfare—and Binga was a major reason why.

SIX MONTHS AFTER BINGA'S WEDDING, THE STATE STREET CARNIVAL OPENED on a Saturday night, August 17, 1912. Thousands of electric lights were lit along a strip of State Street to inaugurate "the most gigantic enterprise of this kind ever given in this city and the only one exclusively by the [black] race," according to the *Chicago Defender*.[46]

A parade kicked off at 9:00 P.M. from the Binga Bank and was led by the Eighth Regiment Band, followed by an elephant carrying the queen of the parade, Miss Hattie Holliday, and her four "little girl attendants." The parade went north to Thirty-First Street and then circled back to Thirty-Sixth Street, where the crowning of the queen took place before a roaring crowd of ten thousand.[47]

This State Street Fair in 1912 was more than just a carnival attraction with its merry-go-rounds, $20,000 calliope, and Chiquita, the "world's smallest lady." It was a statement of equality, "through brash displays of black profit and pleasure, it undermined many of the myths that had been presented as scientific fact," according to historian Davarian L. Baldwin.[48] Through these "parades and carnivals, they created moments of social parity," Baldwin asserted.[49]

Binga was a symbol of that parity. He was a self-made man and a success in an area that seemed reserved for whites—banking. Binga represented free will and self-realization. He wasn't the richest man in the Black Belt, the most successful, or the most popular, but he was one of the most important, right up there with newspaper editor Robert Abbott. There were plenty of businesspeople—men and women—in the Black Belt, including bakery owners, cab company proprietors, small barbershop owners, and rising newcomer Anthony Overton, a cosmetics manufacturer, but no one was more a symbol of black economic power than Jesse Binga. The State Street carnival proclaimed a new day for the Black Belt, a step into a world of black achievement and pride.

"The crowning of the 'most beautiful woman of Chicago' (never mentioning race), by vote of the people, topped off this utopian celebration," observed Baldwin.[50]

Dressed in a tailored suit with starched shirt, Jesse Binga made his way to the front of Hattie Holliday's throne, where he was greeted with cheers and applause as he presented the queen with the carnival prize—a crisp hundred-dollar bill. Binga had organized the State Street Carnival, handled the logistics, and helped finance it.[51] Hattie Holliday was the new queen of the carnival, but Jesse Binga was the new king of State Street.

CHAPTER 11

12

State Street

When a young white man named Ben Hecht was a fledgling newspaper-man for the *Chicago Daily Journal* from 1910 to 1914, one of his duties was to chase down news photos. One day, after retrieving a picture of a woman who had been "held up by two bandits," he heard screams as he walked toward the corner of Thirty-Fifth and State Streets. A black man was run-ning toward him waving two fists stuffed with cash.

"I was to learn in a few minutes that the Negro was full of hashish and that he had walked through the plate glass window of Jesse Binga's Negro bank, terrified a dozen men and snatched a bundle of money from the teller's cage." As the man ran toward Hecht screaming and laughing, Hecht saw a big man in a butcher's apron nearby. "He sprang forward swinging a meat cleaver. The Negro's head vanished suddenly. His trunk remained erect for several instants spouting blood like a fireworks piece. Then it fell."[1]

All the buildings on what was known as "The Stroll," which ran from Twenty-Sixth to Thirty-Ninth Streets, including Binga's Bank, were part of the vibrant "Downtown" of the Black Belt. It was part of a blend of commerce and enterprise, but also vice. With that mix came risk and a certain degree of menace. The world of Jesse Binga's State Street could be a harrowing place.

DESPITE THE GAMBLING AND PROSTITUTES, THE DANGERS, THE POVERTY AND housing woes of the Black Belt, Jesse Binga was one of a growing class of people who were bringing business to State Street, the main commercial strip of the Black Belt. Binga was the future. Binga represented success.

And in that respect, he was similar to the most celebrated man on State Street: heavyweight champion boxer Jack Johnson, who had a restaurant and nightclub five blocks from Binga's Bank.

Both Binga and Johnson were fearless. Johnson was also enormously popular in the Black Belt as the man who defeated white champion James L. Jeffries in the "Fight of the Century" in 1910. Johnson acted as an unfettered free man. He drove expensive cars, married a white woman, and in 1912 opened his "black and tan" Café de Champion right off State Street at 41 West Thirty-First Street, where black and white patrons mixed freely as couples.[2]

Both Binga and Johnson attracted white anger, but in different ways—Johnson for defying racial norms with his lifestyle and by vanquishing white boxers; Binga for defying racial norms with his assault on real estate boundaries set by whites seeking to isolate and contain the Black Belt.

Both were what came to be called "New Negroes." They were self-confident men who stood up for their rights and set their own course. However, while many men in the Black Belt knew they couldn't become a champion fighter like Johnson, they saw that it was possible to become an entrepreneur like Binga, or at least own their own home as Binga said they should.

Binga was the king of State Street, at least during the day. His State Street control extended south of Thirty-Fifth Street, with pockets of frontage all the way to the "Binga Block," which ran from Forty-Seventh to Forty-Eighth Streets along State. At night, however, music ruled.

Two worlds occupied State Street in the Black Belt: business by day, pleasure by night. During the day, State Street was filled with shoppers buying shirts, boots, dresses, chairs, beds, and rugs. Along the Stroll one could find funeral homes, bakeries, barbershops, and beauty parlors. You could get your nails manicured, your shoes shined, and a suit tailored to order and available the next day. Fine clothes were one of the reasons to take a walk down the Stroll. It was a place to meet, to be seen, and to do business. At night, crowds jammed into its cafés, nightclubs, and theaters. If the Black Belt were a country, the Stroll was its capital.

On summer Sundays, church people, businessmen, and "old settlers" in their suits and lace took leisurely walks during the afternoon, occasionally stopping to chat. At night, men in loud suits of red or yellow hustled down the Stroll with women in colorful dresses or short skirts with dangling fringe for shimmying at the local clubs.

While whites owned some of the shops on the Stroll, many were owned by blacks. Encouraged by stories in Robert Abbott's *Chicago Defender*, tens of thousands of southern blacks migrated north to Chicago to seek jobs and a better life away from the confines of Jim Crow, and that meant more opportunities for black entrepreneurs. When Binga was married in 1912, there were 526 black-owned businesses in Chicago. By 1921, that number had more than doubled to 1,260.[3] Binga owned only a couple of those businesses, but his bank and real estate operation were two of the most significant along the strip. In fact, Binga, particularly with his control of the "Binga Block," was shaping the Black Belt as he pushed its borders farther south. And true to the Binga family's entrepreneurial spirit, Jesse's sister Martha Winchester now had an employment agency four blocks north of Binga's bank at 3233 South State Street.[4] Like her brother, she also operated a loan and real estate office.

Around the Binga Bank, State Street was a twenty-four-hour world. Some work shifts ended at 11:00 P.M., midnight, or later, sending workers into State Street's round-the-clock action. Many businesses stayed open during the night to cash in on the after-work crowd of porters, swing-shift factory workers, waitresses, waiters, busboys, and bellhops. These customers found more than shopping: they found inspiring entertainment and lively dancing on and around the State Street strip. There was also plenty of gambling and prostitution. It was the "Mecca of Pleasure," as the *Chicago Defender* called it.[5]

When the sun set, State Street became so crowded and energetic that the poet Langston Hughes once said it was a place where "midnight was like day."[6] As the saying went, on State Street, "You could get anything you wanted, from a foot race to a murder."[7]

MORE THAN TWO CENTURIES BEFORE THE STROLL HUMMED WITH COMMERCE and inventive forms of music, Binga's bank's location was part of an ocean of prairie wilderness running up to Lake Michigan in a four-mile strip extending from the Chicago River south to Hyde Park.[8] It was the only place where the prairie met the lake along Chicago's shoreline. Native Americans from the Miami tribes once traipsed through its grass and the light purple flowers of Nodding Wild Onion, padded around shallow swamps and through an occasional stand of oak. Two well-worn trails made by the Miami and later Potawatomi ran to hunting grounds and villages to the south in an area that eventually became known as Cottage Grove and Vincennes Avenues.[9] (In the twentieth century, Binga often hosted his annual Christmas Twilight Party on one such path, at the Vincennes Hotel at 601 East Thirty-Sixth Street.)

The broader area went through many phases ranging from greystone residential luxury to breweries, meatpacking operations, light industrial use, and even a Confederate prisoner of war camp during the Civil War. Two parallel railroad tracks running north and south helped define the area: the Illinois Central to the east along the lake and the Rock Island to the west.[10]

At one point, a strip west of State Street along the Rock Island track became known as the Federal Street slum when it was occupied largely by Italian immigrants.[11] To the east there was a mix of Anglo Protestants, German Jews, and Irish Catholics of varying economic class.[12]

At first only a few blacks "trickled" into Chicago onto these streets. They settled in the south Loop and slowly spread south in a straight line down State Street. The trickle became a flow during World War I,[13] and it accelerated each decade.

The Black Belt became outlined as a thin sliver of land with State Street as its spine. Eventually some three hundred thousand blacks would live in this "narrow tongue of land" seven miles long and one and one-half miles wide.[14] Binga helped shape it.

While there were smaller black neighborhoods scattered around the city, the Black Belt was by far the largest. Some of the old housing of the area along Douglas and Grand Boulevards reflected the economic divisions of these newcomers, with the western edge and the ramshackle housing of the Federal Street slum attracting the poor and the greystones and mansions to the east attracting the wealthy. But as the Black Belt bulged with increasing numbers, its residents were packed tighter into this compact area hemmed in by unofficial racial borders dictated by the antagonism of surrounding white neighborhoods. By necessity, the Black Belt became self-sufficient, a city unto itself, with the State Street strip as its downtown and the Binga Bank as its cash register.

As the businessman and author Dempsey Travis described it, State Street was both the Wall Street and the Broadway of the Black Belt.[15] It was the capital of black capitalism. But it was also the capital of vice, and Binga as much as anyone knew that brought its share of danger. Once when Binga was opening his bank in the summer of 1910, he was approached by a man who flashed a revolver and demanded money. The man grabbed Binga by the throat and forced Binga to give him about $2,000. The man fled, only to be chased by a "mob," captured, stabbed, and "about to be lynched to a lamppost when police interfered." The mob was outraged because they initially thought Binga had been killed. Police had to fight their way through the angry crowd to rescue the robber.[16]

DESPITE BEING A CHURCHGOER WHO DIDN'T SMOKE AND DRANK LITTLE IF AT all, Jesse Binga wasn't averse to mixing with the "shadies," particularly when it came to business. He was a friend to Robert T. Motts, the dapper owner of a gambling operation and saloon. And he was connected to policy people through business deals and through fellow congregants he met at the three Roman Catholic churches where he worshipped over four decades.

Motts founded the popular Pekin Theatre, a cabaret, saloon, and music hall at 2700 South State Street. Motts, who came from a small town in Iowa, was a protégé of Eudora Binga's brother, John "Mushmouth" Johnson, and he got his start much like Mushmouth—as a porter. Motts worked at Johnson's gambling operation on State Street and eventually bought his own place, with his own political connections to insure he had protection from police and by police. Motts gave money to local churches, promoted race advancement, and was a natural political operator who organized black women to knock on doors for candidates. He also stuffed dollar bills into pockets of saloon regulars to get them to register and vote—his way.[17]

There was no reason to doubt that political funds and gambling profits found their way into Binga's vaults and safety deposit boxes. Binga was a realist. In fact, eventually the Binga Bank's board of directors would come to include Charles S. Jackson, the brother of Dan "The Embalmer" Jackson, a South Side gambling boss and a Second Ward committeeman. Dan Jackson would also later partner with Binga on a banking venture.

Binga's Catholic world also provided more contacts. Dan Jackson's wife, Lucy Lindsay Jackson, who was Motts's sister, was a member of the same parish (St. Elizabeth) as the Bingas in the 1920s.[18] Lucy, like Eudora, eventually inherited her brother's wealth. And Julian Black, Dan Jackson's collector and eventually a policy king himself,[19] donated the holy water fonts at St. Anselm Catholic Church, Binga's church in the 1930s.

Despite these tangled connections, Binga publicly spoke against wasting money chasing a dream and a hope that one's policy numbers will come up: "I never gambled. I was always against that red-light stuff. I worked hard against it, for I was really interested in the uplift."[20]

Two years before Binga opened his bank, Motts enticed entertainment seekers, politicians, and the sporting crowd to his legendary music hall nightclub at 2700 State Street. In 1906, he offered gambling, theater acts, and dancing to blacks and whites alike. Amid the smoke, drinks, and laughs at the bar were factory workers and immigrants slamming down shots shoulder-to-shoulder with politicians, actors, and rich young whites out for a night of thrills. Floating above the din were the strains of rag-time. Binga also spent time at the Pekin.

Around the time of Binga's 1912 wedding, the fabled pianist Tony Jackson, who wrote "Pretty Baby," became a regular performer at the Pekin. Jackson, who sported a diamond stickpin in his tie and garters on his sleeves, began his career in Storyville, the red-light district of New Orleans, where he wowed customers with his ivory skills.[21]

A new kind of music was evolving in the Black Belt, one that started in New Orleans and spread north. Improvisation was key, and dancing seemed mandatory. It started with ragtime and was eventually replaced by *jazz*, a word first used within Chicago as early as 1915[22] and elsewhere before that. The exact origins of the word are still debated by jazz historians, but it has a slang origin with various similar spellings meaning pep, vitality, energy, or verve. When jazz got rolling, the dance floor filled, fueled by gin and the appetites of youth. Jelly Roll Morton, an early jazz pianist and also a Storyville import, had his five-piece band get the crowds swaying in 1914 at the Elite Café at Thirty-First and State Streets, and the Creole Band with cornetist Freddie Keppard got it bumping at the nearby Grand Theatre at 3110–3112 South State Street. Places such as the Deluxe Café, 3503 South State Street; Elite No. 2, 3502 South State Street; and Dreamland Café, 3518–3520 South State Street (where trumpeter Louis Armstrong played in 1926) were just a few of the fabled clubs of the era. On the State Street strip alone there were close to a dozen jazz clubs.[23]

State Street was a magnet for young musicians on the move. By the end of World War I, jazz had taken over. It was such a part of the atmosphere that white jazz personality Eddie Condon claimed that if you held a trumpet up in the air on the Stroll, it would play itself.[24] On State Street, even the rain seemed to fall in syncopation.

Some of these clubs saw mixed couples, black and white, engaged in "coarse and vulgar dancing."[25] White and black newspapers attacked these "Black and Tan Resorts" for outlandish and immoral behavior; white papers always emphasized the mingling of races. And "of all the northern cities, Chicago was probably the most notorious for racial mixing,"[26] according to historian Kevin Mumford.

One white paper, headlined " 'Lid' a Joke as Pekin Shimmies Defiance of Law," leveled its attack at the Pekin with its " 'Lawless liquor,' sensuous 'shimmy,' solicitous sirens, wrangling waiters, all the tints of the racial rainbow, black and tan and white, dancing, drinking, singing, early Sunday morning."[27] The paper described the charged atmosphere inside the Pekin:

The crowd began to arrive. In came a mighty black man with two white girls, a scarred white man entered with three girls, two young and painted, the other merely painted.

Two well dressed youths hopped up the stairs with two timid girls. Seven young men—they looked back o'the Yards [ed. Note: a neighborhood next to the stockyards]—came with two women, one heavy footed, the other laughing hysterically.

Two fur-coated "high yaller" girls romped up with a slender white man. An attorney gazed happily on the party through horn rimmed glasses. The waiters called, shouted, whistled when each party arrived—a full table meant big tips.

At one o'clock the place was crowded. Meanwhile a syncopating colored man had been vamping cotton field blues on the piano. A brown girl sang. . . . All the tables were filled at two o'clock, black men with white girls, white men with yellow girls, old young, all filled with the abandon brought about by illicit whisky and liquor music. . . . The Pekin is again the Pekin of years ago. Only more so.[28]

Robert T. Motts didn't live long enough to hear Jackson play or watch jazz develop; he died in 1911. Yet Motts had created a unique theater of music and vaudeville for black patrons—although whites were welcome too. Motts was a founding partner in the lure and lore of the Black Belt's State Street Stroll. His gambling connections were obvious to the four thousand people who attended his funeral.[29] Funeral director Daniel M. Jackson handled the arrangements at Quinn Chapel; Jackson even ran some of his own gambling operation out of his funeral home.[30] Also sitting in the pews for the funeral was Motts's "bosom friend" Henry Teenan Jones,[31] who ran a lucrative policy operation with his brother Charlie "Giveadamn" Jones.

And there was another Motts friend in the crowd, a quiet, distinguished-looking man in a tailored suit with a pious demeanor. He was an honorary pallbearer named Jesse Binga.[32]

BINGA'S STATE STREET WORLD WAS MOSTLY OF THE DAYTIME VARIETY, BUT HE was no stranger to commerce of the night. His bank held some money from nightclubs and policy operations, like those of his wife. Eudora's brother Elijah H. Johnson leased property near the Binga Bank and built the Dreamland Café at 3518 South State Street.[33] And Binga was close to people like Dan Jackson and Motts, and successors, those in the center of the night world.

Binga's daily routine sometimes included late-night stops on State Street. In 1912, Robert Abbott's *Chicago Defender* laid out "One Day in the Life of a Banker" that went like this:[34]

7:45 A.M.–Honk! Honk! of waiting automobile.

8:30 A.M.–Home mail, breakfast, newspapers.

8:40 A.M.–Bank, Mail, conference with secretary and cashier. Early appointments.

9:00 A.M.–Conference with Manager of Real Estate Department.

10 to 11:30–Downtown appointments Clearing House Association.

12 O'Clock (sharp)–Appointment with wife at Spiffing-Aulding & Co.

12:30 P.M. Lunch at Lectors

1:10 P.M.–Back to Bank.

3:00 P.M.–Honk! Honk! Again.

3:15 P.M.–Meets wife at Mrs. Sabine's Afternoon Reception and then to Mrs. Clay's informal affair for "Dorothy." Englewood next to meet my old school chum "Bill" in town for an hour or two en route to Denver.

5:00 P.M.–Home.

5:30 P.M.–Evening newspapers and a few neglected telephone calls.

6:00 P.M.–Dinner in honor of President B. of Antelope.

8:15 P.M.–Entering Box at the Pekin.

10:50 P.M.–Reserved Table at Betts.

Whether Binga was more of an observer or a participant in the illicit business of the Black Belt, he knew there was money in the night.

When Binga wasn't being chauffeured about in his "Red Devil" automobile or his wife's Detroit-built electric car with blue upholstery,[35] he would often walk the streets searching for real estate opportunities and soaking in the atmosphere. He saw men and women shopping and chatting on State Street; the men were dressed in suits, work clothes, and uniforms, with pepper in their step and purpose in their eyes, and the women wore long dresses and formal hats.

But Binga increasingly saw a different crowd. There were some women hanging out of tenement windows with heads tied up with brightly colored rags and men sprawled out on front stoops drinking and talking loudly. All economic worlds mixed in the Black Belt, and Binga wasn't keen on living amid the lower elements.

While the Stroll was full of commerce and life, it had its share of danger and strife. As black migrants from the South jammed into the already crowded housing of the Black Belt, it was difficult to move outside the neighborhood without the hassle of white hostility. While it was tough to move out, it seemed easy for drugs, gambling, liquor, and prostitution to move in.

Binga could see changes near his home on Vernon Avenue, once the province of the well heeled. Right around the corner and a half block west was a house of prostitution, and another one was operating a half block east.[36] And down the street there were signs of overcrowding as single-family houses were cut up into tiny apartments and packed beyond their design limits. In 1914, just a couple blocks south of his home, Mrs. Grace Garnett, an "old settler," bought a three-story house at 3627 Vernon Avenue and subdivided the apartments into two-room units, which included a kitchen. These came to be called kitchenette apartments, and the cut-up design made more room for renters. And more room was needed. Thousands were pouring into the neighborhood. People from the South "sent for their relatives as soon as they got here," explained Garnett.[37]

Ironically, Binga had done much the same in his early years as a real estate agent when he started out by operating rooming houses. He filled as many beds with renters as the property could handle, as many white immigrants did.

Like many other self-made men, Binga felt he worked for something better; he wanted to move up and live a life he felt he earned. Wealth and poverty lived next door to each other in the Black Belt, a tight, confined area outlined by white attitudes. In the Black Belt, a middle-class merchant could live next door to a noisy saloon or a house of prostitution. Crime and chaos would come and go, the sound of glass breaking, yells from a fistfight, the sight of someone urinating in the alley.

Binga wanted a change, and he decided he needed to move out of the Black Belt to get it.

STATE STREET BECAME A WORKSHOP AND OFFICE FOR ANOTHER ASPIRING entrepreneur, newspaperman Robert Sengstacke Abbott. After Abbott founded the *Chicago Defender* in 1905, he became a fixture along the Stroll. He walked up and down the busy thoroughfare, stopping to chat in hopes of getting items for his paper. He was a constant presence while prospecting for new business openings, gossip, and sports news. Every day he was on the beat, walking the street in his signature black derby, white shirt, white tie, and blue suit. But it was a struggle. At the beginning, his overcoat was lined with paper for insulation against the cold, and his shoes had worn heels with cardboard stuffed inside to cover the holes in his soles.[38]

Despite having a law degree from Chicago's Kent College of Law, he never practiced—he was advised that he was too dark-skinned to develop even a good black clientele. When he founded the *Defender*, he was close to being penniless; he owed money and was living in a cheap, second-floor room at 3159 South State Street where at night he could hear the roars of white men playing craps in a club next door.[39]

Abbott, much like Binga, didn't gamble, swear, drink, or smoke.[40] Despite his insatiable thirst for information on State Street, he was somewhat of a loner. By day he forced his way into dozens of conversations, yet by night he often stayed to himself in his rented room and developed his dream.

Nobody really thought Abbott should start a newspaper;[41] in fact, many people thought it was laughable. First off, his English was poor.[42] Abbott mangled the language and talked with a thick southern accent. And if it weren't tough enough to write for a newspaper, it was even tougher to make money owning one. There were already several local black newspapers in Chicago, including the *Broad Ax* founded by Julius Taylor and the *Conservator*, run by Ida B. Wells's husband, Ferdinand Lee Barnett. There were also several big-name national black newspapers, including the influential Indianapolis *Freeman* and the *New York Age*. Even if hired for one of those papers, many black reporters had to supplement their income with other jobs.

Perched on State Street, Abbott, like Binga and other black entrepreneurs, could see that Chicago blacks were creating a city within a city, and they saw there was money to be made from this separate city. The increasing segregation was creating this new place now known as the Black Belt, a miniature version of the city with its own business infrastructure of bakeries, real estate offices, music shops, taxi services, and grocery stores. Only here, virtually all the customers were black.

Abbott not only saw his newspaper as a way to make money, he also saw it as a way for him to have a voice, a way to showcase his views, to state the case of the African American or, as his paper's name suggests, be a "defender of his race."[43]

Abbott talked with everybody on State Street, but he targeted the black elite. He wanted to be with the leaders, he wanted to be part of them, but they didn't seem to want him, at least at the beginning. Abbott was excluded by some of the old settlers simply because of his dark skin and southern ways. Even at his own church, Grace Presbyterian, Abbott felt rejected.[44] There, light-skinned Chicago-born blacks looked down on his kind and blamed southern blacks for the increasing problems blacks were having in the city. Binga, who himself was never too concerned about acceptance by the black elite, accepted Abbott early on. That was probably not lost on Abbott, a man who was used to being excluded.

Abbott and Binga were both a constant presence on State Street, Abbott working the sidewalks and Binga working inside his busy real estate office and bank. Binga was a man of commerce, Abbott a man of opinion. Both were strong-willed and unbowed. And both were loners.

When he began, Abbott tried to raise money for his newspaper dream, dangling the lure of jobs and excitement to those who invested. Nobody bit. Eventually Abbott decided to go it alone. Hoping to make a success for himself, he figured he could write about people he knew, such as the 150-member Choral Study Club choir in which he later sang tenor. Maybe that way, at least the choir members would buy his paper.[45]

With a makeshift office of a folding table and a borrowed kitchen chair, he put together the first issue of the *Chicago Defender*. On May 5, 1905, his paper hit the streets. The first printing of three hundred copies cost Abbott $13.75. His first issue was four pages of six columns each.[46] The *Defender* would grow over the next two decades to become the largest black newspaper in the country and endure into the twenty-first century.

Abbott "packed the paper with names."[47] If somebody saw his or her name in print, he or she might buy the paper, but more important, Abbott believed that "names make news."[48] One name that was in Abbott's headlines for years was that of a man who bridged the day and night world of State Street: Jesse Binga.

Binga's wedding was on the front page of the *Defender* in 1912.[49] A year before that, Binga made the front page after he attempted to help his chauffeur fix a flat tire. When Binga tried to inflate the tire, it exploded in his face. The rim cracked Binga in the forehead and opened a gash in his leg, but a couple days later, "he was able to be at his desk and about his official business," the *Defender* reported. "We are glad to state that our only [black] banker was not more seriously hurt than he was."[50]

Binga's name appeared weekly, sometimes daily. His letters were printed, his speeches were covered, his vacation itineraries were recorded, and his opinions were coveted. For Binga, the *Chicago Defender* gave him what he needed: publicity.

JESSE BINGA MAY HAVE SEEN ETTA JOHNSON AT MASS AT ST. MONICA CHURCH. She certainly stood out. She was a tall, attractive woman who looked frail, fidgety, and nervous. She was also white. Etta, age thirty, was married to Jack Johnson, the first black world heavyweight boxing champion, and on

September 11, 1912, she put a revolver to her head and pulled the trigger. She died in Provident Hospital after being given last rites by Rev. John S. Morris of St. Monica.[51]

Binga was devoted to St. Monica Church, and he must have been saddened by the death of a troubled soul and horrified by the scandal of it all. Etta, a Brooklyn socialite, was a free spirit who along with her husband shared an interest in theater and the arts. Jack Johnson loved opera, as did Binga and Abbott. Etta also had a history of depression, and after marrying Johnson, pressures mounted. She was ostracized by whites, deserted by friends, viewed as an opportunist by both blacks and whites, and ignored by her black neighbors in Chicago. She was an outcast. Her husband was "her only friend," according to the *Chicago Record-Herald*, but he "sometimes went out with other women and left her with her books."[52]

Three months before Etta's suicide, Johnson opened the Café de Champion. Etta and Jack lived in an apartment above his nightclub, and Johnson had hired two maids "who prayed with Etta" that night. Before shooting herself, Etta reportedly told a black woman neighbor, "I am a white woman and tired of being a social outcast. All of my misery comes through marrying a black man. Even the negroes [sic] don't respect me. They hate me. I intend to end it all."[53]

The world of Jesse Binga's State Street could be a harrowing place. Eventually Binga decided to move out of the Black Belt, but it would be tricky, and dangerous.

13

5922 *South Park Avenue*

BY 1916, PATRICK GRIMES HAD DONE PRETTY WELL FOR HIMSELF. THE SON OF Irish immigrants, Grimes ran a bar and he owned a roomy redbrick house across the street from the lush green of Washington Park. He owned his house free and clear—not bad for the son of a day laborer.

The house at 5922 South Park Avenue was built in 1893, and Grimes and his wife, Nellie, bought it seven years later.[1] Novelist James T. Farrell, who as a youth lived at his uncle's house a block north on South Park Avenue, once wrote that "Paddy Grimes" was a saloon keeper and "the neighbors griped because a sloon [*sic*] keeper was in their midst. So he sold it to Binga."[2] Jesse Binga, that is.

But not exactly. Here's where it might seem a bit complicated, although not in the racial calculus of 1916.

Grimes, who had no mortgage on his house, sold it to a woman named "Viola Canty," according to Cook County real estate records. It just so happened that Jesse Binga's top aide was a black woman named Inez Cantey. She did most everything for Binga at the bank, and she would assist him in other ways, including traveling to Canada to visit Binga's son and his family and buying gifts on Binga's behalf for his grandchildren.[3] She ran the administration of the Binga Bank and kept his daily schedule; she was also his auditor. She was a trusted, long-term employee on whom Binga counted for efficiency and discretion. It seems likely that Inez Cantey was the actual buyer of the house at 5922 South Park Avenue, with the misspelling of her last name a clerical error; an apartment building next door was also bought in her name.[4] There are two facts worth noting here that would support this idea. First, Inez Cantey was very light-skinned and could easily pass for white—and often did. Second, her middle name was Viola. Another possibility, albeit a less likely one, was that Inez's mother, Viola Cantey, was the "buyer."

It seems likely that Inez Cantey was a straw purchaser, perhaps causing Grimes to think he had sold his house to a white woman. The sale was completed on July 17, 1916, and a little over a year later, the real estate records show that the owner "Canty" sold it to Eudora Binga—on August 8, 1917.[5] Eudora already owned several pieces of real estate she had inherited from her late brother, John "Mushmouth" Johnson, and was a savvy real estate owner in her own right.

Given the rising racial tension of the time, it would seem that a black family moving into a house on this all-white block might have caused problems. It did not, however, at least not at the beginning.

Ever since the Bingas moved into their new home, "they have been extremely carful [*sic*] to maintain all of its outer surroundings in a healthy or sanitary condition so that it would be impossible for anyone to tell from outside appearances that a small colored family quietly lived within," the *Broad Ax* reported in 1920.[6]

Jesse Binga, for his part, was always a polite, quiet, low-profile resident of the 5900 block of South Park Avenue. He kept his lawn trimmed, kept his house tidy, and kept his distance—he never once set foot in a neighbor's house.[7] Jesse and Eudora Binga and their maid, Alabama-born Hattie Williams, lived quietly inside their house on South Park, and they liked it that way. Even Eudora's car—an electric runabout—ran with a whisper.[8]

Jesse Binga, like his neighbors, was simply trying to live the dream, make money, buy a nice house, and be successful. In fact, Binga was doing it better than most, if not all, of his all-white neighbors. His neighbors were German, Russian, Irish, Greek, and Jewish, mostly second generation. They were also ambitious. They included a meatpacking superintendent, an accountant at one of the new automobile dealerships, a jeweler, a minister, a doctor, and a bunch of salesmen. Still, only three of the men on the block—a coal merchant, a self-employed warehouse operator, and Binga—owned their house. Everybody else rented.[9]

Binga's house was arguably the nicest on the block, with two stories and an elegant wraparound front porch overlooking an expansive view of the emerald-tinted Washington Park. It wasn't a mansion, but it was swank. It encompassed 2,500 square feet, with three bathrooms, paneled hallways, and a banister and landing of polished wood. The first floor had a parlor with embroidered chairs and hand-painted lamps, and there was a music room and library between the dining room and parlor. The library was packed with books on Catholicism, said Carolyn Louise Dent-Johnson, a relative who once lived in Binga's house. She remembered sitting on the library floor as a little girl, paging through the books and seeing drawings of children in Purgatory, which caused her frightful dreams.[10] On the second floor there were the bedrooms and a gym room outfitted with a medicine ball, small weights, and a punching bag anchored from the ceiling.[11]

The elevator Binga installed behind the house's elegant staircase wowed visitors almost as much as what was in the basement. There, walled in metal, was a huge dryer the size of a small room outfitted with an electric system that rotated a massive rack of clothes on hangers as they dried in the heat.[12]

But perhaps the room which made the longest-lasting impression—because of its elegance, not its innovation—was the dining room, with the china service for twenty-four people. Around the edge of each cream-colored plate was a band of twenty-four-karat gold. And in the center of each plate was a big gold letter: *B*.[13]

JESSE BINGA TALKED SPARINGLY ABOUT HIS FAMILY; ULTIMATELY, HE WAS A private man with a public persona. Occasionally he would tell reporters about his upbringing in Detroit or credit his success to his mother, Adelphia, and his wife, Eudora, but most of his personal life remained largely hidden.

In the dozens of newspaper stories and magazine articles written about his rise and his life, there is little or no mention of his first marriage or his son from that marriage, Bethune. For a faithful Catholic like Binga, divorce would have been a particularly uncomfortable topic. And certainly a divorce didn't do much for anyone's social status at the turn of the twentieth century, particularly if one was a rising business entrepreneur and banker held up as an example of the future promise of the black community. Binga always appreciated that role, and he protected the power of his name and was not hesitant to comment on his achievements.

Robert Abbott's paper, the *Chicago Defender*, which quoted Binga frequently, also reported that Binga rarely sat for interviews, and when a *Chicago Tribune* reporter interviewed Binga in 1927, the white reporter wrote, "He had to be drawn on to talk about himself, and when I urged that surely there was profitable discourse in the story of a man who had begun as a barber and Pullman porter and now was a millionaire banker," Binga merely responded with "Yes, there's a volume in every man—I often say that."[14]

But there was one Binga family story he was happy to be associated with, and that was the one of his handsome and dashing young cousin, H. Binga Dismond.[15] Dismond, whose parents died in his youth, was virtually adopted by Jesse Binga and Anthony Binga Jr., who was Dismond's grandfather and Jesse's first cousin.[16]

Dismond, who for several years lived with Jesse and Eudora Binga in their house on Vernon Avenue and possibly at 5922 South Park Avenue, attended the University of Chicago—within walking distance of Binga's South Park house. He was an excellent student and a star of the track team as a standout quarter-miler. The quarter mile is an exhausting all-out sprint even on the inside lane, but Dismond "was required to run on the outside of the pack, all the way around, so as to avoid any physical contact with any white," a white rival once said, but still, "Binga could beat any man alive at 440 yards."[17] Many reports of his races, however, seem to indicate he wasn't routinely forced to run in the outside lane.

Binga Dismond was one of the earliest black athletes to become a nationally recognized track star. In February 1916, he beat a field in Brooklyn that included national champion James E. Ted Meredith of the University of Pennsylvania, and Dismond won by six yards.[18] Dismond, who was also the only black member of his team, was a critical part of the conference champion one-mile relay team in 1915. Jesse Binga would sometimes put his work aside and board a train to go across the country to watch Dismond compete.

As described by Gerri Major and Doris E. Saunders in their book, *Black Society*, Henry Binga Dismond was bright and good-looking, with a chiseled physique. When he entered a room, women swooned. He was from one of the "FFVs"—first families of Virginia—and had a swashbuckling air about him.[19] While a student at Howard University, before transferring to the University of Chicago, Dismond caused a stir when he eloped with an older woman who was a member of a socialite family in Boston. Dismond had three marriages after that.[20]

He served with distinction in the infantry during World War I as a first lieutenant, and he later became a prominent physician in New York, where he was the head of the physical therapy department at Harlem Hospital. He was also a published poet with his book *We Who Would Die*.[21]

WHILE JESSE BINGA OFTEN HAD HIS NAME IN THE PAPERS LINKED TO THIS DAZzling University of Chicago track star and outstanding student, Binga's son, Bethune, was never part of that public conversation. Despite being his father's only child, Bethune occupied a more distant part of Jesse Binga's life.

Born in 1885, Bethune lived only a few years with his father. Three years after he was born, Jesse hit the road to the West, never to return. Bethune was sent to live with his mother's parents in Canada, although as a young adult he lived briefly with his mother, Frances, in Chicago. (He was sixteen in 1901, the year his parents were divorced and his mother remarried in Chicago.) Even then, when he lived near his father, their relationship never seemed close. Dorothy Binga Taylor, one of Bethune's two daughters, said she saw her paternal grandfather only twice: once when he gave her a silver dollar at his bank when she was three years old, in 1914, and then at his funeral in 1950.[22]

While other more distant family members worked for Jesse Binga in various jobs from cashier to armed truck driver, Bethune was apparently never hired by his father, choosing instead to live in Canada. His was a blue-collar life. Bethune, who lived to be one hundred years old, drove a taxi, worked for an electric company, served in the Canadian army, worked as a carpenter, and delivered mail on a bicycle. Bethune was married twice. Bethune married Mary E. Smith in Chicago in 1909, but he didn't reside long in the city, and Mary died in 1914. As for how Bethune viewed the man exalted as the first black banker of Chicago, Bethune and Mary's daughter Dorothy said, "My father never said too much about him," and "they didn't correspond."[23]

When Frances died in Chicago in 1914, Bethune apparently was living in Chatham, Ontario. Prior to that, Frances lived at 2966 Vernon Avenue, less than four blocks from Jesse. It's unclear whether this was by design or whether Jesse helped finance his son's arrangements. When Frances died, maybe Bethune felt there was nothing more to bring him to Chicago and it was best to remain with his Canadian relatives.[24]

In 1920, Bethune married Mary Lucas, and their daughter, Inez, was born the following year. As an adult, this daughter, Inez Johnson, said all she remembered about her grandfather Jesse was that the family said he owned a bank, "but I never heard anything negative about him." Still, in her family, she added, "If you can't say anything good about someone, don't say anything." Inez said the only time she saw Jesse was at his funeral.[25]

Bethune was baptized Roman Catholic but later became Methodist. When Bethune's second wife gave birth to twin boys in 1923, Jesse sent word to him that he would like the twins to be baptized Catholic, but they had already been baptized as Methodists. Still, Bethune's choice of names for his two sons seemed to indicate that he had feelings of respect for his father. The twins were named Jesse and Bethune.[26] Their mother died in 1924.

While Jesse Binga's grandchildren were growing up in Canada, Jesse once sent his trusted assistant Inez Cantey to check on them. Dorothy Taylor remembers that Cantey bought her two dresses. Describing their long-distance relationship with Jesse Binga, Taylor said, "We always cherished him as our grandfather but never contacted him."[27]

Throughout Binga's life in Chicago, he doted on his other relatives and on the children at his church. He was active in Catholic charitable work and often made and served breakfast to the church's children after they received their first Communion. He occasionally entertained and hosted relatives from all over the country and routinely traveled to visit them. Yet Binga rarely saw his son or his son's family.

SHORTLY BEFORE JESSE AND EUDORA BINGA MOVED INTO THEIR NEW HOUSE on South Park Avenue, there were plenty of warning signs of increasing racial animosity and resentment manifesting in violence against blacks—for example, when a crowd of close to a hundred white boys surrounded the homes of two black families on Forty-Sixth Street.

It was February 1917, six months before the Bingas moved into their South Park home, when these two black families moved into apartments at 456 West Forty-Sixth Street. The day after they moved in, the crowd of boys, ranging in age from twelve to sixteen, came from surroundings schools to throw a hail of stones at the black families' second-floor apartments, breaking many of the windows and letting in the cold winter air. When police arrived, the boys scattered. After the police left, the boys returned and finished breaking every window on the second floor. The two black families moved out.[28]

This wasn't the first such incident, and it was far from the last. By 1917, racial tension in Chicago was building up an uncontainable head of steam. It would eventually blow out into the worst race riot in Chicago history. Competition for jobs was one source of friction. The other main pressure point was housing. And Jesse Binga was in the middle of all of it. By 1917, he could see the warning signs. He was, after all, making deals that brought blacks into white neighborhoods. He was charging higher rents and making money, and he saw and heard the anger from both blacks and whites.

At home, the Bingas kept to themselves. They seldom had visitors, and those were often family and out-of-town guests. As a real estate agent who moved black families into white neighborhoods, Binga certainly felt the tension. He didn't cower, but he didn't broadcast his presence. In neighborhoods where he made his deals, such as Hyde Park and Englewood, pressure rose as blacks "invaded" the leafy enclaves of white homeowners. Angry talk sometimes turned to beatings, broken windows, and ultimatums. Eventually all this strife would land at Binga's front door.

14

Distant Thunder

It seemed to Studs that his mother wiped away a tear. She turned towards the back of the house to ask the girls if they had all their things packed. "Hell, there is scarcely a white man left in the neighborhood," Studs remarked.

—The Young Manhood of Studs Lonigan

ON SUMMER WEEKENDS, JESSE BINGA COULD LIKELY SEE AND HEAR TROUBLE from his own front porch on South Park Avenue. Sometimes white teenagers would suddenly rush into Washington Park and black teenagers would run out. Or there would be a loud group of white teens pushing and shoving one another, taking up all the room on the sidewalk, while everyone else had to get out of the way. From Binga's front porch he could hear yells and shouts coming from across the green fields and see dust rising from scuffles on baseball diamonds. Two spots were particular problems. At the Washington Park Lagoon Boat House, a block or two east of Binga's place, there seemed to be fights every Sunday.[1] And at the tennis courts, some right across from Binga's house, "difficulties between the races" were a problem.[2]

As early as 1913, there were occasional scuffles between blacks and whites vying for parts of Washington Park.[3] By 1919, it was routine.

White teenage "athletic clubs"—such as Ragen's Colts, a group named after Cook County commissioner Frank Ragen, who helped pay their clubhouse rent[4]—would roam the park harassing young black couples sitting on park benches or waging war on black kids over use of the park's more than a dozen baseball diamonds.[5] These white "clubs" operated like gangs and were out to protect "their" turf from the steady stream of black youth coming into the park. With 370 acres, there seemed to be plenty of room for blacks and whites to segregate themselves on their own fields, if they wanted to. In fact, sometimes blacks and whites played baseball together—with white spectators on the first-base line, black spectators on the third-base line.[6] But that didn't last long.

With daily trains from the American South bringing more southern blacks into the city, it would stand to reason that parks and playgrounds would be an attractive oasis for newcomers to a big northern metropolis. The numbers of blacks and whites started to even up in some Chicago parks, Washington Park being a particularly choice destination. Every day more newcomers used the park. With this growing presence of blacks, one white property owner sarcastically said that Washington Park should be renamed "Booker T. Washington Park."[7]

Playgrounds were now battlefields.

BINGA KNEW IT WASN'T JUST TEENAGERS CAUSING THE PROBLEMS; THEY WERE learning this attitude from their parents who increasingly felt under siege. Whites felt pressured by the black "invasion" to move out of their apartments—or houses, which were their biggest investment, the very places where they raised their families and lived their lives. Racial change was shaking them to their core; they felt uncertain about the one thing that gave the most stability to their lives—their homes. Binga may have been reminded of that a month before Eudora officially closed on the deal to buy their home at 5922 South Park Avenue on an all-white block in an all-white neighborhood.

On Sunday night, July 1, 1917, at 10: 45 P.M., the wife of Rev. Eugene Robinson was sitting in the front room of their first-floor flat at 5320 South Maryland Avenue when she heard a noise in the vestibule, as if somebody had dropped a newspaper. Then she smelled smoke. She looked out the front window and saw a white boy—a teenager, maybe about fifteen years old—scurrying down the stairs. She quickly woke her husband, and they went to rouse their four children. By the time they stepped into the adjoining room, a bomb exploded, showering them with plaster while "blowing out part of the parlor wall and wrecking the vestibule and porch completely."[8]

Mrs. S. P. Motley owned the Maryland Avenue building. Mrs. Motley's family was the first black family on the block when they moved there in 1913. After the Motleys were joined by other black families, including the Robinsons in 1917, the neighbors criticized them for bringing more blacks into the neighborhood and "operating a rooming house," and everybody knew that rooming houses meant crowded living quarters and nothing but trouble. Threats came first, then the bombing.[9]

The Robinsons escaped unharmed, but this attack marked the beginning of a more aggressive and dangerous shift in tactics.

When Binga first began in Chicago real estate, he'd seen and heard of assaults and attacks on blacks over housing, but it was isolated and sporadic, nothing organized, nothing like what he was seeing during and after World War I. Still, Jesse Binga was always a forward-looking man. He was in the center of the racial housing storm, but he was also sitting by the cash register. Housing was how he made his living, and his living was good. Chicago had become a huge shifting buyer's market, and Binga was one of the biggest buyers in the Black Belt. While he spoke out against segregation in the black newspapers, it was also in his self-interest to do so. He knew there was plenty of business to be done. He would buy buildings or lease them and then rent out the units at a profitable markup. Money flowed. He started planning for a newer and bigger bank, and beyond that, he eventually dreamed of a gleaming new office building in the Black Belt, like the skyscrapers downtown.

Being in the center of all this real estate activity meant that Binga was also increasingly a target for both sides. On the one hand, newly arrived blacks sought to blame someone for the high rents, and they accused landlords like Binga for charging them more than the white renters who had just vacated the same units (an accusation with some validity). On the other hand, uneasy whites wanted to blame someone for the "Negro invasion." Somebody, they thought, was encouraging blacks to think they could live wherever they wanted. The white finger of blame always seemed to point at one man: Jesse Binga.

He was the bull's-eye. He could handle it, but it was unnerving. An automobile engine backfire could cause a shudder. Everyday Binga had to be mindful of where he was and who was around him. But he showed little fear. Eventually, however, even as he remained tough and unapologetic, his wife hired an armed guard. Binga believed that what he was doing was merely what many Americans aspire to: make money, get ahead, and be their own boss. Binga felt he could take on anybody, and he couldn't care less what any of them thought, black or white. Of course, the color of skin in America was like a billboard, and with it came a pile of assumptions about who you were. A man like Binga had to deal with it every day, as did the people of the Black Belt. Even though some blacks despised Binga for being cold and arrogant, many also saw him as a "race man," unbowed and outspoken on behalf of blacks. Even to a few whites he was a hero, a "pull yourself up by your own bootstraps" success story, but to most whites he was an agent of doom, bringing unwanted racial change—and something had to be done about him, they thought.

EFFORTS TO SYSTEMATICALLY CONTAIN THE BLACK POPULATION IN CHICAGO began at least as early as 1897 in the aftermath of the great Chicago world's fair of 1893. Hotels and rooming houses were built for the overflow crowds attracted to the fair, and many were "quick builds" of cheap materials and shoddy workmanship, particularly those next to the elevated rail line ("the El," as Chicagoans call it) at Sixty-Third Street and along the Illinois Central tracks. After the fair, housing demand dropped, and with the Panic of 1893, a depression followed. With fewer renters, landlords looked to blacks to fill those empty rooms. White residents of Woodlawn were outraged and "declared war" on the managers of these hotels. A committee of Woodlawn community leaders calling themselves "The Society of Woodlawn" organized to stop the black "invasion." Soon Chicago police with orders from building inspectors were confronting building owners. The containment held.[10]

As the black population grew, so did white resistance.

Streets became boundaries, color lines across which blacks would cross at their peril. In 1907, blacks didn't go much past Thirty-Ninth Street.[11] Wentworth Avenue became a color line, and later, it was Forty-Seventh Street and Grand Boulevard, and many more after that. Color lines were always being redrawn as neighborhoods shifted.

When a black kid crossed the border, a beating could be expected, or at least a heart-pounding chase. When the black poet Langston Hughes first came to Chicago, he thought he'd explore his new world and innocently walked west across Wentworth Avenue, where he was soon punched in the face and beaten by white boys who said, "they didn't allow niggers in the neighborhood."[12]

One day in 1918, a huge banner was stretched across Grand Boulevard. It proclaimed, "THEY SHALL NOT PASS."[13] Later in 1919, "move out" posters were slapped on telephone poles, streetlamps, and the walls of El stations. "EVERY COLORED PERSON MUST LEAVE HYDE PARK," one urged.[14] White groups organized to maintain segregation sprang up in Hyde Park, Kenwood, and Grand Crossing. A race war was declared, and Binga was a named enemy. He was threatened by phone and given cold offers to buy his home.

In February 1920, the Hyde Park and Kenwood Association's *Property Owners' Journal* contained this declaration: "The Negroes' innate desire to 'flash,' to live in the present, not reckoning the future, their inordinate love for display has resulted in their being misled by the example of such individuals as Jesse Binga and Oscar De Priest. In their loud mouthing about equality with the whites they have wormed their course into white neighborhoods, where they are not wanted and where they have not the means to support property."[15]

When blacks moved into white neighborhoods, they were subjected to taunts, slurs, and threats.[16] Parks and playgrounds became de facto islands of segregation: whites controlled some, blacks controlled others. And in the heat of Chicago's notorious summers, blacks had just one main beach to use for cooling down in Lake Michigan.[17] It was a tiny strip of craggy lakefront between Twenty-Sixth and Twenty-Ninth Streets swirling with industrial runoff so potent it could "temporarily bleach a black person white."[18] This beach would soon trigger a week of murder and destruction.

BY THE END OF 1917, BOTH JESSE AND EUDORA BINGA WERE FOCUSED NOT only on the growing tension within white neighborhoods like their own but on the sorrow of Cecelia Johnson Mozee, one of the few people who was close to the Bingas. It had to do with her husband, Dr. Theodore Mozee.

Theodore Mozee grew up poor in St. Louis. During sixth grade he left school to help support his family and later worked on and off after he resumed his studies. The hard work paid off in 1909, when he graduated from the University of Illinois Dental School.[19] While tending to his practice in Chicago, he also helped found Kashmir Chemical Company, a cosmetics and hair care firm catering to African American women. Eventually Kashmir, headed by entrepreneur Claude A. Barnett, launched a powerful and pointed advertising campaign that focused on the inherent beauty of black women instead of their "need" for skin whiteners and hair straighteners. Their advertisements showed photos of attractive young women, each called a "Kashmir Girl," and its treatments were described as the "Kashmir Way." Barnett, who also founded the Associated Negro Press, effectively used his contacts in journalism to advertise and promote Kashmir's products. Dr. Mozee, however, would never live to see the growth of Kashmir or even its incorporation.[20]

His trouble began on Monday, November 12, 1917. He likely woke up feeling extraordinarily tired and sluggish. Every movement was labored, as if his body was filled with sand. He probably developed a hacking cough and a body-shaking chill. After a couple of days, his cough might have become thick and bloody and his breathing shallow and labored.

By Saturday he was dead of pneumonia.[21] Dr. Mozee was just thirty-five years old. He and Cecelia had been married only five years. Similar deaths would become commonplace the following year.

The worst epidemic in Chicago history came in late 1918 as thousands of people died of influenza and pneumonia. In the fall of that year, at least 8,510 people died—381 in one day. The city scrambled to stop the pandemic's spread. Public funerals were banned, along with smoking and spitting on streetcars and El trains.[22] For those few months the growing racial turmoil of the city was sidelined (but not halted) by the unifying crisis of the flu. In 1919, that turmoil would return, and it would be much worse.

AT CLOSE TO 2:00 A.M. ON FEBRUARY 28, 1919, A BOMB EXPLODED IN THE hallway of a three-story brick building at 3365–3401 Indiana Avenue. The blast blew out a stairway and shattered windows of the two side-by-side rooming houses and on buildings across the street. The explosion was so strong that it threw many of the thirty tenants out of their beds, including six-year-old Ernestine Ellis. The little girl was sleeping with her grandmother when she was catapulted into the ceiling with such force that it fractured her skull and ruptured her internal organs. She died on the way to Provident Hospital.[23]

At first a gas leak was suspected, but an investigation quickly seemed to dismiss that possibility. While one tenant reportedly said there had never been any problems with their white neighbors, "the only theory advanced by the police for the setting off of a bomb was that it was the violent result of prejudice against the Negro occupants."[24]

The following months would reinforce that theory.

Again, at close to 2:00 A.M., on a Monday in early April, a bomb exploded about two feet behind the headboard of the bed of Mrs. Joseph Davis in a first-floor apartment at 3212–3214 Ellis Avenue. It splintered most of the furniture in her front room and blew a hole through the floor down into the basement and up into the ceiling and the second-floor parlor of another tenant. Despite that damage, Mrs. Davis, was deeply shaken, but unharmed. Six families lived in the building, and miraculously, no one was injured.[25] Black businessman J. C. Yarbrough owned the Ellis Avenue property; he had bought it three months earlier from Jesse Binga.[26]

Only weeks before that, at 11:00 P.M. on March 20, a bomb was tossed from a roadster. It shattered the doorways of Binga's real estate office on the ground level of a three-flat at 4724 South State Street, and another tossed bomb blew a hole in an apartment building managed by Binga.[27] As reported in the *Chicago Daily Tribune*, "Windows in the buildings on both sides of the street were broken. Binga's office was wrecked, furniture was overthrown and a door on the third floor . . . was wrenched from its hinges."[28]

Some people believed the bombers were hired by white real estate agents, and in one instance, it was suggested that Binga was targeted because he hired nonunion janitors.[29] The *Chicago Daily Tribune* suggested a different motive: Binga "is colored and has been leasing apartments formerly occupied by white families to colored people."[30] The *Chicago Herald-Examiner* was more direct, indicating that the Ellis Avenue bombing was part of a "Race War."[31]

A pattern was developing. The three bombings in three weeks had one thing in common: Jesse Binga.

15

"Barefooted and Bareheaded"

Standing at the corner of Thirty-First Street and Michigan Avenue in the summer of 1919, a white reporter for the *Chicago Daily News* saw something so strange to him that he said it seemed like something out of "a movie play."

A "colored woman and three of her children" were walking down the street, he observed. She was two months up from Alabama, where she had lived "in a two-room hut with a dirt floor and no running water," Carl Sandburg wrote in a series for the newspaper.[1] Chicago meant the hope of a better life and so here she was, living in the heart of the city's Black Belt. "Barefooted and bareheaded, the children walk along with the mother, casually glancing at Michigan Avenue's moving line of motor cars," when suddenly "a big limousine swings to the curb."

"A colored man steps out, touches his hat to the mother and children and gives them the surprise of their lives. This is what he says:

"We don't do this up here. It isn't good for us colored folks to send our children out on the streets like this. We're all working together to do the best we can. One thing we're particular about is the way we take the little ones out on the streets.

"They ought to look as if they're washed clean all over. And they ought to have shoes and stockings and hats and clean shirts on. Now you go home and see to that. If you haven't got the money to do it, come and see me. Here's my card."

Sandburg, already a published poet, doesn't name the man except to describe him as a banker and a real estate broker who owned property with more than a thousand tenants—a description that fit Jesse Binga.

"From all sides the organized and intelligent forces of the colored people," Sandburg wrote, "have hammered home the suggestion that every mistake of one colored man or woman may result in casting a reflection on the whole group."

Binga was one of those hammers.

JESSE BINGA WAS NEVER SHORT ON ADVICE. ADVICE TO NEWCOMERS AND UP-and-comers, it didn't matter; Jesse Binga had a way of doing things: the Jesse Binga way. In fact, around 1924 he published a pamphlet of his advice called *Certain Sayings of Jesse Binga.*[2] His advice included the following:

"Learn a business and then mind it."

"Save, save, save, and when you've got it then give, give, give."

"Nothing is so easy or so wasteful as the work of hating—except hating work. And that goes for races as well as for individuals."

"Get a competency. Then the world—white or colored—will concede that you are competent."

"Learn business: Establish a credit: Provide for your own wants. That is my message to our group."

"Life is pretty much what you make it—and making it big means using it every day."

"Be honest."

Outwardly, Binga seemed to live by those words. He knew how to run a building, fix a furnace, and repair a leaky roof. He was taking in thousands of dollars every month in rent—$4,000 a month from just one block and $1,500 from another[3]—and he eventually owned more than one thousand feet of frontage on State Street from Thirty-Fourth to Seventy-Fourth Streets.

And he did "give, give, give." He gave thousands of dollars to the Roman Catholic Church, to Provident Hospital, to promote State Street, and to buy Christmas gifts for children of the Black Belt.

As for Binga's honesty, black and white businesspeople and real estate agents said the same. When a *Chicago Tribune* reporter called white businessmen for a story on Binga in 1927, they all commended Binga for his integrity. They said when they called the First National Bank in downtown Chicago to learn about negotiating with Binga, the message was clear: "You can't do better" than Jesse Binga.[4]

The Binga name had become a beacon of hope in the Black Belt, a symbol of promise and potential for his community. Yet Binga himself remained elusive.

He had a high public profile, but he was a very private man. Publicly, beginning in 1919, he hosted a huge gala called the Christmas Twilight Party at which Jesse and Eudora Binga would give Christmas tokens to hundreds of guests who waited in lines winding through a ballroom at the Vincennes Avenue Hotel or the St. Elizabeth Assembly Hall. And always, somewhere, suspended from the ceiling or on a big frosted cake, there would be the big illuminated letter *B*.[5]

But the rest of his social calendar was largely filled with business lunches, private family dinners, and celebrations with his or Eudora's family or events at St. Monica or St. Elizabeth Catholic churches. As he grew older and more successful, he still got to work early and put in full, long days and then spent evenings at home with Eudora and their books and music, with occasional trips to the opera.[6]

To those who met him in business or at the bank, where he worked behind a massive desk the size of a loading dock while making calls and working deals, Binga could seem distant, and some people viewed him as arrogant and condescending. Certainly he was not a man to be crossed. He was known to take people to court or cut them out of future deals if he felt betrayed. No mere bystander to his deals, he would not hesitate to speak up when his interests were on the line.

For example, in 1915, when one of his clients, a black man named Charles A. Davis, was blocked by whites from moving into his newly bought house on the all-white block of 4700 South Forrestville Avenue, Binga drove up in his bright yellow car and confronted the crowd. They were all sent to a police station, where Binga, who was assumed to have financed the purchase, said he often had to do this to "defend the rights of negroes."[7] He wasn't one to back down.

Some suggested his terse manner was merely a mask to cover up the fact he didn't have a higher education, as did such competitors as Anthony Overton, who founded the Overton Hygienic Manufacturing Company in Kansas City, a cosmetics operation catering to black women with products including "nut brown" face powder. Overton brought his company to Chicago in 1911, a year before Binga's wedding. Overton was a polished man with a regal bearing, a college education, and a law degree. Eventually he would vie for the savings of the Black Belt when he opened the Douglas National Bank down the street from Binga.[8]

Binga might not have had a strong formal education, but he had a natural intelligence and a fierce confidence. He was quick with numbers and could take the measure of a deal as fast as a downtown grain trader. But there were signs of another side of Binga.

He was a skilled dealmaker, and he could negotiate a lease or sale to his lopsided advantage—which could cause resentment among his tenants and lessees. Earl Dickerson, who was a lawyer, business executive, community activist and first African American Democrat to be elected alderman, once waged a ferocious legal battle with Binga, whom he described as "a mean son of a bitch." Dickerson said Binga "used all the means he could on people. He had no sympathy at all."[9] Binga was "bluff, rough and tough," Dickerson said. "He had no interest in racial ideology but was interested exclusively in acquiring money and power."[10]

Binga was no doubt feared, but also respected. He was "Mr. Binga" to his customers and people on the street. Any association with him was considered an honor, a brush with celebrity. Once, a young African American doctor was called by Binga to come to his house for an "emergency." The young doctor was both stunned and thrilled, so he straightened his tie, smoothed his suit, grabbed his bag, and hustled to Binga's house. When he arrived, he was disheartened by what he found: the patient wasn't Binga; it was Binga's dog.[11]

The *CHICAGO DEFENDER* long extolled the virtues of life in Chicago to its readers in the South and eventually helped encourage them to move up north. Pullman porters would drop off papers along railroad stops in Mississippi, Louisiana, Tennessee, and other parts south and southeast. "Come North, where there is more humanity, some justice and fairness!" exclaimed *Defender* publisher, editor, and founder Robert Abbott.

On May 15, 1917, Abbott launched a formal campaign called "The Great Northern Drive."[12] This campaign to escape Jim Crow and live "like a man" echoed throughout the South and helped bring train cars loaded with field workers from Georgia and farmers from Mississippi to the North. For many of them, Chicago was their first destination.

In virtually every *Defender* that made its way to a cotton field in Georgia or a saloon in New Orleans, there was an ad or a story about Jesse Binga's bank and real estate operation. Jesse Binga was famous; when he opened his first bank, it made national news in the black press. Even New Yorkers took note of it, reading a story in the center of the front page of the *New York Age*.[13]

And now he was in the catbird seat, poised to profit from the historic migration of blacks to northern cities.

From 1916 to 1918, about half a million southern blacks migrated north.[14] In an eighteen-month period spanning 1917 to 1918, more than

50,000 came to Chicago,[15] although some used it as a mere stopping-off point before moving on. From 1910 to 1920, Chicago's black population soared from 44,103 to 109,458; it doubled in just the five years from 1915 to 1920.[16] This influx further intensified the density of the Black Belt, that narrow sliver of land then roughly more than three miles long and a few blocks to a mile and a half wide—from Twenty-Second Street south to Forty-Eighth Street and from Wentworth Avenue east past State Street to the Alley El, (elevated rail line) with parts a mile or so farther east. The migration was prompted by a conflation of rising unemployment, a scourge of boll weevils' damage to cotton crops, Jim Crow restrictions, World War I and eventually the urging of the *Chicago Defender.*[17]

Chicago was the end of the northbound railroad line. The *Defender* called it the "top of the world."[18]

When World War I ended in late 1918, black veterans joined the already full-throttled migration of black men and women from the South as they too headed back home to northern cities like Chicago. Jesse Binga's younger cousin Henry Binga Dismond of the 370th U.S. Infantry (once the fabled Eighth Illinois National Guard Regiment, an all-black division, including its commanding officers), was one of them. A letter he wrote home was published in the *Defender* in 1918 that gave a sense of his life in the trenches: "The rats, the grenades and the automatic rifles awoke me several times. It rained just before we arrived and all is mud. As [the English war poet John] Masefield says, the trenches are damn dirty, damn dull and damn dangerous. . . . Give my regards to every one. Tell them we have lost no one so far to my knowledge, but, of course, even before this reaches you the entire regiment may be a thing of the past."[19]

Dismond was at that point married for the second time—to black socialite Gerri Major—when he returned to Chicago and went to Rush Medical School, which in 1846 became one of the first medical schools to accept black students. Dismond graduated in 1921 and took an internship at Chicago's Provident Hospital,[20] where Jesse Binga decades earlier had donated fruit and vegetables from his peddler wagon.

With the steady flow of migrants from the South, the streets and street-cars close to the Black Belt had more black and white shoulders rubbing together and jostling for space. Some southern migrants, used to Jim Crow restrictions, were initially shocked to see blacks and whites riding side by side. In the South, a black person could be arrested for sitting next to a white one on a streetcar. Some whites, however, were rough on the newcomers, whom they said would "sit all over the car," engage in "loud laughter and talking,"[21] and behave in a manner they found rude and coarse. The new-comers often felt the same way about rude white behavior.[22]

One thing familiar to the transplanted black southerners was their limited access—by custom rather than law—to Chicago hotels, restaurants, and theaters,[23] unless, of course, they were in the Black Belt, where all races mixed.

But the source of the highest tension between blacks and whites was made of bricks and boards. Housing.[24] It was the key battleground, and Binga stood in the center of its fury.

IN 1917, AS BLACK HOMEBUYERS AND RENTERS INCREASINGLY SPRINKLED INTO white neighborhoods close to the Black Belt, some white real estate agents banded together to stop it.

Although the Chicago Real Estate Board banned black real estate agents from membership,[25] it nevertheless tried to control them. A board committee met with some black leaders—including Binga and Abbott—to pressure black real estate agents to stop selling homes in white neighborhoods. Binga and the others refused.[26]

The Chicago Real Estate Board, which in 1924 would champion restrictive covenants to effectively stop blacks from purchasing in white neighborhoods, called a meeting on April 16, 1917, to discuss its goals. Again black leadership was invited. Abbott's *Chicago Defender* called for black real estate dealers to stay away, and many, including Jesse Binga, refused to attend. Journalist and civil rights activist Ida B. Wells, however, did not. She walked right into that Monday meeting to protest the board's intentions, only to be greeted by the hoots and taunts of white women sitting nearby. Wells left angry and appalled.[27]

In a *Defender* story on the meeting, the first black real estate broker quoted was Jesse Binga. He called it "nothing less than a crime against good government for real estate men of the character and caliber of some of those who met . . . at the Chicago real estate boardrooms to begin an agitation on Race segregation." And, he added, "It would be well for those who are in any way affected by this move to consult their lawyers for there is justice in the state of Illinois."[28]

His statements not only reflected his sincere belief, they also reflected the fact that segregation was bad for business. Binga, however, was measured and even respectful in his language, hoping to persuade rather than pummel. This fight was becoming strategic.

As thousands of blacks from the South poured into the city, the housing situation became increasingly desperate. The *Chicago Tribune* called these migrants "Darkies from Dixie" and offered to pay them to go back where they came from. Nobody bit.[29]

Married black men would often travel alone to Chicago, get a foothold, and then send for family. Single men also rushed to the city. Many families doubled up in rooms and slept on floors so that their other rooms could be rented to lodgers for extra income, which was how Jesse Binga started in real estate. Lodgers, however, sometimes threatened the privacy and safety of families and often led to further deterioration of the property.

In short, black and white owners squeezed the most money possible out of limited square footage. When black families moved into rental units or homes in white neighborhoods, fears of deterioration surfaced and threats and violence followed. There was, however, a tipping point. When a block became 25 percent black, panic usually set in.[30] Some real estate firms specialized in coming in just for that panic period with contracts, deeds, and moving trucks.

Many whites complained about their property values depreciating, which was sometimes true, but as a study by the Chicago Commission on Race Relations in the early 1920s pointed out, any time poorer people moved into the older homes of a neighborhood where people earned more, there was depreciation. "That's true whether Italians move in, or Poles, Negroes, Greeks, etc.," the study said.[31]

For Binga, all this meant more business. He cut deals to handle rentals of apartment buildings deserted by whites, but he also handled deals of all kind. Deals were how he defined himself; they were his specialty. Deals were his talent and his art. They provided him with a good living by getting profitable rents for rooms or apartments or houses, just like his mother's deals had done some fifty years earlier in Detroit.

Black tenants were paying more than $12.00 a week for a place that white immigrants could get for $8.00. Landlords squeezed money out without putting any into the property.[32] Higher rents meant more boarders, and that meant more stress on properties. A survey as early as 1912 showed that only one out of four places in one area of the Black Belt was in good repair.[33] Black housing often had bathrooms with cracked and leaking toilet bowls or no bathrooms at all. Some of the rentals had been deserted for years and often had poor lighting, leaky pipes, and choking heat from wood or coal stoves instead of furnaces. Sometimes there was no heat. There were rat holes in the plaster, paper hanging from the ceilings, and windows missing panes. White resistance and violence made housing so scarce that black tenants had few places to go.[34]

And that meant blacks paid higher down payments, higher interest rates, and higher insurance premiums. And yet, the monthly payment was still sacred.

As several black real estate agents said, "a colored man usually feels that he will go without food rather than not meet his obligations. That is one reason why sometimes his home is run down, because he has spent every dollar he can get to meet the payments on that property. He cannot spare the money sometimes to buy a lawn mower or sprinkling hose."[35]

Although Binga had thousands of renters, his core belief was ownership. "Today we are beginning to realize that to become a good citizen, it is necessary to own a home," he said, "and that those who are renting cannot be considered other than floaters."[36]

But even some blacks criticized the rush to own, as Charles Duke said in a pamphlet on black housing in Chicago: "A very harmful result of present tendencies is manifested in the acquisition of homes by colored people beyond their social or economic advancement . . . it costs a small fortune annually to maintain one of these establishments, and when this is not done the depreciation is both rapid and spectacular."[37]

Binga saw himself as a man apart from all others, a gleaming example of what could be.

"You won't find any other colored people like me," he told a reporter for the *Chicago Daily News* in 1916. "Most of the colored businessmen in Chicago have started with nothing for the race is young as a free people in the nation and still younger in the north. Few of them aside from professional men have got beyond the stage of small business."[38]

And it was tough to get ahead.

White-owned banks, where thousands of blacks had savings accounts, often refused to give mortgages to blacks. And many of the new Chicagoans didn't know how they worked; it was not part of their experience. Binga, however, was willing to help educate, and he was also willing to bet on the newcomers. For him, that was also just good business. It encouraged more black customers to come through his doors. Binga knew that home ownership was one of the loftiest goals an everyday man could aspire to, the brass ring of the full American dream.

"The colored people in Chicago feel this is their last ditch. Here is something to look forward to, in the South they know there are Jim Crow cars, segregation, humiliation and degradation,"[39] Binga said.

BUT LIKE MANY OF THE BLACK ELITE, BINGA WANTED THE NEWCOMERS TO shape up and learn the ways of the North, and he wanted them to do it quickly. Binga saw their behavior as a threat to integration and a mark against all blacks, including himself.

Binga often offered his guidance, sometimes in the form of positive urgings such as his *Certain Sayings* but at other times in a rather blunt, indelicate way. Quoted in the *Defender* in 1920, the year after the incident observed by Carl Sandburg in his *Daily News* piece, Binga said he wanted to "educate the ignorant people who are flooding our city by gaining their confidence, eliminating their suspicions and thus develop a thrifty and desirable person out of an indolent, reckless spendthrift."[40]

Abbott's *Chicago Defender* not only campaigned for southern blacks to move north, the paper also campaigned for the largely rural newcomers to shed their country ways and conform to the norms and manners of city life. The *Defender* sponsored clean-up campaigns, pushed neighborhood clubs to pressure the newcomers to toe the line, and peppered them with lists of dos and don'ts.[41]

Family members would often meet relatives from the South at the rail station and immediately advise them on how to act, as if they were arriving in a foreign country. When relatives met their migrating relations at the station, author and historian Timuel D. Black Jr. said, they were advised, "Don't talk too loud, dress up and look good, take a bath, don't spit on the sidewalk, take work clothes to work and change there."[42]

Certainly, both the newcomers and the old-timers were fed up with being viewed by whites as one black "lump," as the *Broad Ax* had once reported, which meant that "no individuality is to be allowed and the surest measure of judgment is the very lowest."[43] Some of the newcomers further felt that the last thing they needed was to be corrected and chastised by members of their own race. They longed to be treated as individuals, not merely as members of a group.

Add to this world of festering resentment the regiments of black soldiers returning from war in Europe, many of them armed with service revolvers and rifles. After serving their country in Europe, they were not about to be treated poorly at home.

On the streetcars or walking down the street, blacks in Chicago encountered a host of insults and slights. A sneering glance, a demeaning comment, or a two-hour wait for dinner in a restaurant—all this treatment built up an undeniable tension.

In reviewing crime in the Black Belt, the Chicago Commission on Race Relations in its study of African Americans in Chicago offered this insight: "The traditional ostracism, exploitation and petty daily insults to which they are continually exposed have doubtless provoked, even in normal-minded Negroes, a pathological attitude toward society which sometimes expresses itself defensively in acts of violence and other lawlessness."[44]

The study noted, "A desire for social revenge might well be expected."[45]

16

Riot

IT WAS QUITTING TIME, 5:30 P.M., MONDAY, JULY 28, 1919. JOHN MILLS WAS headed home from the Stockyards on the eastbound Forty-Seventh Street trolley car. After traveling only a few blocks, a mob of about fifty white teenage boys appeared and surrounded the streetcar, forcing it to stop. The boys started rocking the car, and Mills could hear someone clomping around on the roof above with the sound of thunder. A white teen on the roof yanked the trolley loose from its wires while a couple of others jumped on board, slamming bats into the wall, throwing bricks at blacks hiding beneath the seats, and clubbing those who tried to make a run for it. Mills was one of the few to get away.

When he stepped onto Forty-Seventh Street, he was met by hundreds of howling whites now lined up along the street. White children had made their way to the front of the crowd, squirming in to get a better view. There were tiny boys and girls, some as young as four or five years old, with faces so twisted by their angry taunts and yells that they looked much older. Mills took off.

He ran to Normal Avenue when the full weight of a hurled brick caught him in the back, knocking the wind out of him. He stumbled and slowed, struggling to get his breath, and soon was tackled from behind and the beating began. He fought to get up a couple of times, but the mob was like a heavy blanket on top of him; their bodies suffocated Mills. As he tried to get up one more time, a man clubbed him with a two-by-four, cracking his skull. Mills's eyes blinked and closed as he lost consciousness. The beating continued until Mills's body lay limp and twisted in the street. Mills was dead.[1]

Twenty minutes later and a mile north, at Thirty-Ninth and Wallace Streets, stones peppered Oscar Dozier as he ran from a mob of close to one thousand screaming whites, until halfway down the block he finally fell. He too was trying to get home from work, and he too was killed—stabbed to death.

An hour and a half later and one block west, Henry Goodman's skull was fractured when a white mob boarded the front of an eastbound Thirty-Ninth Street streetcar and pushed their way to the back, pounding on every black person they could find until they were forced off the rear. Goodman survived the beating but later died of tetanus.

With short intervals of minutes and hours, the beatings and murders continued deep into the night.

Monday, July 28, 1919, was a perilous day to be a black man traveling the streets of Chicago. And it didn't matter where. Inside the Black Belt, whites in speeding sedans drove through, cursing and firing shots. Outside the Black Belt, black workers heading home were confronted by angry whites and scattered into white neighborhoods, pursued by crowds through backyards, alleys, and gangways.

And it continued the next day. Some of the beatings were in the heart of crowded downtown Chicago. Downtown! A mob of white civilians, soldiers, and sailors rampaged through the Loop for several hours early Tuesday, July 29. At one point the crowd charged into a restaurant at Wabash Avenue and Adams Street and tossed food and dishes at black patrons. One black man, Paul Hardwick, managed to escape into the street and took off down Adams. When it looked as though he was getting away, a rioter stepped out of the crowd, pulled a gun, took aim at Hardwick, and fired. Hardwick fell dead, and a couple of people stepped out of the crowd and rummaged through his clothes for valuables. Hardwick's body was left twisted in the street, his pants pockets turned inside out.[2]

AS JESSE BINGA HEARD ABOUT THE MULTIPLE BEATINGS, HE COULD TELL THAT this was a full-scale riot with no end in sight. It began on a hot Sunday, July 27, at the scraggly beach nestled behind a brewery and an ice company between Twenty-Sixth and Twenty-Ninth Streets. Intermittent rioting continued for nearly a week, until Saturday, August 2, when it finally calmed down with the arrival of state militia and a "cooling" summer rain.[3]

During this time, Binga and the rest of the Black Belt grew enraged as they began to feel desperate and trapped. Some of Binga's relatives might have hunkered down in their family bakery[4] at Thirty-Third and State

CHAPTER 16

Streets while roving bands of whites drove through the neighborhood shooting out windows and menacing anyone who dared to appear on the street. Work stopped, wages went unpaid, and supplies ran low. The Black Belt was under siege.

Binga made phone calls and met with businessmen to figure out how to get food and provisions into the Black Belt. It was as if war had been declared, and Binga was the quartermaster.

WHILE THERE WERE PLENTY OF RUMORS, IT WAS BECOMING KNOWN THAT THE riot began with the drowning of a seventeen-year-old black youth named Eugene Williams at that three-to-four-block strip of beach on July 27. Williams and four of his friends hoped to get some relief from the ninety-degree heat that Sunday and headed to the beach and the chilled waters of Lake Michigan. There was a tacit understanding between blacks and whites that the Twenty-Sixth Street Beach (some called it the Twenty-Fifth Street Beach) was the black beach up to Twenty-Ninth Street, and then it was the white beach. An invisible color line in the water kept the races separated.

On that Sunday, however, some black men and women entered the water from the "white side." That prompted some yelling and cursing and stone throwing between blacks and whites. The blacks left and returned with reinforcements and the stone throwing resumed. Then the whites left and quickly returned with more help of their own, and it became a full-scale fight. Williams and his pals were largely oblivious to this conflict as they floated on a large raft made of railroad ties and frolicked in the water a couple hundred yards from shore, where the water was about fifteen feet deep. A white man made his way out to the end of a breakwater about seventy-five feet from the raft and threw stones at Williams. At first it may have seemed like a game, and Williams and his pals dodged the stones while dunking themselves underwater. At one point Williams looked away and a stone clipped him in the forehead, according to one of his friends, John Harris.

Harris saw that Williams was injured and then "just sort of relaxed" and sank into the water.[5] Williams's friends tried to bring him up but couldn't. Finally, white and black swimmers worked together searching for Williams. An hour later, lifeguards pulled out the teen's body. But his autopsy later showed no stone bruises.[6]

A white policeman refused to arrest the white man accused of throwing the rocks at Williams. The officer instead arrested a black man "on the complaint by a white man." That officer's chosen course of action was believed to be a major factor in inflaming the gathering crowd of blacks and whites on the beach.[7] "Hundreds of angry blacks and whites" swarmed to the beach, and when more police arrived in a patrol wagon at Twenty-Ninth Street, a black man shot into the crowd, wounding a policeman. A black police officer returned fire, killing the shooter.[8] Wild stories, both true and false, quickly spread, and "new crowds gathered" in other areas away from the beach. The rage that had been ignited would flare up more violently that night and the next day. Farther to the west on Sunday night, "white gangsters" in "white districts" joined in the violence. According to a report by the Chicago Commission on Race Relations (CCRR), "From 9:00 pm until 3:00 am twenty-seven Negroes were beaten, seven were stabbed and four were shot."[9] Blacks fought back and began to target whites, and the fighting would ebb and flow for days.

JESSE BINGA KNEW THERE WOULD BE MORE TROUBLE AFTER WHAT HAPPENED Sunday and Monday, and he had to know it was fueled by the already strained feelings of whites over their perception of blacks taking their jobs and moving into their neighborhoods. Mostly he knew it was about the color of skin. But as he must have heard beating story after beating story, Binga, like everyone else in the Black Belt, had to have been stunned by the enormity of it all.

The newspapers carried reports reading like scorecards of how many whites were dead or injured versus how many blacks were making the atmosphere more "peculiarly dangerous."[10] The city's newspapers pumped out a variety of stories where facts were frayed, tethered to rumors, and given over to exaggeration. Among the white-owned papers, the *Chicago Tribune* tabulated an early death toll at thirteen whites and seven blacks when just the opposite in numbers was true.[11] The *Chicago Herald-Examiner* reported that several thousand black men broke into the Eighth Regiment Armory and grabbed hundreds of guns with ammunition, and about fifty people were shot, when in fact some windows were broken, but there were no weapons inside, and nobody was shot.[12] Yet black newspaper owner Robert Abbott's *Chicago Defender* had similar problems with presenting the truth. In one story, for example, the *Defender* reported that a black woman was killed with her baby as they tried to get on a streetcar at Forty-Seventh Street and Wentworth Avenue. The story said the "mob beat the baby's brains out against a telephone pole," and the mother was slashed to ribbons, with her breast severed and stuck on a pole carried by a white youngster as the crowd "hooted gleefully." None of that was true. In fact, no women or girls were killed in the riots.[13]

Binga knew the Black Belt was being cut off and isolated by the violence. And the talk on State Street wasn't good. Angry words of vengeance filled the barbershops and street corners. And there was outrage among veterans of the fabled Eighth Regiment, "known as the Fighting 8th."[14] They didn't fight with distinction in France during World War I to be treated like this at home now.

State Street became a meeting point for black anger. The growing rage could be seen from the steps of the Binga Bank, a little before 5:00 P.M. on Monday, shortly before John Mills would be chased down Forty-Seventh Street. There, at Thirty-Fifth and State Streets, a crowd of about four thousand blacks gathered and grew increasingly angry amid rumors of an imminent white attack. That's when Casmere Lazzeroni, a sixty-year-old Italian peddler, came by with his banana wagon, one much like the one Binga himself had driven as a fruit peddler back in the 1890s. Four teenagers in the crowd saw Lazzeroni and rushed out and chased him, hurling stones as they ran. They caught up to him at 3618 State Street, just a few doors from Binga's bank, across the street. They stabbed him repeatedly with pocketknives, and their hands and arms were covered in blood. Soon Lazzeroni was dead.[15]

This would not be the only instance of racial violence instigated by blacks in the Black Belt. In another incident, an angry crowd of about five hundred blacks stopped cars at Thirty-Fifth Street and Wabash Avenue and pummeled white passengers with fists and bricks. One car of whites turned around to escape and a passenger, William J. Otterson, was hit with a brick. His skull was fractured and he died.[16]

As the days that followed were filled with marauding bands of whites and blacks, the Black Belt became marooned. Food and supplies couldn't get through because of the fights, and teamsters didn't want to drive in and face mobs that could suddenly surround delivery trucks and loot their contents.

"My people have no food," Jesse Binga told a reporter a few days into the riot. "Retailers in the district have run out of stocks and outside grocery and butcher men will not send their wagons into the district."[17]

Garbage began to pile up on sidewalks and in alleys. The stench was overwhelming, and the decaying trash posed a major health hazard. Windows were broken, and fires were set throughout the Black Belt and in houses of blacks in white neighborhoods. With few people able to work, the economy of the Black Belt was dying.

By Thursday it was still too dangerous for blacks to go back to work at the stockyards: several who tried were beaten. A black man named

William Dozier showed up for work, and by 7:15 A.M. he was dead. It began when a white worker tried to hit him in the head with a hammer. Dozier dodged the blow, but the hammer hit him on the neck. As he ran east on Exchange Avenue, he was smacked by a broom, a shovel, and other assorted missiles of convenience found handy by white attackers.[18] He fled, and near the sheep pens, he was hit by a brick and died.

People shopping or going to work outside the Black Belt had to be escorted by police to "safe" zones. But no one felt safe. When a food truck finally made it onto State Street—under the protection of armed state militia—it was surrounded by people crowding in to buy badly needed provisions. Some people were able to buy ice from freight cars diverted into the Black Belt.

As a leader and figure of power in the community, Binga felt frustrated, there was so little he could do. But he did what he could. By Friday, he had set up an emergency pay station, established by the packers for stockyard workers. Huge crowds formed to get paid at Binga's bank (fig. 8) and at other pay stations set up at the Urban League and the Wabash YMCA. Fresh food and milk were finally trucked into the Black Belt, and black workers returned to their jobs under the protection of the militia's machine guns.[19] Slowly, commerce once again began to flow.

WHEN THE RIOT WAS OVER, THE TERRIBLE TOTAL CAME TO 38 KILLED, 537 injured, and about 1,000 left homeless. Of the dead, 15 were white and 23 were black. Of the injured, 178 were white and 342 were black; the race of the remaining 17 was not recorded.[20] That's how Chicago counted: by color.

Chicago was one of more than three dozen cities with race riots in the summer of 1919, including Washington D.C.; Knoxville, Tennessee;, Longview, Texas; and Charlotte, South Carolina.[21] In many instances whites attacked blacks, and in a few cities including Chicago, blacks fought back. James Weldon Johnson, a field secretary for the National Association for the Advancement of Colored People (NAACP), called it the "Red Summer" because of the blood spilled during the riots.[22] But it was also a summer where the country was in the grip of a "Red Scare"—a fear of Bolsheviks rising up in the United States to overthrow the government—fueled by the Russian Revolution abroad and by a series of bombings in the United States, including one on Wall Street. Some of these threats were real, many were imagined or exaggerated. The white press and the government stirred those fears by suggesting blacks would be a part of a communist revolution (when in reality the coming years would see a

Fig. 8. *Crowds gather outside the Binga Bank as people wait for news during the 1919 race riots. Jesse Binga also set up a pay station for black workers who could not get to work during that time. Notice the partially blocked words "Jesse Binga" in the large lower window in the center.* CHICAGO HISTORY MUSEUM, ICHI-065481; JUN FUJITA, PHOTOGRAPHER.

huge growth and embrace of black capitalism). Into that already volatile atmosphere add hundreds of thousands of blacks who had migrated to northern cities for work during the recent world war and hundreds of thousands of soldiers who had returned to compete for the few jobs remaining after the war, with the black soldiers returning home only to face disrespect and discrimination as payment for their service. Lynchings of blacks increased to seventy-eight in 1919, and some victims were soldiers still in uniform.[23] America in 1919 was like a powder keg, and in that summer heat, it exploded.

Of all the riots that summer, Chicago's was among the worst. In the aftermath, blacks and whites alike saw a lopsided form of justice. While black victims far outnumbered whites, the prosecutions at first seemed to favor white victims. Finally, an all-white grand jury fed up with hearing riot cases against only blacks stopped their proceedings and demanded that the state's attorney bring some evidence against white rioters.[24]

Ultimately, there were only nine indictments out of the thirty-eight murders in Chicago, and only four convictions.[25] No one was ever charged in the death of the first victim, Eugene Williams. And no one was charged in the deaths of John Mills, Oscar Dozier, Henry Goodman, and William J. Otterson. One person was convicted in the Paul Hardwick case. In the case of Casmere Lazzeroni, two teens were found guilty and sent to the penitentiary. Two people were indicted in the stockyards murder of William Dozier, but neither was found guilty.[26]

SEVERAL DAYS AFTER THE RIOT ENDED, JESSE BINGA RECEIVED A HANDWRITTEN letter in the mail. It came from the "Headquarters of the White Hands," which claimed its territory as being "Michigan Avenue to the Lake Front." It was signed "Respect. Warning Com." The letter read: "You are the one who helped cause this riot by encouraging Negroes to move into good white neighborhoods and you know the results of your work. This trouble has only begun and we advise you to use your influence to get Negroes to move out of these neighborhoods to Black Belt where they belong and in conclusion we advise you to get off South Park Ave. yourself. Just take this as a warning. You know what comes next."[27]

17

"I Will Not Run"

ON NOVEMBER 12, 1919, AN AUTOMOBILE ROLLED IN FRONT OF JESSE BINGA'S real estate office at 4724 State Street and a bomb was tossed out the window. Its explosion blew out windows, splintered wood, and sent contracts and title documents flying. By the time police arrived, the car was gone.

Binga's home was next.

On December 3, a "passerby" near Binga's house heard a "plop" and saw smoke rising from under the front porch. Firefighters were called, and a bomb was found sizzling harmlessly beneath the front steps. It didn't explode; it just charred the steps.[1]

Jesse and Eudora Binga were rattled, but it didn't stop them from celebrating their favorite holiday a couple of weeks later. They might not have realized it at the time, but their Christmas party celebration of 1919 would become their signature annual holiday tradition called the Christmas Twilight Party. It would also be the hottest party ticket in the Black Belt. The first Binga Christmas Twilight Party was held at the spacious black-owned New Vincennes Hotel at Thirty-Sixth Street and Vincennes Avenue.[2] The music, provided by Elgar's orchestra, which was hidden behind palms and ferns in the hotel's palatial ballroom, had a calming effect on the nerves of the guests and the Bingas, now in their fifties. The orchestra made "the music float out in the dreamy soulful way that causes even the old to forget their age and the youthful to become more gay, if possible," according to a *Broad Ax* newspaper story on the party.[3]

The Bingas rented the hotel's reception rooms, parlors, and dining room and filled them with holiday flowers and wreaths of holly fashioned in the letter *B*. Party favors were standard at the Christmas Twilight Party, where women would be given gifts of headbands trimmed in silver or glittering bracelets with tiny silver bells. Men sometimes were given a bow of white chrysanthemums or a black cane decorated with silver trim and tied in red ribbon. Everyone was in formal attire, with Eudora elegantly "gowned" in black iridescent over satin with diamond ornaments.[4]

The first Christmas Twilight Party was in honor of Mr. and Mrs. James Cole, who were visiting the Bingas from Detroit, where Jesse was born.[5] Both couples were in the receiving line, as was Eudora's beloved "little sister" Cecelia Johnson Mozee, now a widow of several years. And no party could be a party of Chicago's black elite without the popular master of ceremonies Julius Avendorph, journalist and bon vivant. *Chicago Defender* editor Robert Abbott was there with his wife, as were cosmetics manufacturer Anthony Overton and funeral director Charles Jackson, who in a few weeks would become vice president of Binga's bank.[6] Medical student Henry Binga Dismond and his wife Gerri made stylish turns on the dance floor, as did many of the several hundred in attendance. The crowd was the who's who of the Black Belt elite. Half a dozen doctors and their wives were in attendance including Dr. Ulysses Grant Dailey, who sharpened his surgical skills under the legendary Dr. Daniel Hale Williams.[7] Also there was Eudora's nephew, poet and author Fenton Johnson. Fenton had published several books of poetry and founded the *Champion Magazine* in 1916 in connection with Renaissance man Dismond, also a budding poet. Fenton dedicated his book of poetry *A Little Dreaming*, to his grandmother, Eudora's mother, "whose life was a poem full of tender sympathy and wholesome striving." Eudora set Fenton up with initial capitalization of $3,000 to start the magazine.[8] Fenton wrote that the magazine would "do all in its power to impress upon the world that it is not a disgrace to be a Negro, but a privilege."[9]

The "younger set enjoyed the pretty new dances and their graceful ways of doing them was a pleasure to onlookers," the *Broad Ax* reported. Dinner was served in the hotel's "pretty little tea room."[10]

The *Broad Ax* story made no mention of the bombings but referenced the struggles of life and perhaps hinted at what the Bingas faced when it stated, "It was truly a lovely gathering in one of the most beautiful spots that could have been selected in this city. . . . Too much cannot be said of this pretty Xmas party and Mr. and Mrs. Binga will long live in the hearts of their friends for it is large hearted, Broad-minded people that hold the old world of ours on a level and keep us feeling that it is not such a bad place to be after all."[11] The last song played at the Bingas' Christmas party was "Home Sweet Home." Two days later, Binga's house was bombed again.

ON THE NIGHT OF DECEMBER 27, A BOMB WAS THROWN ONTO THE FRONT steps of the Bingas' house. This one didn't just sizzle, it exploded, shaking the windows and damaging the large, white, wraparound front porch. An eyewitness, Arthur Curtiss, a *Chicago Tribune* Linotype operator, said he was positive the bomb thrower was a white man. Curtiss said he was "driving by the Binga residence in his twin six when he saw an auto dash up to the curb. A young man wearing a soft hat pulled down over his face jumped out, ran to the porch, tossed a package on it and scooted by to the car." The driver of the car, also white, kept the engine running and stepped on the gas when the bomb thrower jumped back in the car. Curtiss was unable to get a good look at the car, and there were no taillights to illuminate the license plate number.[12]

It wasn't just the color of Binga's skin that drew the attention of the bombers. It was Binga himself. He had become a symbol of racial change, the general leading the black "invasion." For months, Jesse and Eudora had been receiving threats, some by phone, others by mail. The message was clear and blunt: Get Out.

Jesse Binga had become the most hated man in Chicago—at least in white Chicago.

BY CHRISTMAS 1919, BINGA CONTROLLED HALF A MILLION DOLLARS' WORTH OF South Side property.[13] As a banker, he held mortgages on hundreds of black-owned properties that no other banker would touch. He ran a thriving real estate business that symbiotically funneled loans and savings accounts into his bank. One business boosted the other. Armed with those two weapons, he was leading an exodus of black families out of the cramped, crowded, and contaminated housing in the Black Belt. Now, with Binga's help, blacks were moving into white neighborhoods. That led whites to sell, which in turn led to more deals for Binga, and Binga loved deals.

He didn't make the most deals—white real estate brokers handled many more than black ones did—but he was an agent of change, a symbol.[14] He bought and sold and managed buildings in and around the Black Belt. White owners would hire him to handle a "changing" building, and once a building had "turned" black, he collected the rent and hired people to keep the furnace firing, the plumbing clear, and the hallways clean.

Binga straddled the two worlds of white ownership and black renters. He was the highest-profile figure of racial change in Woodlawn, Kenwood, Grand Crossing, and Hyde Park. Now he was also the biggest target.

As much as Binga tried to manage his image in the press, his race defined him far more than did his ambition, his success, or his three-piece suit. His main goal was to make money, but his skin color would cast him into a world of racially charged deals, and he would be accused of "block-busting." Since the early 1900s, he and others had propelled a pattern of buying and selling that would continue in various forms in Chicago for close to a century. Binga always seemed to find a way to rearrange the odds in his favor. Betting on how people would react to his race was a sucker bet; it was a sure thing.

Binga, however, also wanted out of the Black Belt. He moved out of his house on Vernon Avenue to get away from the dangers, noise, and tumult of his neighborhood and into a neighborhood on South Park Avenue in which he and Eudora became the first black residents. When asked by a reporter for the *Chicago Defender* why he moved to a white neighborhood, with an implication he was trying to get away from his own race, Binga was defiant.[15]

"I have just as much right to enjoy my home at Washington Park as any one else to go there and play tennis or baseball or enjoy other advantages of the district," he told the *Defender*. "It is a personal privilege. I went there to live because I liked the house and I had a chance to buy it. During the past twenty years I have often heard the same remarks whenever our people moved into better districts. In time criticism subsided. I do not want to get away from anybody, but absolutely refuse to live in a neighborhood inhabited by the lower class of white trash."[16]

As the Black Belt grew, so did its problems. Since the Black Belt was constrained by white resistance to expansion, overcrowding grew worse. And that caused blight. Some of the "changing" buildings were already in bad shape. Properties were soon exhausted by the overuse of plumbing and misuse of small apartments designed for far fewer people. Prostitution, gambling, and assorted other vices were just doors away or around the corner in many parts of the Black Belt. This environment made it tough for middle-class black families to find suitable property in which to raise their children or enjoy their prosperity. The solution for some was to move to larger, single-family homes in nearby neighborhoods, only to be greeted by threats and violence from the whites living there. To many of these black families, there was a clear hypocrisy to it. After all, hadn't well-meaning whites argued that they didn't object to the color of a person's skin, that it was really just about economics? That is, it was about class, not race. Yet many of the bombings, most of the threats, and much of the mistreatment of blacks moving into white neighborhoods involved middle-class black families—families like Jesse Binga's.

BY EARLY FEBRUARY 1920, POLICE WERE WATCHING BINGA'S HOUSE, patrolling in the back alley, and walking on the sidewalks in front and along the sides. The guards changed watch at midnight, but on February 6, the patrolman on duty left a few minutes early and his relief, oddly enough, came minutes too late. In that gap of time, it happened again. A next-door neighbor saw a "big black touring car" swing around a corner and roll in front of Binga's house; a man leaned out of a window and tossed a bomb into Binga's front yard. A thaw that day had melted snow into slush, and the bomb sizzled and went out. The arriving police officer picked it up, yanked out the dead fuse, and took the bomb to the station, where they found it to be "made of black powder, manila paper, and cotton."[17]

Police investigations continued to explain that "racial feeling" had caused the bombings and that whites said, "Binga rented too many flats to Negroes in high-class residence districts." And that Binga's "home is in a white neighborhood."[18] Yet no arrests were made.

Police were still assigned to Binga's house on June 18, 1920, when a black sedan swung by again. This time the man got out and carefully placed the bomb on the steps. No police were in sight. When the bomb blew, it splintered the front porch and shattered windows up and down the block. The explosion left Binga with $4,000 worth of damage. He had to repair his porch yet again.[19]

Binga offered a $1,000 reward for the arrest of the bombers.[20]

By now, the Bingas and their maid constantly lived on edge. When Jesse was at work, he worried about Eudora. And Eudora always worried about Jesse's safety out on the street. Binga was careful how he got home, and he was perpetually wary of who or what was around him. Even the slap of a newspaper on the front porch could send a shiver. But when the *Daily News* reported that after the June 18 bombing Binga said, "This is the limit; I'm going,"[21] Binga lashed out.

"Statements relative to my moving are all false. My idea of this bombing of my house is that it is an effort to retard the Binga State Bank, which will take over the mortgages of colored people now buying property against which effort is being made to foreclose. I will not run. The race is at stake and not myself. If they can make me move they will have accomplished much of their aim because they can say, 'We made Jesse Binga move; certainly you'll have to move,' to all the rest. If they can make the leaders move, what show will the smaller buyers have? Such headlines are efforts to intimidate Negroes not to purchase property and to scare some of them back South."[22]

Whatever hidden rage Binga had, he probably took it out on the heavy punching bag in his upstairs gym on South Park Avenue. Binga contained his anger; he knew the dangers of losing control, and he was always a man in control.

Novelist James T. Farrell, who lived down the street, later fictionalized Binga as a black banker named Abraham Clarkson in *The Young Manhood of Studs Lonigan.* In his portrayal of the crowd that came out to see the aftermath of the bombing, Farrell wrote:

> Most of the excited and gaping people present also eyed the wreckage with approval, wishing that it would have a proper and fearful effect. But they knew the bomb would teach no lessons and inspire no fear. For Abraham Clarkson had been bombed before, and he had stated defiantly that he would move from his home to another one only in a casket.[23]

Although his tenants didn't universally love Binga, they and others in the Black Belt admired him for his stand. The bombings created sympathy for him and made him a fearless champion of their plight. They could identify with him.

Of the forty black families that were bombed over several years, only two families moved.[24]

A group called the Protective Circle of Chicago was formed by blacks to find and arrest the bombers and to combat such white organizations as the Kenwood and Hyde Park Property Owners' Association in their efforts to stop blacks from moving into white areas.[25]

But the bombings continued. On November 23, 1920, the Bingas were preparing for dinner when they were jolted by a deafening explosion at the front of their house. While this bomb had been loud, it only slightly damaged the Bingas' house, but it shattered and overturned furniture of a neighbor at 5916 South Park Avenue and left pockmarks in the wall made by slugs scattered from the bomb. Windows were broken nearby and a two-foot hole was left in a driveway.[26] It seemed the bombs were getting more powerful. Police said this one was made of dynamite.[27]

When the Bingas went out of town on August 24, 1921, it had been nine months since the last bombing. Nevertheless, they had hired an armed guard, former policeman William McCall, "a Negro employed as a watchman at the Binga home," while they were away.[28]

On August 25, two men in a large sedan were seen heading north on South Park Avenue as a woman near the front of the Binga house yelled,

"Look out!" A bomb was tossed from the car, and the blast that followed dislodged the front pillars of the Binga porch and shattered windows throughout the neighborhood.[29] McCall, who had heard something back by the garage, was looking back there when the blast came.[30]

The Bingas' maid, Hattie Williams, quickly locked herself inside the house and refused to open the door. By the time police arrived, McCall was nervously waving a revolver at the crowd that had gathered near the front steps.[31]

"Back right up or I'll shoot you with this here gun," McCall shouted at the curious onlookers who crowded around, according to a *Chicago Tribune* report. A police detective came forward and grappled with McCall and managed to grab the gun out of his hand. In a *Chicago Defender* article, McCall said that he ordered *Chicago Tribune* reporters off Binga's property and pulled his gun out only when a reporter reached into a coat pocket to possibly do the same.[32]

A *Chicago Tribune* story on this bombing said, "Enmity of a number of white persons against Binga because he had sold property in 'white' districts to Negroes is thought to be responsible for the bombings."[33]

Binga was repeatedly pressured to sell his house, and he repeatedly refused, once saying he would not sell for $100,000.[34]

AND THEN IT ENDED.

The August 1921 bombing was the last of it. The bombings of Binga's property stopped.

No one ever claimed the $1,000 reward. No one ever was arrested for the six bombings of his house and the two bombings of his business.

Binga was there to stay. It would be decades before he moved. By 1930, the racial makeup of his block had clearly changed; at that point, half of his block was occupied by blacks.

The bombers did not defeat Binga, but years later, something else would. Binga's world would come undone not by bombs but by a couple of blank sheets of paper.

18

Stacking Cash

JESSE BINGA QUICKLY AND METHODICALLY STACKED BUNDLES OF CASH ON THE counter in the money cage of his bank—big stacks of bills, everything the bank had. Two trusted employees, Inez Cantey and C. N. Langston, helped him pile the money like bricks in a house. When the pile shifted or looked unsteady, they would gently pat it back in place as if it were held together with soft mortar. They made sure the stacks lined up just right. Hovering over the house of money, all they could smell was linen paper and ink. They finished quickly and then stood back and admired their work. There it was: $300,000 in cash, a thing of banker beauty.

Mr. Herman, a cold-eyed representative of the Auditor of Public Accounts for the State of Illinois, studied the pile and nodded his head. Everything was fine, he said, as he put on his coat to head into the cool night air. The Binga State Bank had far exceeded its requirement of having $120,000 (its shareholder investment). Binga now had a state-sanctioned bank (fig. 9).[1]

FROM THE MOMENT BINGA OPENED HIS DOORS THAT MONDAY, JANUARY 3, 1921, hundreds of people lined up at teller cages to make deposits while others simply took in the atmosphere with pride and a feeling of ownership. Even the weather was in Binga's favor, with an unusual high that day of forty-nine degrees and no snow on the ground. The much-anticipated opening culminated in a crowd of an estimated three thousand people who came throughout the day. Some wore furs, silks, and gingham; others wore overalls or work uniforms. By closing time at 5:00 P.M., an additional $200,000 had been deposited, bringing the total number of

Fig. 9. *Jesse Binga* (center) *standing in the middle of his bank on January 3, 1921, when his bank became a state-sanctioned bank—the Binga State Bank.* BROAD AX, JAN. 8, 1921.

new depositors that day to 1,100. The first proud customer to open an account was thirteen-year-old Miss Marvel Clinksdale, who lived down the block. To mark the opening, she and all first-day depositors received an "artistic souvenir" of a "birthday card of the Binga Bank."[2] One new customer was a local "Jewish merchant" who deposited $6,000, showing that "he has absolute faith in the soundness of the Binga State Bank," according to a *Broad Ax* article on the day.[3]

It was now some time past 6:00 P.M., (the bank stayed open until 8:00 P.M. that day to accommodate depositors) when a slight smile must have crossed Binga's face. Another milestone achieved. While still in the same location at 3633 South State Street, Binga's operation now had state-sanctioned respectability—the first for a black-owned bank in Illinois.[4] It also gave him bragging rights to use against his competition—other private unregulated banks that had opened to challenge him. These competitors could no longer operate as private banks because of new state law, so they had to either change or close. Binga supported the change, which now allowed the state to routinely check on Binga's bank and regulate its operation, since the new law had helped eliminate some of his competition, but not all. (In 1922, his rival Anthony Overton, entrepreneur and cosmetics mogul, would secure a federal charter for his bank, the Douglass National Bank.)

After the cash was counted, and the auditor's approval granted, James P. McManus, second vice president of the First National Bank of Chicago, extended his hand to Binga and shook it while affirming that Binga's newly chartered Binga State Bank could continue to clear through the First National in downtown Chicago.

The 125-foot long main banking room of Binga's bank had been decked out in flowers, ferns, and potted plants to commemorate the occasion. The plants came from the Abbotts, Cecelia Johnson Mozee, Mr. and Mrs. Charles S. Jackson, and other well-wishers. Binga's employees, including Cantey and her two sisters who also worked at the bank, gave Binga an engraved gold-lined silver loving cup as a congratulatory gesture.[5]

Back in 1910, the *Chicago Defender* had predicted it all. Jesse Binga was "not content to stand still and be satisfied with what merely comes his way, like most men."[6]

Binga was a man on the move, and having a state bank was just another step. He was far from finished. He had plans for a new bank building, maybe even another bank. He wanted to expand his real estate holdings, but his biggest dream was to build a skyscraper in the Black Belt. Heady plans.

Times were good on the South Side, the *Defender* said in early 1920: "People are spending money, people are saving money, people are investing money as never before in the history of the race."[7]

And, the *Defender* said, the Binga Bank had arrived at a perfect time.

BY 1921, THE WEALTH OF JESSE AND EUDORA BINGA WAS RISING WITH THE prosperity of the times. One corner of Jesse Binga's State Street property had been valued in 1919 at $500 per front foot, compared with $300 when he bought it.[8] And Binga owned or controlled hundreds of feet of State Street frontage. He also owned multiple three-flats, two-flats, vacant lots and greystone homes.[9]

The newly sanctioned Binga State Bank now had five thousand depositors, though some had as little as one dollar in their passbook.[10] Binga's bank also had multiple accounts of modest deposits from local businesses and from not-for-profits such as churches, including his own, St. Elizabeth Catholic Church. His board of directors included Colonel John R. Marshall, an old friend of Eudora's late brother John "Mushmouth" Johnson who had run as a Republican for the county board, and Oscar

DePriest, the onetime decorator turned blockbusting real estate dealer and groundbreaking politician. A Republican, when most blacks voted for this "party of Lincoln," DePriest became one of the most powerful black politicians in Chicago and an ally of the controversial white mayor William "Big Bill" Thompson. DePriest also knew the terrible downside of the election business. As Chicago newspaperman Finley Peter Dunne once said, "Politics ain't beanbag."[11]

Apart from the bank, Binga sat on numerous boards, some for mixed-race organizations and some for black organizations. But he hated politics and tried to stay away from it. Indeed, Binga didn't have the personality to run for public office, even though in 1910 he ran as an "Independent candidate" on a Republican ticket for the county board and lost. For a man of Binga's stature and connections, it was impossible to avoid politics.

In Chicago, politics was blood sport. As Chicago's first black alderman (for the Second Ward), DePriest had to step down in 1917 when he was indicted on conspiracy and bribery charges connected to a powerful gambling kingpin, Henry Teenan Jones. DePriest hired the famous white lawyer Clarence Darrow, who argued that $1,000 given by Jones to DePriest wasn't a bribe for police protection but merely a campaign contribution. DePriest was acquitted. Binga later said he gave DePriest $2,500 to fight the indictment.[12] Interestingly, DePriest's bondsman was Elijah H. Johnson, the owner of the Dreamland Café and the brother of Mushmouth and Eudora.[13] DePriest, while slowed by the indictment, was far from finished. He went on to become the first black U.S. congressman elected since Reconstruction. Years later DePriest would play a role in one of the saddest chapters of Jesse Binga's life.

The obligations and favors that went with accepting public deposits from government entities was anathema to Binga, who in 1928 would say, "I'm not handling public deposits now and do not contemplate doing so." Shifting to the third person in which he liked to refer to himself, he would continue, "You see, Jesse Binga is a businessman, not a politician. I can't be bothered by the numerous solicitations for this that and the other purpose. It wasn't so bad when they called on me to contribute to a fund for needy black children. The south side knows Jesse Binga doesn't need to be asked to give to a purpose like that."[14] But, he would acknowledge, "when it came to buying meal tickets to some banquet that they were getting up for the Hon. So-and-So, I decided charity begins at home."[15]

Privately, Jesse Binga in the 1920s preferred a quiet and reserved life. He and Eudora gave time and money to the children of the Black Belt. They spent many hours devoted to St. Elizabeth Catholic Church, often helping with bills or first Communion celebrations. On occasion Jesse would surprise the children of St. Elizabeth Catholic School with treats or gifts. One Friday afternoon in December 1926, he gave Christmas gifts to each of the school's one thousand children as nuns handed out ice cream, cake, and candy that he also provided.[16] Eudora hosted separate Christmas parties for children of the Black Belt, one for Protestants and one for the children of the St. Elizabeth parish.[17] The Binga home library was filled with religious books about the lives of the saints illustrated with frightening images of torture and torment and salvation.[18] Catholicism was Jesse's refuge. Jesse and Eudora also donated college tuition for young Chicagoans to attend Fisk University (a historically black university in Nashville, Tennessee), the University of Chicago, and the Chicago Musical College (now a part of Roosevelt University in Chicago).[19]

Apart from her philanthropic endeavors with her husband, Eudora was more of a behind-the-scenes giver. She helped found the Old Folks Home in the Black Belt, and she volunteered at the YWCA. In 1927 she became the first black woman to organize a Salvation Army doughnut drive in Chicago.[20] And she was a tireless volunteer for the Sisters of the Good Shepherd and the Sisters of the Blessed Sacrament.[21]

The Bingas' biggest public event was undoubtedly hosting their Christmas Twilight Party on Christmas Day. Hundreds would vie for an invitation—which invariably had an embossed art deco *B* at the top and reminded all guests at the bottom that it was a "formal" event.[22] The men attended in "full dress evening suits," and the women were attired in elegant gowns and wearing "it is safe to say seventy five to one hundred thousand dollars worth of Diamonds and other costly jewels," according to a *Broad Ax* report on the 1921 party.[23] With a classic Binga touch, the invitations mandated that the party time was precise: "half after five until ten o'clock sharp."[24] As would become typical at each of these successive years' parties, a giant letter *B* was always present somewhere. Sometimes it was suspended from the ceiling of the Vincennes Hotel or drawn in frosting on the top of cakes, or hanging as a wreath fashioned out of holly.

In addition to her philanthropic activity, Eudora Binga was actively involved in managing her own wealth, including a sizable real estate portfolio. She once was reported to have negotiated the profitable sale of one piece of her land to the Santa Fe Railroad for $180,000.[25] Eudora was close to being an equal partner in the new Binga State Bank. She put in $40,000, nearly matching Jesse's $45,000 investment.[26]

When they weren't volunteering for charitable works or conducting business, the Bingas, both now in their fifties, enjoyed a more contemplative life. They became subscribers to the Chicago Civic Opera Company after it was organized in 1922. Jesse Binga was also friends with utility mogul Sam Insull, who, like Binga, had come to Chicago in 1892. Insull headed the Opera Association and on November 4, 1929, unveiled his new $20 million Chicago Civic Opera House with Binga in attendance.[27] The Bingas belonged to the Art Institute of Chicago, and Eudora collected art from her extensive travels to Europe.[28] The Bingas also commissioned paintings for their home and a mural for the bank. A portrait of the couple hung in their home.[29]

WHILE THEY EMBRACED A LIFE OF CULTURE AND REFINEMENT, FOR BLACK elites in the early twentieth century, there were some things money couldn't buy. A reminder of that came when the Bingas' friends the Abbotts decided to go on a three-month tour of South America. Jesse Binga hosted a bon voyage party at the Unity clubhouse for Robert Abbott on January 12, 1923.[30] The Abbotts were on their way to New York, where they would board a steamship headed for Rio de Janeiro. The who's who of the Black Belt were in attendance at the party, including four directors of Binga's bank: C. N. Langston, U. G. Dailey, John R. Marshall, and Oscar DePriest.[31] Several gave toasts—although Abbott didn't drink and Binga rarely did so.

Binga raised a glass, pointed at Abbott, and said, "A just cause of dark hue, is just what God has made of you."[32]

The elite who had gathered for the send-off felt they were a part of newspaper publisher Abbott's success, and they celebrated his wealth and ability to do what a rich man in America was entitled to do: travel and live a life of luxury. But for a wealthy man of color, there was always a catch.

Once, when Abbott tried to buy a Rolls-Royce in a downtown Chicago showroom, the white salesman said he couldn't make the deal. Apparently, Abbott would learn, a $16,000 Rolls-Royce could not be sold to a black man in Chicago. Instead, Abbott had to buy it through a white friend.[33]

Similarly, when the Abbotts got to New York for the South American trip and Robert tried to book the couple's first-class passage with a white ticket agent, he was again denied. Sensing a similar racially motivated snub, he had his light-skinned wife Helen call to try to book tickets on the same ship. She was "mistaken for a white person and was promptly offered first class tickets for the identical ship on which her husband had been refused passage."[34]

These stories were routine among the wealthy of the Black Belt. Jesse Binga and his business friends knew all too well that money and wealth don't free a man of the slights and indignities of being a black man in white America. It didn't matter if you pulled yourself up by your boot-straps, as America preached, and it didn't matter how high your money was stacked.

19

"They Seem Like One"

PROHIBITION, JAZZ, AND BLACK CAPITALISM WERE ALL GOOD FOR THE BLACK Belt in the 1920s—and for Jesse Binga. He saw his wealth and reputation rise with each year, bringing more evidence that the building blocks of his bank were as safe and stable as the more than foot-thick steel doors of his bank vault. Each year seemed to bring another announcement of achievement and success.

In 1921 his bank became the first black-owned state-sanctioned bank in the city. In 1922 it became the first black-owned bank to become a member of the Chicago Clearing House, which clears checks, smooths the way for payment, improves efficiency, and reduces the risk of a member bank failing to meet its obligations. Binga advertised his bank's membership in gold letters on the bank's front plate glass windows.

And then, on October 20, 1924, Binga unveiled his new $120,000 bank building,[1] which looked like a Greek temple and quickly became an iconic symbol of success in the Black Belt (fig. 10). Two white stone Ionic columns flanked the front entrance, and the *Chicago Defender* breathlessly estimated that one hundred thousand people walked through those doors in the opening week to admire the new bank, just north of the northwest corner of Thirty-Fifth and State Streets.[2] Early visitors were each given a souvenir of a "handsome clothes brush with a mirror on the back and a beautifully bound pamphlet,"[3] and some left with a stiff new passbook with the distinctive *B* on the cover. One of the first visitors was Prince Kojo of Dahomey, an African kingdom whose people were once represented in a popular and controversial exhibit on the Midway during the 1893 Chicago world's fair.[4]

B I N G A   S T A T E   B A N K

Founded by Jesse Binga, 1908, as a private bank. Incorporated as a State Bank January 1st, 1921, with capital of $100,000.00. Present capital and surplus, $235,000.00; deposits, $1,268,357.91. Directors 9, stockholders 292, employes 20. This bank has stabilized, through its timely loans, more than $20,000,000 of real estate. The building is of Ionic architecture, suggestive of an ancient Greek temple. Located on State Street, near 35th. Member of the Chicago Clearing House. Jesse Binga, President.

Fig. 10. *Jesse Binga unveils his new $120,000 bank building on October 20, 1924.* SCHOMBURG CENTER FOR RESEARCH IN BLACK CULTURE, JEAN BLACKWELL HUTSON RESEARCH AND REFERENCE DIVISION, THE NEW YORK PUBLIC LIBRARY. "BINGA STATE BANK FOUNDED BY JESSE BINGA, 1908, AS A PRIVATE BANK." FROM THE NEW YORK PUBLIC LIBRARY DIGITAL COLLECTIONS, HTTP:// DIGITALCOLLECTIONS.NYPL.ORG /ITEMS/510D47DE-1A4F-A3D9-E040 -E00A18064A99.

Inside the three-story building, visitors were greeted with "soft colors" and "old ivory ornamental plaster work" decorated in "Italian shades."[5] Each teller cage had individually controlled lights with triangular reflectors. The customer "check desks" were appointed with brass calendar cases, cut glass inkwells, and bronze wastepaper chutes. A stairway of Sainte Genevieve marble led to the mezzanine, and a river of marble flowed through the rest of the bank. A balcony overlooked the foyer of the building, and marble steps led down past a protective grille to the bank's subterranean twenty-ton vault door of sixteen-inch-thick steel which protected a space with four thousand safe-deposit boxes.[6] The bank's exterior and interior exuded safety and permanence.

Binga's bank now had $1.15 million in deposits (close to $17 million in today's dollars) and twelve thousand customers (nine thousand of them with savings accounts)[7] served by a staff of eighteen employees,[8] almost all of whom had college degrees. The deposits may have been modest, but they had more than tripled since 1921.[9] The bank's 202 stockholders had seen their stock rise from $120 to $165 per share in just a few years.[10]

The new bank was in the heart of the Black Belt. It stood like a pillar of economic might amid the strip's theaters, nightclubs, insurance companies, bakeries, barbershops, and beauty parlors. It was a symbol of black achievement, and so was Binga. The bank was a source of community pride, or, as the *Defender* said, it was an "institution that lives exclusively for its community" and a "testimonial to [Binga's] rugged persistency and his championship of conservative but progressive ideals."[11]

When state bank examiners made their annual visit in 1924, "Two of their members were Negroes. It was indeed novel, surprising and thrilling," wrote bookkeeper and teller Richard Mickey in a letter to his cousin, the portrait painter Teddy Harleston. "They handled themselves like old veterans," he said. "That's progress, eh?"[12]

The *Defender* routinely emphasized what Binga and his bank meant. "The same as the bank is interlocked with the community, Mr. Binga's career is so interlocked with the Binga State bank that they seem like one."[13]

Progress was being made. In 1870, five years after the Civil War, only about 8 percent of black families lived in their own home. But by 1920, that number had jumped to almost 23 percent, although still less than half the rate for whites (47 percent).[14] Binga was part of that shift in Chicago, although he was more of an evangelist for home ownership than a provider of it.

While he may not have been as wealthy as *Defender* editor Robert S. Abbott or maybe even his banking rival Anthony Overton, Binga was the enduring symbol of success in the Black Belt. He was feted in both black and white newspapers and praised for his seemingly classic American success story. The *Broad Ax* in 1926 characterized Binga's rapid rise from "a poor street fruit peddler to a man of prestige, fame and affluence" as both "permanent and spectacular."[15] A front-page *Chicago Tribune* feature in 1927 said Binga's story was of a man who began "as a barber and Pullman porter and now was a millionaire banker."[16]

He was also immortalized in a half-length painting by Harleston, which was arranged by Inez Cantey, who also once helped get Mickey his bank job. Harleston had Binga sit for him for an hour a day in 1924, starting at 7:00 A.M., Harleston wrote to his wife, to "catch him when he is fresh

Fig. 11. *Jesse Binga, a success story in 1927. THE CRISIS*, DECEMBER 1927.

and before he is bothered by the day's business." Harleston thought Binga would be "fussy and a little irksome," he told her,[17] but in a later letter said the banker "talks business all the time while sitting but is not a bad sitter and our meetings are very pleasant."[18] With a typical Binga flourish, Harleston said that after one appointment, he was driven home in the Bingas' "real Lincoln limousine."[19] Harleston was taken with the Bingas' home, which he found "very nicely furnished, showing nice taste with a number of paintings, mostly landscapes" but including one of Harleston's own works, *The Bible Student*, which he said "holds its own" on Binga's walls.[20] When a 1927 exhibition called *The Negro in Art* opened at the Art Institute of Chicago (fig. 12), Harleston's portraits of Binga (fig. 13) and *The Bible Student* (fig. 14) were among the paintings featured. Binga was a patron of the exhibition, along with Abbott, George C. Hall, Jane Addams, Carl Sandburg, and other black and white Chicago luminaries.[21]

Binga's name had the ring of success, and he planned for much more—and more was to come.

"NEGRO IN ART WEEK"

Committees

MISS ZONIA BABER
CHAIRMAN

MRS. ELI DAICHES
CHAIRMAN OF PUBLICITY

MRS. IRWIN S. ROSENFELS
SECRETARY

MR. ELDRIDGE BANCROFT PIERCE
TREASURER

MRS. ALBERT GEORGE
Chairman of Music—Tickets

MISS MARY E. McDOWELL
Chairman of Literature & Poetry

MISS BLANCHE V. SHAW
Chairman of Books

MRS. FREDERICK W. GROWER
Chairman of Hostesses

MR. CHARLES C. DAWSON
Chairman of Sub-Committee on Fine Arts

MRS. WENDELL GREEN
Chairman of Sub-Committee on Drama

MISS ELLA BOYNTON
MRS. B. FRANK BROWN
MRS. HARLAM WARD COOLEY
MR. CHARLES C. DAWSON
MRS. ELI DAICHES
MR. W. M. FARROW
MR. A. L. FOSTER
MRS. ALBERT GEORGE
MRS. HERBERT Y. McMULLEN
MRS. GEORGE MEAD
MR. FRED A. MOORE
MRS. ROBERT E. PARK
PROF. ROBERT E. PARK
MRS. JAMES F. PORTER
MRS. NANNIE REED
DR. HERBERT A. TURNER

MRS. WENDELL GREEN
MRS. WILLIAM F. GROWER
MRS. ALFRED HAMBURGER
MRS. WILLIAM HAWES
MRS. KATHERINE IRWIN
MRS. EDWIN L. LOBDELL
MISS MARY E. McDOWELL
MRS. KATHERINE WAUGH McCULLOCH
MR. WILLIAM SCOTT
MISS BLANCHE V. SHAW
MISS MARY ROZET SMITH
MRS. ALBERT W. SPROENHLE
MRS. LORADO TAFT
MISS GRACE TEMPLE
MRS. MAXINE VAN CLEEF
MRS. C. COLE PLUMMER

Patrons

MISS JANE ADDAMS
MR. AND MRS. MAX ADLER
MR. ARTHUR T. ALDIS
MRS. JOSEPH T. BOWEN
MR. DUNCAN CLARK
DR. AND MRS. HENRY CHENEY
JUDGE AND MRS. ALBERT GEORGE
DR. AND MRS. CHARLES GILKEY
MR. AND MRS. WM. F. GROWER
MR. AND MRS. CLARENCE HOUGH
MR. AND MRS. HAROLD ICKES
MRS. BENJAMIN F. LANGWORTHY
MRS. EDWARD LOWENTHAL
MRS. ANDREW MACLEISH
MR. AND MRS. FRANCIS NEILSON
WILLIAM V. O'BRIEN
DR. WALTER DILL SCOTT
MRS. MAUDE E. SMITH

MR. AND MRS. LORADO TAFT
MISS EDITH WYATT
MRS. JAMES WESTFIELD THOMPSON
MR. ROBERT B. HARSH
DR. MAX MASON
CLARENCE DARROW
MR. AND MRS. HERMAN DeVRIES
MR. ROBERT B. HARSHA
MR. AND MRS. JESSE BINGA
DR. AND MRS. GEORGE C. HALL
ALDERMAN AND MRS. LOUIS B. ANDERSON
MRS. IRENE GAINES
MR. AND MRS. GEORGE ARTHUR
MR. AND MRS. ROBERT S. ABBOTT
MR. CHAS. S. PETERSON
MISS HARRIETT VITTUM
MR. CARL SANDBURG

Cooperating Organizations

CHICAGO WOMAN'S CLUB
WOMAN'S CITY CLUB
CHICAGO WOMAN'S AID
CHICAGO URBAN LEAGUE
CHICAGO CHURCH FEDERATION
CITY CLUB OF CHICAGO

NATIONAL ASSOCIATION FOR THE
ADVANCEMENT OF COLORED
PEOPLE, CHICAGO BRANCH
FEDERATED CLUBS OF COLORED
WOMEN
Y. W. C. A.

Fig. 12. *"Negro in Art Week" flyer listing patrons for the exhibition* The Negro in Art *at the Art Institute of Chicago in November 1927. Jesse Binga was among the patrons; among the paintings was the portrait of Binga done by Edwin Harleston.* IMAGE COURTESY OF THE ART INSTITUTE OF CHICAGO, RYERSON & BURNHAM LIBRARIES.

No. 28—"PORTRAIT OF MR. JESSE BINGA"—Edwin A. Harleston

Fig. 13. Portrait of Mr. Jesse Binga, *by Edwin Harleston, as shown in the program for* The Negro in Art *exhibition at the Art Institute of Chicago in November 1927. Harleston painted the Binga portrait in 1924–Binga sat for the portrait at his house on South Park Avenue.* IMAGE COURTESY OF MAE WHITLOCK GENTRY AND THE ART INSTITUTE OF CHICAGO, RYERSON & BURNHAM LIBRARIES.

No. 29—"THE BIBLE STUDENT"—*Edwin A. Harleston*

Fig. 14. The Bible Student *by Edwin Harleston, as shown in the program for* The Negro in Art *exhibition at the Art Institute of Chicago in November 1927. The painting, bought by Binga, was loaned for the exhibition; normally it hung in his home on South Park Avenue.* COURTESY OF MAE WHITLOCK GENTRY AND THE ART INSTITUTE OF CHICAGO, RYERSON & BURNHAM LIBRARIES.

THE 1920S MAY HAVE LIFTED THE BLACK BELT AND BINGA, BUT FOR EVERY STEP forward there were new and inventive ways to contain and isolate Chicago's growing black population. Restrictive covenants were particularly effective, at least for a while. Pushed by the Chicago Real Estate Board, the covenants prohibited sales of land to blacks, and the covenants ran with the property, thereby limiting black ownership into the future. By the late 1920s the covenants stretched like a "marvelous delicately woven chain of armor," encircling the Black Belt, according to the *Hyde Park Herald*, a white neighborhood newspaper.[22] "Even Al Capone's mother, Theresa, signed up to guarantee the 'respectability' of the family home."[23] In 1938, a black man named Carl Hansberry, father of playwright Lorraine Hansberry (*A Raisin in the Sun*), would challenge these covenants tied to his property at 6140 South Rhodes Avenue, just a couple blocks from Binga's house. Hansberry would win his case in 1940 as restrictive covenants would be ruled invalid, at least for that Washington Park subdivision, but it would take another eight years for the U.S. Supreme Court to prohibit racially restrictive covenants, declaring them invalid in the 1948 case of *Shelley v. Kraemer*.[24] In the 1920s, however, these covenants were in full force and put a straitjacket on some of Binga's real estate ambitions. It was yet another racially based complication to his business life, but by this point he was occupied on many other fronts.

Binga regularly invested in stocks, and he was involved in several insurance companies—at one point he tried, unsuccessfully, to take over Liberty Life Insurance.[25] He also planned to enlarge his banking operation while his civic duties were constantly expanding. Although privately he was quiet and reserved, publicly he was forever giving speeches and receiving loving cups and varnished plaques attesting to his leadership in charities and business organizations, some that crossed racial lines. For example, in 1927 he became president of the then newly formed and interracial Mid-South Chamber of Commerce, which was partially devoted to compelling landlords to keep their buildings in good repair.[26] And while Binga was always testing the color line in business, as when he became the first African American banker in Illinois to join the Illinois Bankers Association in 1913,[27] he was above all a practical man. He knew racial animosity wasn't disappearing. He could see it in all the surrounding white neighborhoods that conspired to isolate the Black Belt. As the prominent black twentieth-century sociologist Franklin Frazier said, "The . . . pathological feature of the Negro community . . . grows out of the fact that the Negro is kept behind the walls of segregation and is not permitted to compete in the larger community."[28]

The solution of numerous entrepreneurial "race men," such as Binga, Abbott, Overton, and various policy kings, was to make the Black Belt somewhat self-sustaining. They wanted to create black-owned businesses with black customers spending "Double Duty Dollars," which worked by "both purchasing a commodity and 'advancing The Race.'"[29] Black capitalism was powered by Double Duty Dollars and inspired by practical mantras like "Don't spend where you don't work." Of course, Binga said the banks should lead: "I would say to those aspiring to be of influence in our community, to remember that the banks and the business men are the bulwark of the community."[30]

"A race to achieve its independence," Binga asserted, "must foster its own interests."[31] He explained, "When we support our own business enterprises and patronize our own banks we develop our own civilizations and perpetuate our own Race."[32] And as the *Chicago Defender* later said, Binga was not just a banker: "the big 'B' was a symbol of financial solidarity."[33]

In 1924, Binga, Abbott, and Overton formed the Associated Business Clubs (ABC) as a unified black business movement designed to improve cooperation among business owners and promote black entrepreneurship.[34] Binga introduced a coupon system where for every dollar of purchase, the customer was given a three-cent redeemable coupon to be used for future purchases at participating ABC stores.[35] By 1925, ABC had one thousand businesses as members,[36] within a community of black businesses that Binga himself had estimated in 1922 had grown from five hundred to three thousand over the preceding five years.[37]

This was the "golden decade of black business," according to black studies scholar Christopher Robert Reed.[38] There was so much commerce in the Black Belt in the 1920s, Reed wrote, that the National Association for the Advancement of Colored People (NAACP) "was suffering" because "no organized body could fully attract the attention of the mass of the people during this decade with the exception of business, and in particular, business success."[39]

Binga was a tireless missionary for capitalism, extolling the virtues of thrift and hard work and the need to spend at black-owned businesses. "An afternoon never dreamed of as coming true," for Binga, was the large gathering that he and his bank directors organized in early 1927, where W. E. B. Du Bois spoke on the virtues of thrift and the need for black banks.

The philosophy of self-sufficiency worked well in the 1920s and worked better for black-owned businesses like Abbott's, which specifically targeted a black readership, or the Overton Hygienic Company, which served the specific skin care needs of black women. But there was a limitation to this market. The black-owned businesses in the Black Belt were competing with white-owned businesses that had a broader geography and wider markets with multiple locations that cut costs and fueled its enterprise.

Binga, however, knew there were weaknesses to having an isolated yet self-sufficient Black Belt. Near the end of the 1930s, there were some 2,600 black-owned businesses in the Black Belt, along with some 2,800 white-owned businesses.[40] Yet, as the mid-twentieth-century black sociologists St. Clair Drake and Horace Cayton emphasized, "*While Negro enterprises constituted almost half of all the businesses in Negro neighborhoods, they received less than a tenth of all the money spent by Negroes within these neighborhoods.*"[41]

Indeed, capitalism in the Black Belt was separate but not equal.

Binga himself had thrived on exploiting the racial equation of the city. He made plenty of money through rent hikes and rising prices caused by segregation and neighborhood color lines that increased demand for black housing while limiting it. Binga unabashedly capitalized on black needs and white fears. But he also saw the potential of black buying power beyond the Black Belt. In a telegram to the Illinois Bankers' Association, he said, "You may get the Negro's dollar, but the question is, are you getting all you should from the Negro?" Employing a bit of patriotic self-promotion in response to this question, he said, "The Binga State bank has taken upon its shoulders the task of developing the Negro commercially. We intend that the black man's dollar shall be for the benefit of all the nation and that the black man shall do his share in the commercial development of the land of the Stars and Stripes."[42]

Black capitalism rooted in segregation had its limits, and the next decade would begin with ominous signs for Black Belt business, and for Binga.

DURING THE 1920S, BINGA FULLY ENJOYED THE BENEFITS OF HIS POSITION and wealth. In March 1921, Jesse and Eudora Binga attended the inauguration of President Warren G. Harding and then toured the East Coast.[43] While previously favoring the warm baths of French Lick West Baden, Indiana,[44] by the 1920s the Bingas traveled across the country and summered in such places as Oak Bluffs, Massachusetts,[45] one of the few places that welcomed wealthy black tourists on Martha's Vineyard. Sometimes their trips were designed to improve Eudora's fading health as she was increasingly overcome by fatigue. The Bingas also enjoyed trips to Idlewild, Michigan,[46] known as "Black Eden." Since about 1912, Idlewild had been a respite for wealthy and middle-class blacks to enjoy the outdoors and entertainment. This resort town attracted black elites from across the country ranging from Dr. Daniel Hale Williams, with his house "Oakmere," to W. E. B. Du Bois and Louis Armstrong.

Binga continued to be a key player in his church activities, donating money or organizing events. In June 1926 he helped Father Joseph Eckert organize and prepare for black Catholics coming to Chicago for the Eucharistic Congress in the spacious Chicago Coliseum. Four and a half million communion wafers were readied for masses offered for white and black Catholics coming from across the country. For the congress's Sunday program, Binga gave a speech.[47]

Although by the end of the 1920s he was in his midsixties, Binga wasn't thinking about retirement. He was still dreaming about the future.

In May 1929 he announced plans to open a second bank—the South Park National Bank, 4636 South Park Avenue, about a mile north of his house.[48] As the *Defender*, one of Binga's greatest boosters, wrote at the time, "It is predicted that when the bank has its formal opening it will mark the dawn of a new era in the forward march of a race who for years, down-trodden and scorned, has come into its own."[49] Binga, with "his experience in the banking world, his intimate knowledge of high finance and his integrity,"[50] was the leader of that forward march.

Yet, at the end of the decade Binga heard a chorus of naysayers criticizing one of his pet projects and perhaps his biggest dream—the Binga Arcade.[51]

FROM THE BEGINNING BLUEPRINTS FOR THE BINGA ARCADE IN 1927, BINGA'S friends and colleagues warned him that the neighborhood around Thirty-Fifth and State Streets was fading; the Stroll was old and outdated. With the opening of such places as the Savoy Ballroom, the new action was headed south to Forty-Seventh Street. The nightlife was moving there, and so was business, including that proposed new Binga-run bank. Binga's critics said the Binga Arcade rents would never be enough to sustain the new building.[52] But Binga, being Binga, had his own ideas. He was going to build a magnificent monumental building for the Black Belt on the old strip, and it would help revitalize the sagging fortunes of South State Street. At six stories high, it would be the Black Belt's skyscraper, and it would dominate the northwest corner of Thirty-Fifth and State, right next door to his bank. The cost: $400,000.[53]

Designed by Joseph Scheitler,[54] the Chicago bank architect who also designed the Binga State Bank, the Binga Arcade opened in February 1929 (figs. 15, 16). It was Tudor and Gothic in style, with the first two floors anchored by a second-story row of arched windows running on the east

Fig. 15. *The Binga Arcade, opened in 1929 at the corner of Thirty-Fifth and State Streets. The Binga State Bank next door is barely visible at the far right.* ILLINOIS INSTITUTE OF TECHNOLOGY ARCHIVES.

and south faces of the building. Straight, vertical lines of stone running from the building's base to the decorated parapet drew the eye upward while giving the impression of soaring height. Inside were forty-eight offices, twenty-one stores, and space for the new Trust Department of the Binga State Bank.[55]

The exterior was clad in marble, the interior woodwork was warmed by American walnut, and the foundation was capable of adding three more floors if Binga's expected crush of business called for it.[56] Binga, a friend and business ally of utilities mogul Samuel Insull since 1910, likely parlayed that relationship into leases for his new enterprise. Indeed, Commonwealth Edison, Illinois Bell Telephone Company, and People's Light and Gas signed ten-year leases to have branch offices in the Binga Arcade.[57]

Fig. 16. *The Binga Arcade, with the pillared Binga State Bank to its right. This photograph was taken long after the bank closed. Both buildings were later demolished.* ILLINOIS INSTITUTE OF TECHNOLOGY ARCHIVES.

Entering the building from State Street, a visitor was greeted by a long arcade extending the full depth of the first floor, with rows of shops on either side.[58] Two "modern, fast elevators" whooshed visitors up to the spacious fifth-floor reception hall, which was two stories high, flanked by tall narrow windows, and designed to hold crowds of up to seven hundred people. Suspended from the twenty-foot-high ceiling with its eight different designs were twenty Belgian glass chandeliers. An inscription on the ceiling read, "Let peace and contentment enter into the hearts of all who gather here." The reception hall floor was made of black-and-white Linotile, perfect for dancing. And there was a stage outlined with "cherry-red velvet draperies" for performances and a "Seebert electrical organ for background music." The view out the windows would stretch for miles east over the lake and south over apartment buildings and businesses past the city borders. The Binga Arcade became a symbol of racial pride in the Black Belt.

"I could see a 'skyscraper' built by a black banker named Jesse Binga," wrote the black *Chicago Tribune* columnist Vernon Jarrett fifty years after the Binga Arcade opened, recounting his first trip to Chicago in 1942. "Coming from the small-town South, the impact of seeing that building was indescribable."[59]

The building was magnificent; the timing wasn't.

ON CHRISTMAS EVE OF 1928, JESSE BINGA CALLED ONE OF HIS TENANTS LIVING on the Binga block (4712–4752 South State Street) and asked him to meet him at the bank. Binga said he had a proposition.

Charles Worthington was a photographer, married with three children, who lived at 4744 South State Street. His father was an old friend of Jesse Binga, and Worthington had known Binga all his life.

Worthington came to the bank, but Binga never told him about the proposition. Instead, he asked Worthington to sign a blank piece of paper. Binga said he was collecting signatures from tenants but didn't tell him why. Nonetheless, Worthington was "tickled to death" to help Mr. Binga. After all, this was Jesse Binga of the Binga Bank. Worthington felt honored to help him. In return for the signature, Binga gave Worthington a "Christmas present" of a month's rent, worth sixty dollars.[60]

The reason for the signature would not become known to Worthington until years later.

ON JUNE 21, 1929, JULIUS ROSENWALD WROTE A TELLING LETTER TO JESSE Binga. Rosenwald, who ran Sears Roebuck & Company from 1908 to 1924, was a wealthy white philanthropist who endowed Chicago's Museum of Science and Industry and established the Rosenwald Fund with his gift of $30 million. Rosenwald was passionate about racial equality and helped finance the construction of some 4,977 schools for black children throughout the South. He built YMCAs in twenty-five cities and funded the construction of a model low-rent housing project at Forty-Sixth Street and Michigan Avenue, which would serve as homes to Nat King Cole, Gwendolyn Brooks, Quincy Jones, and Joe Louis.[61] Rosenwald's 1929 letter to Binga read as follows:

My dear Mr. Binga,
 I have been given the ungrateful task of collecting the outstanding pledges of the Hampton-Tuskegee Endowment Fund which were made several years ago. Among them is one of yours for $1,000.00.

Won't you be kind enough to send me your check for that amount. By doing so, the Fund will gain $2,000.00 because of my agreement to contribute dollar for dollar up to $150,000 raised in Chicago. Yours is among the few still unpaid pledges from responsible persons.

Yours very truly,

Julius Rosenwald[62]

IN ESSENCE, THIS WAS A DUNNING NOTICE, ALBEIT AN EXTREMELY POLITE ONE. It was sent to have a promise fulfilled, a promise that was now several years old and meant to help fund scholarships, a girls' dormitory, and teachers' salaries for black students at Hampton and Tuskegee Institutes.[63] Binga had failed to make good on his promise.

Now, in 1929, he was building a huge addition to his empire, yet he apparently didn't have the cash to pay a thousand-dollar pledge. It was becoming clear that the secure and stable world of Jesse Binga was beginning to crack.

20

Trust and Devotion

TOWARD THE END OF 1929, IT STARTED TO BECOME OBVIOUS TO THOSE INSIDE the Binga Bank that something was wrong; its finances were shaky. Few on the outside could see this, but Binga knew, and so did his board of directors, some of whom resigned.[1] As those problems grew, two people close to Binga would now play an even more crucial role in his life. One was his trusted aide, Inez Cantey, and the other was his parish priest, Father Joseph Eckert.

BY THE 1920S, INEZ V. CANTEY WAS JESSE BINGA'S MOST IMPORTANT EMPLOYEE. No one besides Binga knew more about the bank's operation, and no one was more trusted than Cantey. When Binga first hired her in 1910, she was already long connected to one of the most important black men in America, albeit through the keys of a typewriter.

Day after day in the summer of 1902, the pecking sound of a typewriter could be heard coming from the front porch of a Victorian house on Twenty-First Street in the Rose Hill section of Columbus, Georgia. Cantey, a young, light-skinned black woman, sat with her back straight and her eyes focused on a dog-eared manuscript as she efficiently tapped the keys on a typewriter set on a wooden table. She surely realized the words she typed were important, and she likely thought they were groundbreaking, maybe historic. She was nineteen years old, smart and capable, and although she would never finish college, she completed three years at Atlanta University,[2] the historically black university now known as Clark Atlanta University.

Cantey was typing the manuscript of W. E. B. Du Bois's seminal work *The Souls of Black Folk* (1903). She was using Du Bois's new upright typewriter at the house of her cousin Alma W. Thomas, who was then only ten years old but would grow up to become a renowned African American expressionist painter. The young typist was just starting her career with the heady job of secretary for the brilliant Dr. Du Bois, a professor of history and economics at Atlanta University from 1902 to 1907. The city of Atlanta, however, lacked opportunities for Cantey, and she eventually moved to Chicago with her family.[3]

She first worked at Marshall Field's,[4] but felt displaced and traveled back and forth between Chicago and Atlanta. She wasn't eager to stay in Chicago, but with weak job prospects in Georgia, "I see nothing left for me to do but to return North," she wrote in 1908 to Edwin "Teddy" Harleston, a friend from Atlanta University.[5] She took a job at the Binga Bank in 1910.[6]

Working with Binga for more than two decades, Cantey learned the intricate details of his business and personal finances while serving as his secretary, cashier, auditor, and bank director. She became his sounding board and his confidant. She knew close to everything about the bank and the people who worked in it. Cantey became an indispensable employee. Harleston called her "the seat of power behind the throne."[7]

When Inez started as a cashier in 1910, it was quite a position for a woman of any color in the early twentieth century. This was the beginning of a close working relationship with one of the most powerful men in Chicago's Black Belt, and it would benefit her and her family. Cantey used her connections to hire family and friends as employees at the Binga Bank, and she often helped fund the education of her relatives. By most accounts, those "connected" employees were all well educated and hardworking.[8]

Cantey usually worked out of a first-floor office in the bank, the one with "Mr. Binga's name" on it, she once explained, but everyone in the bank called it her desk. "Upstairs there was an office we called Mr. Binga's private office, nobody else occupied it except when I was there taking dictation or working for him,"[9] she said.

Cantey was in charge of the bank books, Binga's real estate accounts, and his private records.[10] While the two worked closely together, there was always a sense of formality between them, a relationship of employer and employee. She called him "Mr. Binga" at work, and in private correspondence she referred to him as "The Big Boss," "Mr. B.," or "The Chief."[11] Binga seemed to echo that formal relationship when he wrote to Du Bois that "Miss Cantey has always been skeptical about saying things without authority."[12]

Cantey was proud of her work with Binga; she felt purpose in it. "The last year and especially since last June I have worked harder, undertaken more—and perhaps I may add accomplished a <u>little</u> something—than ever before in my life," she wrote Harleston in 1911.[13]

Eventually, Inez helped hire Harleston's cousin, Richard Mickey, and two of her younger sisters, Bessie and Marvelyn, who at one time were rent collectors for Binga's real estate firm.[14] As a Binga employee, Marvelyn was once his witness in a lawsuit over a real estate commission in a 1913 deal. The trial resulted in a win for Binga, allowing him to keep a disputed fifty-dollar commission.[15] Binga never liked leaving money on the table.

The two families grew tighter when Marvelyn and Bessie each married a nephew of Binga. Marvelyn married John C. Cotillier, the son of Jesse's sister Adelaide, and Bessie married John's brother James C. Cotillier.[16]

Work and marriage weren't their only connections. Inez Cantey had an important network from her school days and her family life in Georgia. She kept in touch with Harleston, a rising portrait artist; Truman Gibson, later a successful insurance executive; and Du Bois well after their years at Atlanta University. At Du Bois's request, she wrote a short biography of Binga for the NAACP's magazine *The Crisis*, which DuBois had helped found in 1910. Binga, who had "deep feelings of gratitude" for the story, reacted with modesty. "To be frank, it was about all that could be said that was good about me," he wrote to Du Bois.[17]

Cantey nurtured Binga's relationship with Du Bois, and for years he and Du Bois corresponded on business matters. Du Bois, who was also the editor of *The Crisis*, admired Binga and made that clear in his magazine, and on February 27, 1927, Du Bois came to Chicago at Binga's invitation to speak to a Sunday afternoon gathering of three thousand people at Wendell Phillips High School. Binga met him at Northwestern Station, and Du Bois was his guest for the duration of the visit,[18] presumably at Binga's home on South Park Avenue. Du Bois, the event's marquee speaker, said, "The Proudest Hour in the Life of a colored boy should be when he can stand on the corner of the street and boast about the amount of money he has in some progressive colored bank."[19] Du Bois's speech, "The Part Banking Is Playing in the Modern World," was well received, as Binga, writing for his board of directors, said it "was an address that so deeply impressed Chicago that its echo is still being heard"[20] (fig 17). Binga's esteem for Du Bois was such that ten months later, Binga sent him a coveted invitation to the Bingas' Christmas Twilight Party (fig. 18), the Black Belt's social event of the year.

CAPITAL $200,000.00   SURPLUS $35,000.00

Binga State Bank

ESTABLISHED 1908
INCORPORATED A STATE BANK 1920

SOUTH STATE AT THIRTY-FIFTH STREET

Chicago

March 5, 1927.

Dr. W.E.B. DuBois,
69 Seventh Avenue,
New York City.

My dear Dr. DuBois:-

      The Board of Directors of the Binga
State Bank desire to express their gratitude for the
remarkable address on "The Part Banking Is Playing In
The Modern World," delivered by you at the Wendell Phillips
High School, Sunday afternoon, February 27th.

      It was an address that has so deeply
impressed Chicago that its echo is still being heard. Its
constructive import is that part which is so deeply appreciated and which we daresay, will cause it to live when
every obstacle in the economic development of our lives has
crumbled.

      Thanking you for your inspiring
message, we remain

      Yours very truly,

      Board of Directors

      BINGA STATE BANK

JB/EG

Fig. 17. *Letter written by Jesse Binga (note the "JB" dictation marks at the bottom), on behalf of his bank's board of directors, to Dr. W. E. B. Du Bois to congratulate him for his speech and visit to Chicago to promote banking in the Black Belt.* COURTESY OF THE DEPARTMENT OF SPECIAL COLLECTIONS AND UNIVERSITY ARCHIVES, W. E. B. DU BOIS LIBRARY, UNIVERSITY OF MASSACHUSETTS AMHERST.

Fig. 18. *Invitation to attend Mr. and Mrs. Jesse Binga's annual Christmas Twilight Party, sent to W. E. B. Du Bois in 1927.* COURTESY OF THE DEPARTMENT OF SPECIAL COLLECTIONS AND UNIVERSITY ARCHIVES, W. E. B. DU BOIS LIBRARY, UNIVERSITY OF MASSACHUSETTS AMHERST.

Inez Cantey also possessed a unique characteristic that proved useful in Chicago's treacherous real estate world. Since Inez and other family members could pass for white, they helped Binga with "straw purchases." And when Binga's wife Eudora put up $3,000 to start a monthly magazine to highlight black achievements, Cantey helped there too. She worked as an associate editor of the *Champion Magazine* with Jesse's cousin Henry Binga Dismond and Eudora's nephew, the poet and author Fenton Johnson.[21] It seemed Inez could do it all.

Her relationship with Binga was so close it included running highly personal errands such as making the trip to Canada to buy gifts on his behalf for his grandchildren, whom Binga rarely saw.[22] But Cantey didn't seem to be very socially involved with the Bingas. She was rarely invited to Binga's house,[23] and her name didn't appear in the list of attendees at many of the fabled Binga Christmas Twilight Parties—although she may have been invited but simply chose not to attend.

Cantey, the oldest of eight children, had a close and loving family of her own, and she spent much of her time with them. After they moved to Chicago from Georgia, Inez lived with her mother, father, three sisters, and a brother—including a stay at 5830 South Wabash Avenue in 1920.[24] Interestingly, that was one of John "Mushmouth" Johnson's old houses, the same one where Eudora and Cecelia Johnson once lived, the one Eudora Johnson Binga inherited and still owned. When the Canteys were renters in 1920, neither parents were working, but the three sisters worked for Jesse Binga. A brother, Charlton, a laborer, also lived there. Inez, however, was the go-getter.

Inez Cantey dressed well—but not flashy—and as she grew older, she rarely wore makeup.[25] Publicly she seldom showed emotions and routinely carried herself in a businesslike manner. She was a disciplined manager for whom efficiency sometimes trumped social niceties, which made her come off as confident, but aloof.[26]

"She was "a very elegant woman, kind of airy," Binga's granddaughter Dorothy Binga Taylor recalled later of Cantey's visit to Canada, "but she was a nice person."[27]

Cantey's private life had more than a hint of heartbreak. For years, she saw her friend Teddy Harleston as much more than a friend.[28] Harleston was a handsome young artist, whom Du Bois, Harleston's former teacher at Atlanta University and lifelong friend, would later call the "leading portrait painter of the race."[29] Back in Atlanta in 1908, Inez wrote Harleston, then an art student in Boston, "You needn't be grieving over <u>having</u> to stay there alone next winter. Find me a good position and I will come stay with you."[30]

Later, while working as a librarian at Atlanta University in 1910, Cantey wrote, " 'My dear Teddy:—You will write soon if you still love me.' Loved you. I always have since the morning long ago I walked into my Elocution class and saw you standing by the organ:—and always shall."[31] Her letter continued, "Ah! Ted, if I take what you say as a test of real love, then you are the only one who ever loved me. 'The saddest words—it might have been.' " She signed it, "Lovingly, Nez."[32] Harleston apparently saw their relationship differently, and later that year Cantey was back in Chicago, but her unrequited affection for Teddy would last for years.

When she received word that Harleston had married in 1920, she gave somewhat reluctant congratulations to Teddy and his bride, but she added, "(Perhaps too, I'm a little peeved over your leaving me—I think

I am the only one left of our crowd who is still single and as long as you were—why there was a little consolation there.)"[33] She signed this letter, "Sincerely, Nez."

Inez Cantey never married.

JESSE BINGA FIRST MET FATHER ECKERT IN SEPTEMBER 1921, WHEN THE German-born priest was assigned to Binga's still unbuilt church, St. Monica. Binga couldn't help but be impressed. The young white priest with a mop of curly hair and an energetic gait seemed to be everywhere on the streets of the Black Belt in the 1920s. He was tireless and ambitious with his faith. He spent many days knocking on doors and talking to as many people as a policy salesman, but Father Eckert wasn't selling tickets for a game of chance. In his mind he was selling a certainty: Roman Catholicism.

Father Joseph Eckert was called the "Great Evangelizer" because he converted thousands of blacks to Catholicism—some accounts have said he converted more than any priest in America, three to four thousand converts by most reckonings.[34] And he did it using a tried and true method—face-to-face contact. He talked to people, shook their hands, looked them in the eye, and invited them to church. And after every Mass, he stood by the front door in the narthex shaking hands and asking parishioners how they were doing.[35] On one spring day in 1929, Father Eckert presented a class of more than "500 colored converts" for confirmation to Rev. Bernard Shiel, auxiliary bishop of Chicago.[36]

People in the Black Belt, however, were justifiably wary of white Catholics on Chicago's South Side. Some of the white ethnic groups that were hostile to blacks were also Catholic, and black Catholics often felt unwelcome in white Catholic churches as they were ushered to pews in the back of the nave or into an alcove. Sometimes if a black parishioner sat next to a white woman, the white woman would pick up her purse and move to another pew. But Father Eckert wouldn't stand for that.[37] To begin with, he wasn't from Chicago. He was born in Germany and ordained in Vienna, Austria. He was known as a militant largely because he was a champion of the black race. As Father Eckert wrote in 1936, the "Negro is just another human being who, as they (whites), thinks American, reads American and talks American."[38] As one black leader said, "If the Roman Catholic Church had a hundred such men as Father Eckert, it would sweep the Negro race."[39]

Father Eckert's calling came early. Born on January 17, 1884, Joseph Eckert was just thirteen years old when he decided to enter the Society of the Divine Word at Holy Cross Mission House in Silesia, Germany.[40] The society, founded in Holland in 1875, was at first composed mostly of

German priests at a time when Catholics in Germany, primarily Prussia, were being harassed and discriminated against in what was called "Kulturkampf" (culture struggle), during which Otto Von Bismarck tried to assert government control of the activity of priests.[41] The Divine Word was founded as a missionary society to spread Roman Catholicism, and Father Eckert's first assignment sent him thousands of miles away to the United States, specifically to St. Mary's Mission House in Techny, about twenty miles north of Chicago. At St. Mary's he taught and conducted retreats for about twelve years, then he was sent to the South Side.[42]

In September 1921, Father Eckert was assigned to St. Monica Church, Jesse Binga's church. St. Monica's services were then being held in the church basement at Thirty-Sixth and Dearborn Streets, since the church was still under construction but remained underfunded and unfinished. But once Father Eckert took over, the congregation quickly outgrew the basement and needed a larger church and a school other than the makeshift classrooms then housing its three hundred children. In 1924, Cardinal George Mundelein ordered St. Monica to merge into St. Elizabeth Catholic Church at Forty-First Street and Wabash Avenue. St. Elizabeth had been founded in 1881 as an Irish parish, and it had a massive Gothic church with a spacious school building. Over the years, as black southern migrants continued to flow into Chicago and moved into white neighborhoods such as the one where St. Elizabeth stood, whites moved out. Thus only a few white parishioners remained at St. Elizabeth by the time Father Eckert took over on December 7, 1924.[43]

St. Elizabeth was a perfect fit to meet the expanding needs of a parish run by a persuasive priest with a strong constitution. Prior to Father Eckert's arrival, St. Elizabeth had two schools: an academy for the remaining white girls, run by the Sisters of Mercy; and the main school for black children, operated by the Sisters of the Blessed Sacrament. The dual school system ended in 1925, leaving one thousand children in the parochial school. Half the students were not Catholic, but Father Eckert viewed those youngsters as potential converts.[44]

Not everyone, however, welcomed Father Eckert. As he wrote in 1925, "Through the malicious agitation of dissatisfied parishioners, partly supported by an irresponsible press, the colored Catholics were made to believe that Archbishop George W. Mundelein intended to segregate the colored Catholics in Chicago, a thing that was never thought of by any leader of the Church in Chicago."[45] The previous dual school system heightened those fears, as did the discrimination of blacks at white Catholic churches. Father Eckert agonized over slights made to his black parishioners when whites were still attending their old church. When there were white children in the school, he watched them on the playground and sadly noted that "the whites would be by themselves as would the Negroes. They would never play together."[46]

Belying his missionary zeal, Father Eckert, with his thick German accent, was a stern taskmaster with a strong, square jaw and a piercing gaze, yet he had a handsome face with a distinctive dimple in his chin. At five feet six inches tall, he was a squat, barrel-chested man and as immovable as a block of granite. He didn't take any guff. Once when a "gang of ruffians" hassled his parishioners at a St. Monica Church New Year's Eve party, he grabbed a couple of the smirking "gangsters" and threw them down the stairs so hard that he "feared their bones would be broken."[47] He then turned them over to police.

He ran the parish much like Jesse Binga ran his bank—in a strict, no-nonsense way. And through it all, Father Eckert was well loved by his parishioners.[48]

Binga was a constant presence first at St. Monica and then at St. Elizabeth churches. He gave money to the school, bought supplies, provided food for the schoolchildren, and supplied coal for winter heat. Jesse and Eudora Binga helped at the school and often gave the children gifts for Christmas and treats for Easter. Jesse's devotion to the church began before the complexion of parishioners changed completely, as mentioned in James T. Farrell's fictionalized version of the bombing of Binga's house in *The Young Manhood of Studs Lonigan*. Farrell wrote of the Binga-based character Abraham Clarkson, "Some of the Catholics wished only that it [the bomb] had wounded him un-mortally, for didn't he always give Father Gilhooley a hundred dollars in the annual Easter and Christmas collections."[49]

Father Eckert depended on Jesse Binga. He knew he could always call Jesse for help or financial guidance, and he deposited church funds in Binga's bank. Father Eckert and Jesse Binga could often be seen huddled in Father Eckert's office or in a school hallway discussing challenges for the church or problems at the school. Father Eckert would talk with his passion and emphatic energy, and Binga would nod or interrupt in his calm and measured way. They trusted each other.

WHEN THINGS LATER WENT TERRIBLY WRONG FOR JESSE BINGA, THEY ALSO went terribly wrong for Inez Cantey. Father Eckert would prove to be unbreakably loyal to Binga; Inez Cantey would not. But for Cantey, it would be much more complicated.

21

"Your Daddy Would Not Have Said That"

AT THE AGE OF SIXTY-FOUR, WHEN MANY MEN LOOK TO SLOW DOWN OR retire, Jesse Binga was fighting for his future. Sitting behind his enormous three-by-ten-foot glass-topped desk at his bank, Binga opened his mail and grabbed his ringing candlestick phone only to receive a steady stream of bad news. He was being dunned, sued, and pressured.

First, in the spring of 1929, his ambitious plan to open a new bank, the South Park National Bank at 4636 South Park Avenue, was crippled and eventually doomed by death and illness. And it soon became apparent to insiders that the new bank was not just an addition to the Binga empire; it was a desperate attempt to save it.

Dan Jackson's death was the first major setback. The personable undertaker, political power broker, and Black Belt policy king planned on playing a role in Binga's new bank venture.[1] Jackson, who was also a friend of Congressman and Binga State Bank director Oscar DePriest, was a key player in the Black Belt's politics and business, and he was someone with ready cash to invest. Since the return to power of Republican mayor William "Big Bill" Thompson in 1927, gambling and vice enjoyed a resurgence on the South Side after the city's brief flirtation with reform under Democratic mayor William Dever. With Thompson in, Jackson's fortunes were rising. He was the "czar of the colored underworld," smart, strategic, and generous to the people of the Black Belt.[2] He was a powerful ally for Binga, but by 1929 Jackson was also under indictment for conspiracy to protect gambling. Then in May 1929, the popular gambling king died of pneumonia before the bank's launch.[3] He was just a year shy of sixty.

Dan's brother Charles, a longtime Binga associate and onetime vice president of the Binga State Bank, was also an intended investor, and it was planned he would be the new bank's president.[4] But after the strain of his brother's death, Charles was hospitalized. Eventually, Charles and his wife, who was also in poor health, left town to recuperate at their country home in the tiny town of Sparland, Illinois, on the Illinois River. Jackson was reported to have promised to invest $60,000 in the new bank.[5] Now that was in doubt.

Then in October, shortly before the stock market crash of 1929, Eudora Binga became sick and was confined to a hospital for months as she was "hovering between life and death."[6] Jesse Binga, who was reported to have a $50,000 interest in the new venture, was making daily trips to the hospital, spending four to eight hours a day with his wife.[7] He said "Dora" would not eat unless he personally fed her.[8]

Binga's new national bank would never get off the ground.

At about the same time, Binga was sued for $55,000 for allegedly failing to complete a contract to buy controlling interest in Century Life Insurance Company of Little Rock, Arkansas.[9] Other lawsuits would follow.

Most people in the Black Belt could hardly think Binga was in trouble—after all, it was only February when Binga formally opened the gleaming Binga Arcade—but what the public didn't know was that money was getting extremely tight for Binga. And behind conference room doors of the Binga State Bank, pressure was mounting.

The bank's board of directors was nervous and weary of Binga's tyrannical ways and secretive rule. Binga wouldn't listen to criticism, and he often dug in on even the smallest issues, prompting some directors to say that Binga himself was the bank's biggest problem. His once illustrious name was now a liability. Several directors resigned in protest. Some thought Binga should go. His name, which once suggested safety and stability, was now "a personal detriment to the bank." Directors called the bank a "one-man organization" and said Binga was "domineering and arrogant."[10]

Binga's trusted assistant Inez Cantey also felt the strain. "I have not been as well as I might have been this past year," she wrote to her friend Edwin "Teddy" Harleston. Earlier in the letter she mentioned that Binga wanted to buy another Harleston painting, as though he had no financial cares, but Cantey felt the clock ticking. "I shall stay at the old bank for the next year and then—well I hope to leave altogether—two decades at one place are about enough don't you think?"[11]

Cantey's talk of leaving would prove prophetic. Although few outsiders knew it, the bank was teetering.

BY 1929, THE BLACK BELT'S STATE STREET STRIP HAD SEEN JAZZ RISE AND BUSI-
ness surge. Prohibition made for good business in the Black Belt. You
could always get a drink in State Street hideaways. Police raids added to
the excitement and were so routine that when musicians saw police coming, they hustled out to the patrol wagons to get good seats.[12] While the
election of reformer Mayor Dever slowed the clubs down, they always
seemed to bounce back, and when "Big Bill" Thompson became mayor
again, the spigots opened wider, the dice rolled, and the music roared.

By now there were more than 230,000 blacks in Chicago, crammed
mostly into the crowded Black Belt. Despite Prohibition gains and the popularity of late-night entertainment, business on State Street was moving
south to Forty-Seventh Street, and "The Stroll" was looking worn and old.

When the stock market crashed in late 1929, the average family didn't
immediately feel anything except apprehension. Less than 2 percent of
Americans owned stock,[13] and many people didn't see any immediate
change in their everyday life. Of course, the October crash was just the
beginning of a series of events that would prove catastrophic. It would
take a year or two for everyday people to really feel its effects. Except in
the Black Belt. There the pain came much quicker, and Binga's bank was
part of the reason.

When the Great Depression started to take root, the Black Belt was
hit first and hardest. As thousands lost jobs, black workers were often the
first to be laid off and last to be rehired. Unskilled jobs were particularly
vulnerable. By January 1931, unemployment in seven northern U.S. cities,
including Chicago, bulged to nearly 28 percent for white males, yet for
black men it was nearly 42 percent. Unemployment for black women was
worse, more than twice that of whites (45.6 percent to 16.9 percent).[14] As
unemployment rose, real estate values plummeted and rents went unpaid.
None of this was good for Binga's bank, which was largely dependent on
Black Belt mortgages and rental properties. Even before the crash, Binga
was in deep trouble.

Behind the public curtain of the Binga Bank's seeming success and stability was a fragile infrastructure of unsecured loans—of 686 loans, 438 were
unsecured—and unorthodox banking procedures.[15] In fact, "the largest single block of securities held by the bank was issued by the Binga Safe Deposit
Company." Those shares were now worthless. (There were only three
shareholders in the Safety Deposit Company: Binga and two of his friends,
Chicago Defender editor Robert Abbott and Colonel John R. Marshall.)[16]

Binga's bank held $800,000 worth of mortgages made on black-owned
property. White downtown bankers wouldn't touch them as collateral for

a loan to Binga's bank, however, because they couldn't or didn't know how to sell these mortgages.[17] The Black Belt market was foreign to them.

Binga's bank liabilities outnumbered its assets by $500,000 or more.[18] And one of the bank's biggest assets—the bank building itself and its equipment, valued at about $175,000—was, with its declining bank business, a stagnant piece of property that wasn't earning interest or bringing in revenue.[19]

Then there was the demise of Binga's plan for a new national bank. He apparently thought he would transfer the frozen assets of the old bank—like unsecured loans—to the new bank, in order to give the old bank a cleaner balance sheet. While that process was questionable in itself, Binga had already collected about $29,000 for the sale of stock in the new bank, and that money was gone.[20] It got humiliatingly worse.

Binga tried to borrow from his competitor and sometime business associate Anthony Overton through the Douglass National Bank, just one and a half blocks south on State Street. Overton offered a deal, but Binga, apparently in the delusion of hubris, rejected the terms.[21] The besieged banker then turned to utilities mogul Sam Insull, a friend since 1910.[22] Insull, who like Binga came to Chicago in 1892, made his fortune as the head of Chicago Edison Company. Insull came up with a check for $200,000, but state auditors said that wasn't enough. Binga needed $400,000 more.[23] That was too much for Insull, who was already under his own increasing financial pressures and in a few years would become a fugitive and the target of political attacks.[24]

Binga was stuck.

Running out of options, he went to the office of Melvin Traylor, the white chairman of the board of directors and president of the First National Bank of Chicago, which held most of the Binga State Bank's securities as collateral for bills payable.[25] Traylor had built the First National into a financial powerhouse and would go on to make the cover of *Time* magazine in 1932 and be briefly considered a presidential contender. Traylor shuttled Binga off to Edward Brown, a first vice president, who was also white. [26]

Binga later explained that visit to a reporter: "When I went to Brown he derided me, saying, 'Why, you are no banker.' I had known his father. The words hurt me and confused me. I replied, 'Your daddy would not have said that.' The interview ended with Brown taking a position against me and [he] blocked every effort I made afterward to save the bank."[27]

Brown's boss, Traylor, was later quoted as saying, "The Binga Bank was a little nigger bank that did not mean anything."[28]

22

A *Life Unravels*

AT NOON ON FRIDAY, JANUARY 3, 1930, A NURSE WALKED INTO THE SANCTUARY of St. Elizabeth Catholic Church for a moment of prayer. She wasn't Catholic, but she often stopped here for a moment of peace and reverie. St. Elizabeth was always open to non-Catholics; this was, after all, the church of the "Great Evangelizer"—Father Joseph Eckert, the charismatic white priest whose flock of predominantly black parishioners included Jesse and Eudora Binga. On this day, however, as the nurse knelt down to pray, she saw smoke "curling up from behind the main altar of marble."[1]

She ran out, rushed to the rectory and alerted Father Eckert. Fire alarms were sounded as Father Eckert and two young assistants, Rev. Ladislaus Pawloski and Rev. Paul Thunick, hurried to the front of the church. Father Eckert was only two weeks away from his forty-sixth birthday, yet he was described by a *Chicago Tribune* reporter as an "elderly man of frail constitution," which may have said something about the strain of his mission. Seeing the smoke, Father Eckert started to charge into the church to retrieve the "sacred host from the main altar."[2] Reverend Pawloski held him back, and once Eckert was calmed, Reverend Pawloski rushed in himself. About five minutes later, firefighters carried out a coughing Reverend Pawloski, who tried to get to his feet but collapsed in the snow in the street.[3]

Then Fire Department chaplain Rev. William J. Gorman went in and disappeared into the smoke for several minutes. When he came out, he opened his slicker and showed that he had retrieved the sacrament. Soon a raging 4–11 fire consumed the church, and some two hundred parishioners gathered out front, kneeling between "the tangle of hose lines in the street."[4]

Father Eckert watched his church's stained glass windows tumble as the roof began to collapse on the three-story stone building. "I began to cry like a child," he later said.[5] Father Eckert looked around him and saw the firefighters and many of the parish nuns—Sisters of the Blessed Sacrament—coated in ice from the spray of the hoses. The large Gothic church was ruined: its windows were now dark holes, and the church looked like a hollowed-out skull. The damage was estimated at $150,000 plus $35,000 in contents. Insurance paid $135,000, but since whites were leaving many nearby Roman Catholic churches, it was decided not to rebuild St. Elizabeth but instead move its parishioners to one of those other half-empty churches. The insurance proceeds were used to pay off the mortgage on St. Elizabeth.[6]

An investigation failed to reveal where or how the fire started. Father Eckert had overhauled the furnace only a few months before and it was working fine. But he was haunted by the memory of a few letters he received shortly before the fire. One said that "if you continue to let Niggers come to the services in the Church and their children to the school, something will happen." At the time, he recalled, "I considered these coming from a crank, tore them and threw them into the waste basket."[7]

The cause of the fire was never determined.

AN INTRIGUING PHOTOGRAPH ON THE FRONT OF THE "ALL AROUND THE Town" section of the *Chicago Defender* ran on January 18, 1930,[8] and an identical one ran in the *Chicago Tribune*. It was taken at a dinner gathering in the English Room of the Blackstone Hotel, where "the city's foremost Loop executives and financiers" pledged $414,500 in just twenty minutes for a "Colored Hospital" and a medical teaching center. Seated at a round table covered in a linen tablecloth were seven people, including white utilities mogul Samuel Insull and, one chair to his left, Jesse Binga. Insull, who already knew he was in deep financial distress, said he'd give $50,000 to the hospital. Binga, who looked his usual calm, dignified self, promised he would give $5,000 "if I have to take off my coat and get a new job in order to earn it."[9] This was a racially mixed crowd of businessmen at the dinner, and there were big names among the contributors, such as the white department store namesake Marshall Field III, who gave $15,000, and the German-born State Street clothier Maurice Rothschild, who gave $6,000.[10]

It all appeared to be business as usual, but it wasn't. Soon Insull would see his own finances fall apart, and Binga was struggling to meet his own obligations. How could Binga, a man being dunned and sued as his bank was underwater, pledge $5,000? Perhaps there was a tiny bit of fear in Binga's eyes in the photo at the Blackstone Hotel, or a bit of resolve; it was difficult to tell with Binga. In the photo he seems to be distanced from those gathered at his table, alone even in a banquet crowd. The *Tribune* and *Defender* pictures were posed and taken together. But perhaps Insull was feeling the pressure of his own financial worries when he snapped at photographers, "Hurry up, don't spoil the dinner, Take 'em and get out." When asked to pose for a second photo, he nearly blew, causing everyone to fidget in their chairs in discomfort and embarrassment.[11] One photographer said they were used to it.

Jesse Binga's friend and ally Insull wasn't the only one feeling pressure. Binga saw his own carefully built life unraveling on several fronts. First, his business was collapsing. Second, the destruction of his beloved St. Elizabeth Catholic Church meant that more money was needed for the parish, and Binga knew he couldn't keep supporting all his charitable urges. And third, his wife was still in the hospital at the end of January. Yet Binga nevertheless appeared to maintain his usual calm and reserve and seemed to believe he could pull himself out of the financial mess at his bank. Either that or, as some of those close to him thought, he had lost touch with reality.

On January 30, 1930, Binga wrote a letter to his second cousin Anthony Binga Sr., who was then a student at West Virginia State College (now West Virginia State University).[12] Jesse wrote that he was busy and still making daily trips to the hospital to visit his wife,[13] but he did not indicate that he was in trouble. With his usual confidence and reverence for his family honor and status, he wrote, "I trust you are getting along splendidly and will do honor to the name of Binga." His cousin later called the letter "inspiring," given Jesse Binga's troubles at the time.[14]

Jesse also wrote in that same letter to his cousin Anthony that he had received a letter from his athletic younger cousin Henry Binga Dismond, who was "doing well. I usually see him when I run down East but due to the fact that we are planning to open a new National Bank in the near future I could not get away last summer."[15]

There was not a hint of worry, and maybe none should be expected in a letter to a cousin. Certainly by then, however, prospects for the new bank had to seem bleak at best. Binga knew there were no bailout loans coming his way, and every deal he touched seemed to turn to dust.

The Binga State Bank held many mortgages of black-owned homes that were quickly dropping in value. Building prices were relatively strong and stable when white neighborhoods were being vacated and those homes sold to blacks. The market inventory kept refilling as more whites panicked and moved out, but as the prominent black twentieth-century economist Abram L. Harris explained, once the borders of the "Negro population become fixed, it is difficult to find purchasers for property occupied by Negroes."[16] The Depression magnified those problems.

Jesse Binga saw it all around him. "Why there is a house I once offered $22,000 for and could not get it," he said. "Today it could not be sold for $6,000."[17] Harris also pointed out that while Binga previously could borrow from white banks, the economic downturn now blocked those avenues for cash flow.[18]

And Binga had more problems than a down market.

He had authorized some questionable loans that seemed to benefit just one person—Binga himself. It was also soon learned that Binga largely ignored the advice of his bank's loan committee, which was required by law to review all bank loans. Like many self-made men, he viewed what he built as his own, but this was a bank owned by shareholders; it was not his personal asset. As he saw it, however, the bank wouldn't be there without him.

These questionable loans were negotiated by Binga, possibly for his own benefit, and without proper security. The loans were eventually found to total $379,000.[19]

It was also discovered that Binga apparently overdrew his own account by more than $7,000, and he received another $3,073 by using his chauffeur Harry Scott to make a withdrawal through an overdraft. More than $50,000 was apparently received by Binga through notes or loans made by an assortment of people apparently used as proxies or "dummies" for Binga. The notes were made starting in the late 1920s and were still being made all the way through July 1930.[20]

Binga certainly knew he was in trouble, and he had known it for some time.

LATE THURSDAY AFTERNOON ON JULY 31, 1930, THE BINGA STATE BANK WAS ordered closed and a state seal was placed on the front door by order of Illinois state auditor Oscar Nelson. An initial audit had raised enough questions about the bank's operation that the state auditor decided to close it "temporarily" for a more complete review and a thorough audit.[21]

Worried depositors soon began to gather in front of the bank. By now some had lost their jobs in the economic panic. Some knocked on the door, some yelled their protests, others seemed to line up as if the bank would soon open. By Saturday, August 2, there was a big crowd in front.

Depositors were growing frantic about their money. Why couldn't they make a withdrawal, they asked? After all, it was their money.

The bank never reopened.

Two other banks nearby quickly closed, and within a month almost all the banks of the Black Belt were shuttered.[22]

Binga's bank was Chicago's first black-owned bank. Now it was the city's first bank to close in the Great Depression. In fact, the Binga State Bank was the first Clearing House bank to close in twenty years.[23] Several hundred more would follow. C. N. Langston, the Binga State Bank's vice president, who had recently lost an election as a Republican candidate for county commissioner, issued a statement that "the closing was the result of insufficient cash and frozen assets."[24]

Many Binga customers would lose most of their life savings. His rival Anthony Overton's Douglass National Bank, which suffered three runs, would close in early 1932. Together the Douglass National Bank and the Binga State Bank had represented "36 percent of the combined resources of all Negro banks in the United States."[25]

An editorial in New York City's *Opportunity, a Journal of Negro Life*, said that "the closing of the Binga Bank in the city of Chicago will have repercussions throughout black America. For a Negro bank is more than an institution for financial savings and transactions—it is a symbol of the Negroes' aspirations to enter the commercial life of the nation and it is a mark of his faith in the ability and competence of his own."[26]

These banks not only represented life savings, they also were icons of racial pride. The once growing confidence of the Black Belt was deeply shaken.

THE QUESTION OF BINGA'S MENTAL HEALTH COULD VERY WELL HAVE BEEN raised when he refused to relinquish control of his empire. Or perhaps it was his outsize ego. He didn't think anyone at the bank, or maybe anybody in the Black Belt, was capable of stepping in. Once he even said that the bank was in such condition that he would step down only if a white financier was chosen "to guide it to safety."[27] Binga's intransigence was extreme, and soon his mental health became an issue, either as tragedy or as a tactical ploy. Binga would later say that he told his bank board, " 'I am incapacitated, and you must appoint somebody and take my station.' I said 'I have arthritis in my feet, I have heart trouble, and a nervous breakdown.' "[28]

On October 5, 1930, Eudora Binga, still weak from her long hospitalization, went into probate court with her attorney and asked Judge Henry

Horner to declare her husband incompetent to manage his own affairs. Eudora's lawyer called a doctor to the witness stand who testified that Binga was not himself; he was suffering from "agitated depression."[29]

Interestingly, or perhaps suspiciously, this action came after the Great Lakes Elks Lodge sought to have Binga arrested to force him to turn over an $18,000 insurance payout he received after fire damaged a building he was in the process of selling to the Elks. An insurance company paid the money to Binga, the legal owner of the building, but the lodge said it repaired the damaged building and deserved the insurance money. The lodge asked the judge to force Binga to pay its contractors. Mrs. Binga countered and sought to have a conservator named to handle her husband's estate. She also said Jesse had signed over nearly a million dollars' worth of assets to one man since the bank closed.[30]

Judge Horner, who later became the first Jewish governor of Illinois (serving from 1933 to 1940), heard a few witnesses and then said, "Mr. Binga, come up here." After he told the courtroom that "I know Jesse Binga better than any of you," he motioned for Binga to take the stand.[31]

"What is the matter?" the judge asked.

"Your Honor, I am all done. I am incapacitated," Binga said.

The judge then asked Mrs. Binga to approach the bench. Judge Horner told Eudora, "Put him in a sanitarium and then bring him back later."

Nonetheless, Judge Horner denied Eudora's petition for a conservator for the estate of Jesse Binga.[32] The judge refused to rule that Binga was incompetent, saying merely that "Jesse Binga was just a sick man."[33] Questions raised in this lawsuit would soon be overrun by more powerful legal developments at the end of the year.

Some people said Binga was using the question of his competency as a ploy to place his assets out of the reach of creditors. Others thought Binga truly was acting strangely.[34] Whether Jesse Binga had become mentally impaired would be a debate that would last for years.

In a letter to a Chicago friend, Mildred Jones, a couple of months earlier, W. E. B. Du Bois had expressed sympathy and support for Binga. While Du Bois bemoaned the failure of the bank, he asked Jones for "any inside dope" about what happened. But, he commented, "I assume that it was simply the general depression and not rascality." Du Bois then closed his letter by urging Jones to take a vacation and get out of Chicago, adding, "That town is enough to kill anybody."[35]

A CASE FILED ON DECEMBER 3, 1930, MADE FURTHER ALLEGATIONS THAT BINGA had transferred property out of his name. It was alleged that he had transferred personal property over to Eudora.[36] But the transfer issue went well beyond his wife; it was widespread. All this was learned after the John J. Dunn Coal Company began involuntary bankruptcy proceedings against Binga to recover a debt of $15,868, an action which marked the beginning of a process that would dismantle the Binga empire and ultimately take ten years.

One part of the case moved quickly, however: Binga was declared bankrupt on December 17, 1930.[37]

This adjudication of bankruptcy was humiliating for this very proud and public man with his very private life. A bankruptcy cracks open the door on what people like to keep most private: their finances. In Jesse Binga's case it literally counted his coins—39 gold pieces, 104 silver pieces, all the way down to 16 pennies. And it counted his and Eudora's jewelry— their diamond pins, gold watches, lockets, fobs, and wedding rings.[38] All creditors were listed, including their plumber ($117.82), decorator ($61), and maid ($348),[39] along with their night watchman service ($80), phone service ($78.12), and even a mattress ($15) apparently bought for a sister.[40] It was an excruciating array of details of how the Bingas lived.

Eudora claimed four items exempt from bankruptcy: a watch, some "wearing apparel," a mahogany rolltop desk, and a small gray safe.[41]

As the case wore on and Jesse Binga's empire was whittled down, several facts splintered off to indicate that Binga may have transferred as much property as possible before his complete financial collapse. On August 4, 1930, Jesse and Eudora had conveyed their interest in an apartment building at 6528–6530 Champlain Avenue over to Jesse's sister Martha Winchester. The quitclaim deed was filed on December 2, the day before the involuntary bankruptcy action was started.[42] Another apartment building just south of the Bingas' house, right next door at 5924–26 South Park Avenue, was held in the name of Inez V. Cantey, Jesse's assistant, but effectively it too was in Jesse's control.[43] And Jesse and Eudora also quitclaimed their home at 5922 South Park Avenue, Eudora's house at 5830 South Wabash Avenue, Eudora's brother John "Mushmouth" Johnson's old house at 3324 South Vernon Avenue where the Bingas had gotten married, and another property at 3734 State Street to a William S. Bradden, whose identity and relationship to Binga are unclear.[44]

There were other similar problems with titles. In fact, Binga owned several dozen parcels of property, sometimes in his name and sometimes in the names of others. They included his fabled "Binga block" of properties running from 4716 to 4746 South State Street, properties up and down the South Side, and a piece of property in Gary, Indiana. It was a thick tangle of deeds, mortgages, and rentals.[45]

Binga later dismissed all these findings about his properties by saying, "So far as putting property in other people's names, that has been the practice during the career of the bank. The bank was fostered by me, and I let the real estate carry all of that."[46]

Oscar DePriest, the bank's onetime director and Binga's old friend and colleague, had to sort it all out when he was appointed trustee in bankruptcy on May 27, 1931. It took him years to get through it. DePriest, who was a congressman at the time of his appointment, found that many of Binga's properties had mortgages held by the Binga State Bank, where Binga was the largest shareholder. But DePriest also found that "the Bankrupt's affairs were mixed and intertwined in a most complicated manner with the affairs of the Binga State Bank."[47]

Whether this practice was fraudulent or just Binga's way of doing business became a persistent question.

A petition of Edward H. Morris, a well-respected black attorney who was appointed receiver for the Binga State Bank, said in a petition dated July 31, 1931, "It would appear that said Jesse Binga owned certain real estate and interest in real estate, when in truth and in fact, the said Jesse Binga placed the money of said Binga State Bank in said real estate transactions and took title in himself."[48]

In other words, Binga seemed to manage and control bank property as if it were his own. On the other hand, he seemed to own the property as agent for the bank, and he never refused to transfer title to the bank when the deed was issued, according to the petition filed by Morris.[49] This form of ownership muddied the legality of Binga's actions and raised plenty of questions.

Binga, however, also blamed Morris for having a vendetta against him dating back twenty-five years concerning some vague "trouble over defamation of character, some subterfuge," Binga said. "I made them go in and settle that for $5,000. Then I told him after I was married 'If you ever do anything toward defamation of my wife I will give you plenty.'"[50]

"We have always been at enmity," Binga added. "'He would say old Binga ought to be dead.' I was a bad character."[51]

For his part, Binga said he turned over his assets, "everything I had," to the bank including 613 shares of bank stock, real estate, and other stocks. He called himself a "a victim of vicious circumstances and my associates."[52]

Among these circumstances, one huge one stood out: the Great Depression. It had taken root by the early 1930s, and as Binga's bankruptcy proceedings wore on, his real estate "was not only rapidly depreciating through obsolescence, but was also depreciating through inability of tenants to pay rent,"[53] according to DePriest's "Trustee's Final Account and Report."

Binga's world was mired in foreclosures, lawsuits, and multiple claims of creditors. His financial empire was reduced to a tangled mess of unexplainable deals, debts, and legal complexities. And then it got worse.

23

Two White Men in Fedoras

ON A CHILLY THURSDAY AFTERNOON ON MARCH 5, 1931, TWO WHITE MEN IN
fedoras and long cloth overcoats climbed the front steps of Jesse Binga's
house and knocked on the front door. No answer. They knocked again
with the same result and they left. After dark, they returned and waited
near the front porch, concealed in the shadows. Eventually Binga's doctor
arrived, walked up the steps, and knocked on the door. When it opened,
the two men, Cook County deputy sheriffs, hustled up the stairs and
arrested Jesse Binga. The aging banker was unable to immediately make
bond and, as the *Chicago Defender* reported, "He spent the night in the jail
hospital, broken in health and spirit."[1]

Binga was indicted for embezzling between $250,000 and $300,000.
Four others were indicted, including his trusted aide and secretary Inez
Cantey, whom the *Defender* called "one of the brains of the then pros-
perous real estate and banking operation."[2] The other three were Harry
Scott, Binga's chauffeur and "right hand man"; Thomas R. Webb, a bank
director and former head of the Pullman Benevolent Association; and
DeWitt Curtis, a bank guard and vault custodian.[3]

The *Defender* article on Binga's arrest said that when the bank closed
back in July 1930, a "deathlike pall" had hung over depositors milling
around the front door, but the article was quick to add, "not so much
that they had any love" for the banker but that "it was the pride of seeing
their own race behind the [teller] cages that led them to 35th and State to
do their banking."[4] Binga's bank and its approximately twenty employees
represented something more than a symbol of progress and hope; after

more than twenty years, they had become an icon not just of possibility but of expectation.

Only a couple of weeks before Binga's arrest, Webb was at Pilgrim Baptist Church talking optimistically about a reorganization of the bank; it seemed that this closure might just be a temporary setback.[5] But with Binga's arrest, any hope of the bank reopening was all but gone.

Binga was charged with taking bank money without putting up any collateral and using promissory notes of his employees and others who were unwittingly used as "dummies" to put through some of his real estate deals.[6]

By October 1931, the bottom line for depositors would look dismal. The Binga State Bank paid out $138,000 to its 17,000 depositors.[7] That was an average of $8.12 per depositor.[8] When the bank had closed in July 1930, however, deposits amounted to $1,280,000.[9]

That accounting also showed how the Binga State Bank's accounts were spread: the vast majority—16,274 accounts—had balances between $1.00 and $100.00. There were only eleven accounts with balances between $5,000 and $10,000, and only two accounts with more than $10,000.[10]

Over the course of his bankruptcy, Binga turned over most of his property to the bank and Edward H. Morris, the bank's receiver, to pay depositors back. His real estate and other property was said to be worth as much as $750,000, but by the time it was sold and reduced to cash, it was a fraction of that amount. Depositors were ultimately paid about twelve cents on the dollar.[11] Binga later claimed this drop in value was due to mismanagement by Oscar DePriest, the appointed trustee in bankruptcy. DePriest, who was also a stockholder, countered and said the low value was because of uncollected rents, deteriorating property, and the general economic downturn of the Depression.[12]

THE WHOLE BANKRUPTCY PROCESS AND NOW HIS MARCH 1931 ARREST WERE wearing Binga out. He saw his sixty-sixth birthday go by while sitting in the Cook County Jail, unable to make his $5,000 bond.[13] While locked up, he was often light-headed and nauseated, and he was largely confined to the jail's hospital, living on "a soup and milk diet" because of his "delicate" stomach.[14]

And then, strangely, he made his bond on April 16, 1931, through the help of an Irish couple he never met and didn't know. Martin and Honore McNally put up a large strip of vacant land (423 feet by 133 feet) they owned at Eighty-Eighth Street and Stony Island Avenue to guarantee Binga's bail.[15] The property was valued at $175,000, according to the signed bond, but why the McNallys did this can't be determined from court documents. Martin McNally may have been connected to one of Binga's longtime political friends—the powerful Democrat Thomas D. Nash, who would eventually testify for Binga. McNally listed his occupation as "Securities," and his estimated net worth was declared as $250,000 on the bond questionnaire.[16]

Once home, Jesse spent most of his time with Eudora in their South Park Avenue house in seclusion. Binga's mental health continued to be poor, and he often seemed emotional and bewildered by what was happening to his life. His block had changed quite a bit since they moved there. In 1917, the Bingas were the only blacks on the block; by 1930, there were only three whites. While there were plenty of renters on the block in 1917, there were also three owners, including Binga. Now Binga was the only one on the block who owned his own place.[17] The jobs of his neighbors were decidedly different, too. In 1917, while Binga may have been the wealthiest man on the block, his neighbors were rising economically as well, with jobs such as salesman, jeweler, accountant, stockyard manager, and doctor.[18] By 1930, his neighbors were maids, waiters, an elevator operator, a garage attendant, a porter, and a houseman at a men's club.[19]

The Bingas had now lost the trappings of wealth, including their live-in maid. They were mired in lawsuits, buried in debt, and filled with frustration. They both suffered the physical deterioration that comes with age and great loss. Jesse's memory was unreliable, and he was depressed. Eudora was worried about her husband, and she was still weak after her earlier prolonged illness and hospitalization. The Bingas kept to themselves even more than before, and their wealthy friends rarely visited.

The *Defender* still mentioned Binga in the paper; his editor friend Robert Abbott was all about names and personalities in the news. In fact, even years after his heyday, Binga was one of the people who received the most front-page attention from 1933 to 1938: Binga ranked fourth, with sixteen mentions; only Oscar DePriest (twenty), Haile Selassie (twenty-four), and Joe Louis (eighty) received more.[20] But now the stories weren't filled with praise and glory; instead, they were about criminal charges and the dismantling of his business and his reputation. And the tone was different, more critical. Understandably so: Abbott had been a depositor, stockholder, and director in both the Binga State Bank and Anthony Overton's Douglass National Bank, and he lost savings at both banks when they closed and found himself potentially liable for some of their problems, so he was forced into long and expensive litigation.[21]

Binga's relationships were strained with many friends and investors. For example, Binga's physician, Dr. U. G. Dailey, was also a small investor in the Binga State Bank and one of its directors, and Dailey suffered deep financial reverses with the collapse of the bank. Born in 1885 in Donaldsonville, Louisiana, Dailey grew up with a father who was a bartender and a mother who was a teacher, yet Dailey managed to come to Chicago in 1902 to attend Northwestern University Medical School and later became a surgical assistant to the legendary Provident Hospital founder Dr. Daniel Hale Williams. Dailey founded his own Dailey Hospital and Sanitarium in 1926 in two remodeled mansions at Street and Michigan Avenue. After the crash and the bank closure, Dailey lost his Binga State Bank savings and cash reserves for the hospital and had to close it in 1932. He rented out the upper two floors of his house until he was able to financially recover.[22]

Amid this turmoil, one part of the Bingas' lives stayed constant—the support of Father Joseph Eckert and the Sisters of the Blessed Sacrament.

AFTER FIRE DESTROYED ST. ELIZABETH CATHOLIC CHURCH IN 1930, FATHER Eckert was forced to hold services in what used to be the St. Elizabeth Assembly Hall, the same place Jesse and Eudora Binga had sometimes hosted their dazzling Christmas Twilight Parties before the collapse of the bank. The Assembly Hall was also used for dances and other church parties for parishioners, and Father Eckert knew his parishioners didn't like to worship where they once "danced to their hearts" content. Some never returned to St. Elizabeth church after the fire.[23] Eventually he was assigned to another church, twenty blocks south on Michigan Avenue.

Cardinal Mundelein told Father Eckert he wanted his black parishioners to have a well-appointed church, not a dilapidated hand-me-down. St. Anselm Catholic Church at Sixty-First Street and Michigan Avenue fit the bill. It was built in the 1920s for $375,000, and it was a gorgeous Romanesque church made of Toronto brick and Bedford stone, with stained glass windows imported from Munich, Germany. On June 2, 1932, it was turned over to Father Eckert's Society of the Divine Word and his black parishioners. About 150 white families were then still members of St. Anslem, but not for long. After letters of protest and objections made to the church chancery office, Cardinal Mundelein remained steadfast in his decision. "Our good Colored Catholic people must also have nice churches," he told Father Eckert. "Generally when the churches are dilapidated they were turned over to the Colored Catholics. That will not happen in Chicago."[24]

St. Anselm was Father Eckert's third South Side church, and he knew what to expect, but he was always shocked by it nonetheless. White parishioners asked for some form of segregation at St. Anselm; they suggested that maybe whites and blacks could be assigned separate sections of pews. Father Eckert refused. When he saw white parishioners move away from black parishioners who sat next to them, Eckert found the white parishioners after church and privately told them that if they came to St. Anselm, he expected better behavior.[25] He was clear: there would be no segregation.

When the Sisters of Saint Mary of the Woods, the nuns who taught grammar school at St. Anselm, learned that black children would be attending, they asked to leave the parish. Father Eckert objected, but in vain, and they left. The Sisters of the Blessed Sacrament then took over instruction at the parish school.[26]

While some whites stayed, Father Eckert would shake his head in disbelief as he watched the children self-segregate—the black and white children never played together on the school playground. Eventually almost all of the white families left.[27]

St. Anselm Catholic Church became Binga's new church. As Binga had helped the church for much of his life, now the church would help him. All along, Father Eckert and the nuns kept in contact with Binga as his troubles unfolded. Their care and attention would continue for the rest of his life.

AFTER BINGA MADE BAIL, THE CRIMINAL COURT PROCESS LUMBERED THROUGH multiple continuances until September 1931, when a celebrity entered the courtroom of Judge John Prystalski.

Prystalski's courtroom was where Jesse Binga would be tried in the relatively new, two-year-old Criminal Court building at Twenty-Sixth Street and California Avenue. Its massive limestone columns and heroic sculptures give an appearance of strength and stability, not unlike a large downtown bank. When it opened, on April Fool's Day, 1929, the *Chicago Tribune* called it "the new $7,500,000 de luxe Criminal court building."[28]

The courthouse is known to lawyers, police, prosecutors, and defendants as "26th and Cal" because of its Near Southwest Side location at Twenty-Sixth Street and California Boulevard. It still has wide decorative courtrooms largely looking the same today as they did in 1931. The judges still sit behind high, dark wooden desks, or "benches," elevated to impress on anyone who comes before them that serious business is taking place. The ceilings are still lined with a latticework of white beams outlined in dark brown wood, and behind the judges are expanses of wood-grained paneling flanked by fluted columns and smooth walls of cream-colored stone.

Family and visitors in the gallery still sit on long, high-backed wooden benches that look like church pews, and bailiffs patrol the main aisle barking warnings to all that there's "no talking when the judge is on the bench."

For more than eight decades the courtrooms and hallways of "26th and Cal" have been filled with heard-it-all judges and seen-it-all prosecutors; rows of sarcastic street-weary cops waiting to testify; and an endless assortment of sociopaths, con men, pedophiles, thieves, and killers—and a few lost souls who stood wrongly accused. Binga likely thought he had arrived at the edge of humanity.

But it wasn't Jesse Binga causing a stir of murmurs and excitement in Judge Prystalski's courtroom on September 15, 1931; it was Clarence Darrow. At seventy-five years old, the famous lawyer was "resuming" active practice by appearing on behalf of Inez Cantey, Binga's longtime assistant and one of Binga's codefendants. Darrow was talked out of "retirement" by Walter White, according to Cantey family stories. White, a civil rights activist and graduate of Atlanta University, had recently become the executive secretary of the NAACP. White's brother was married to Inez Cantey's sister, Minnie. Darrow told reporters he hoped to do much for Miss Cantey. His first move was not exactly spellbinding: he asked for a continuance.[29]

Not only was Cantey's future clouded by the criminal charges, but her friend Teddy Harleston (whom she had once hoped could have been more than a friend) died of pneumonia at the age of forty-nine on May 5, followed in death not long after by a close family friend and her mother's oldest sister. "The last four or five weeks have been so full of trouble and grief for us that I just could not compose myself long enough to write," she said in a letter to Harleston's widow, photographer Elise Forrest Harleston. At the close of her letter she delicately asked for a favor: "Am I asking too much by begging for a recent photo of Ted?"[30]

THE CONTINUANCE REQUESTED BY DARROW WAS GRANTED, AND THE TRIAL was postponed until July 1932. Even though Binga was never called to testify in this trial,[31] at one point he broke down and sobbed[32] while asserting his innocence before Judge John Prystalski. Binga's lawyer John Cashen said that "severe nervous strain" made Binga incapable of remembering or discussing the transactions of the bank, so "I refused to let him testify knowing the difficulty I had discussing matters with him."[33]

After a trial in which Cantey testified against Binga, the jury deliberated for twenty-four hours only to end deadlocked, and the case was dismissed without a verdict.[34] After this mistrial had been declared, there were conflicting stories as to how the jurors had leaned; one version had it as eleven to one in favor of conviction, while another had it as a majority in favor of acquittal.[35]

Now Binga would have to go through it all over again.

24

Blank Pieces of Paper

WHEN JESSE BINGA WALKED INTO THE HALLWAY OF THE COOK COUNTY CRIMI-
nal Courts building on Friday, May 19, 1933, he heard the familiar sounds
of his footsteps as they echoed off the marble floors, much like sounds he
had heard during his years of walking through the Binga State Bank. But
any warmth of familiarity quickly faded when he entered the sixth-floor
courtroom of Judge James F. Fardy. By now, Binga had lost his business,
his livelihood, his money, and most of his assets. He felt besieged standing
in this neoclassical temple of justice, a serious place designed to process
the innocent and frighten the guilty. Soon it would be determined into
which category Binga fell.

State auditors and bankruptcy officials had pored over the details in
Binga's bank books and raised a host of questions about the Binga State
Bank's operation, particularly the myriad of names used for bank property ownership and Binga's purported misuse of its cash. But most of
those questions never rose to the level of criminal charges. Even though
Binga was originally thought to have embezzled more than $250,000, by
the start of his second trial, the charges were narrowed to only a fraction
of that, and many people in the Black Belt thought his race was the true
target.

Binga's guilt or innocence would now be placed in the hands of twelve
jurors, all of them men, all of them white. Eleven of the jurors were from
Chicago, and one was from west suburban Maywood. They included
a railroad clerk, a bookkeeper, a hardware salesman born in Germany,
and a picture frame sprayer whose parents were from Poland. Many were
young, in their twenties or thirties.[1] While embezzlement generally needs

a bit more of a legal road map than more violent crimes, the jurors' verdict, in part, would revolve around sheets of plain, blank paper.

BINGA WAS NOW SIXTY-EIGHT-YEARS OLD. HE HAD A HEART CONDITION, arthritis, and a fragile state of mind. Shortly before a trial hearing earlier in the year, he was slightly injured when an explosion in his basement lacerated his arm.[2] And then, close to the day of his court appearance, his beloved wife Eudora died.

On Saturday, March 25, Eudora Binga started to feel disoriented, her eyelids fluttered closed, and she slipped into unconsciousness in her home. She never revived. Twenty-four hours later she was dead. The cause of death: a cerebral hemorrhage.[3]

Despite the gossip and suspicion surrounding the Bingas' marriage, Eudora had been the base of Jesse's world, his foundation, and it was clear he was devoted to her. She had been with him through the bombings, the bank closing, and the loss of both their fortunes. After the collapse of the bank and even though her own health was poor, Eudora became Jesse's caretaker. She fussed over his meals and worried about his mental well-being. Beyond that, she had a true partnership with her husband. She understood what he went through, because she went through it with him. Even with the later hardships, Eudora was known for "her gentle disposition" and as someone who always had a "kind word even for little children in the streets."[4] Just weeks before her death, she played the role of "Lady Bountiful" as hostess for three parties, one "to the little protestant [*sic*] children, one to the little Catholic children and one for her social friends."[5]

Eudora's funeral was a High Mass at St. Anselm Catholic Church at Sixty-First Street and Michigan Avenue, with four limousines lined up in front. Father Joseph Eckert officiated, assisted by two priests from St. Elizabeth Catholic Church, the Bingas' former church. Eudora was buried next to her mother, Ellen Johnson, and her brother John "Mushmouth" Johnson in Oak Woods Cemetery, the oldest cemetery in Chicago.[6]

Eudora's death left Jesse Binga alone in an empty house, facing a handful of felony charges and possible prison time. As the trial began, he was weak and grief stricken, certainly not in the best shape for what he was about to endure.

JUDGE JAMES F. FARDY DIDN'T SEE MANY CASES LIKE BINGA'S WHILE SITTING on the bench in his sixth-floor courtroom. Embezzlement was pretty tame business compared to the shootings, stabbings, and other forms of mayhem that littered his docket. In fact, in the same month of the Binga trial,

CHAPTER 24

Fardy sentenced William "Three fingered Jack" White, "one of the 'toughest' gunmen in Chicago," to a year in prison for carrying a concealed weapon.[7]

Judge Fardy also didn't see many defendants like Jesse Binga, an elderly gentleman in a tailored suit with a quiet, distinguished demeanor. Fardy, a 1907 graduate of Chicago-Kent College of Law, where he also now taught as a law professor,[8] was more accustomed to seeing sleepy-eyed defendants fresh out of the lockup, with torn jackets, stained shirts, and matted hair.

While Binga's case didn't have the gore and sensationalism of Chicago street life, it did hold the fate of a man who was once the pride of the Black Belt, a man known for his pluck and first-of-a-kind achievement. What was left of that reputation was now on trial.

The prosecution would portray Binga as a scheming banker out to save his fortune by playing a shell game with promissory notes, loans, and mortgages designed to make the books look balanced while pocketing cash. They would assert that Binga treated his bank like a personal savings account, and they would say he did it by betraying friendships, taking advantage of trusted employees, and manipulating people unsophisticated in financial matters.

Binga now stood accused of embezzling $32,000 from his bank in four separate transactions (a fifth charge, accusing Binga of embezzling $500 through a note signed by the Cottage Grove Manufacturing Company, was dropped before the trial began). The prosecution would attempt to show that the four transactions involved employees, tenants, or friends subject to Binga's autocratic control. They included, among others, the Binga Arcade's elevator operator, the bank janitor, and the bank's switchboard operator.

There was also a star witness for the prosecution who was one of the few people who knew all about Binga's bank habits and practices: Inez V. Cantey.

Binga's lawyer, a white man named John F. Cashen Jr., was a seasoned defense attorney. A graduate of New York University Law School, Cashen was admitted to the Illinois bar in 1912.[9] Before he became a successful and connected lawyer, he started out like many smart up-and-comers in the loyal Democratic Party ranks; he began as an assistant Cook County state's attorney trying criminal cases. Later in life, as a liquor license hearing officer for Mayor Richard J. Daley, he would handle the obscenity case of stand-up comedian Lenny Bruce when the liquor license of Chicago's Gate of Horn nightclub was threatened after Bruce's arrest there on criminal charges in 1962 for using "four letter words" in his act. Cashen had to help determine whether Bruce was a "social critic or a social menace."[10] Menace got the nod, and the nightclub's license was suspended for fifteen days.[11]

As a former prosecutor, Cashen was comfortable in the criminal courts building, and as the Binga case wore on in Judge Fardy's courtroom, he became increasingly combative, at one point snagging an objection for loudly complaining about the prosecutors to his client during the trial.[12] At another point he announced to the court that the lead prosecutor, D. L. Thompson, "gives me the creeps."[13]

THE FOUR EMBEZZLEMENT CHARGES SPANNED A PERIOD FROM 1928 TO THE first half of 1930, shortly before Binga's bank was closed. One of those charges came out of a meeting Binga had with Charles Worthington on Christmas Eve in 1928.

Worthington was a photographer who lived on the "Binga Block" at 4744 South State Street. Married, with three children, he had been a tenant of Binga for fourteen years.[14] Binga was an old friend of Worthington's father and knew the son since the day he was born. On December 24, 1928, Binga called Charles Worthington and asked him to come down to the bank. Binga told Worthington he had a proposition for him and he wanted him and other tenants to sign onto this proposition, Worthington testified. Binga didn't tell him what the proposition was, nor did he give any other details.[15]

"Well, being one of his old tenants," Worthington testified, "and knowing him so long and he knowing me so long, my signature helping him to do anything, I was tickled to death to do it." He said he had "great confidence" in Binga, and since "he has been a lifelong friend of my father's, I had no doubt or no thought of anything wrong. I said 'All right.' I just signed a piece of paper."[16].

There was "no printed matter" on the paper and no writing of any kind, Worthington testified.[17] Binga, however, gave Worthington something in return for his signature: credit for a month's rent, worth $60. Worthington viewed it as a "Christmas present"[18] for helping Mr. Binga with his undefined "proposition." As it turned out, that blank piece of paper later became a promissory note for $8,000, and Worthington only learned what it was when Edward H. Morris, the bank's receiver, contacted him for payment.

Later, as she would do for most of the trial, Binga's former trusted assistant Inez Cantey testified about the purpose of these transactions. On Worthington's note, she said, a loan check for $8,000 was issued, and

Binga told her to cash it at the bank and put the money into his own safe-deposit box, which she said she did.[19] She said she later put $2,000 of that money in Binga's real estate account and $3,500 to the credit of the bank as a loan commission.

Worthington testified that he unknowingly signed two other pieces of paper and said he didn't know they became promissory notes or anything else until notified by the receiver of the shuttered bank. When the bank closed, the $8,000 note was found along with a collateral note and second mortgage signed by Binga's deceased nephew Adolph Dandridge and his wife. The prosecutors presented testimony that indicated the collateral was not enough security for the value of the $8,000 note.[20]

Cashen's cross-examination of Worthington did little damage. Cashen reaffirmed that Worthington had signed three blank pieces of paper, and that one of those notes was brought to him by Harry Scott, who was Binga's chauffeur, according to the state's witnesses, or just a friend, as Binga later explained. The other two he signed at the bank.

Cashen hammered away at Worthington. Wasn't it strange for a man to sign his name on a blank piece of paper, not once but on three different occasions?

"Without examining it or without reading it or without looking what was on the piece of paper?" Cashen asked.

"No suspicions of anything," answered Worthington.

"Up to that time you held Mr. Binga to be a reputable person?" Cashen asked.

"Absolutely," Worthington replied.[21]

AND SO IT WENT. THIS WOULD BECOME THE PATTERN OF THE STATE'S CASE. The prosecutors presented a string of witnesses who said they signed notes but never received money. Each witness presented a variation on that theme. In many instances, the final element—what happened to the money—came through the testimony of Cantey, who had worked for Binga for twenty-three years and was a bank director and supervisor at the time of the alleged crimes. She had charge of Binga's real estate books and private records, and she was authorized to sign his name. Now she was the chief witness against him.

A deal similar to Worthington's Christmas Eve "proposition" was done a little over a year later with another longtime Binga acquaintance, Fountain Thurman, a janitor at the Binga State Bank. Thurman first met Binga some fifty years earlier in Canada, when Binga was a teenager; Binga's uncle had married Thurman's aunt, and that's how they met, Thurman testified.[22] Thurman was raised on his aunt's farm in Canada and came to Chicago two years after Binga, and eventually became a janitor at the bank. He also had an account at the bank, and he always referred to Binga as "Mr. Binga." Thurman trusted his boss completely, at least before Mr. Binga's arrest.

Thurman said he once told Binga that he was tired of the city life and wanted to move to the country, get a small farm, and live out his life there. He was looking for just "forty or fifty acres." Binga told him that he frequently had farm property come through his bank for sale, and "he said as soon as I get one I will let you know," Thurman testified.[23]

With that in mind, Thurman went to see Binga at the bank on February 11, 1930, at which point Binga asked him to sign a piece of paper. Thurman testified, "As I supposed, it was an application that he was going to get me a farm, and I thought he wanted my name to keep me on record. That is why I signed that piece of paper."[24]

Prosecutor Thompson showed Thurman "Exhibit 8"—the signed piece of paper—and revealed that it wasn't an application at all but a promissory note dated February 11, 1930, for $6,500.

"Was this amount $6,500.00 on there at the time you signed it?" Thompson asked.

"There wasn't any writing on there at the time I signed it," Thurman replied, adding that he didn't know it was a promissory note until it surfaced as a bank asset when the bank's receiver Edward H. Morris sought collection.[25] The paper he signed was just a blank printed form, Thurman said.

The prosecutor then showed Thurman a loan check apparently endorsed by Thurman, but Thurman said it wasn't his signature.[26] Thompson asked if Thurman ever received $6,500 from the Binga State Bank.

"No sir," Thurman replied.[27]

Prosecutors linked Thurman's transaction to another deal Binga had made more than a year earlier with the Pyramid Mutual Life Insurance Company. John Holloman, chairman of the board for Pyramid, testified that in 1928 he needed to provide the state insurance department an additional $6,500 in securities to keep his company in state compliance. He went to Binga, who provided them with securities in exchange for a note for $6,500 signed by Pyramid's officers and dated December 14, 1928.[28]

Again, Cantey later tied up the loose ends. She said the securities given to Pyramid included mortgage papers signed by Charlotte Smith, a switchboard operator. Cantey said Smith signed them as she sat at the bank's telephone switchboard, even though Binga was the real owner of the mortgaged property. A loan check was cut and endorsed by Philip M. Grant, Pyramid's treasurer, but no money was given to Pyramid. Instead, the check was deposited in Binga's real estate account, Cantey said.[29]

Binga later demanded the return of the securities he had given Pyramid, after which Binga surrendered the note.[30] That meant the bank's list of assets was now short $6,500 since, as Cantey testified, that money was put into Binga's real estate account. To cover that missing note, according to prosecutors, Binga placed Thurman's phony $6,500 note among the bank's assets to balance the books. This was the pattern throughout, the prosecution contended: money taken out, bogus notes or securities put in.

Prosecutors called John H. Minor, president of the Commonwealth Burial Association, to the stand. Minor said his company sought a $10,000 loan. On June 20, 1929, Minor, along with Maurice Anderson, the company's manager; R. A. Armstrong, the company treasurer; and C. L. Duprey, the company secretary; signed two notes of $5,000 each to support the loan. Loan checks were issued and endorsed, but no money was paid to Pyramid, according to testimony. After two months, the association's officers asked Binga for their money or the return of their notes. Binga told him that his lawyer advised him not to make the loans, and so he destroyed the notes.[31]

Later Binga called the company officers to the bank and said he was ready to make the loan after all, with the condition that the company put a Dr. Wilson on the board of directors as treasurer. Two notes were signed, $5,000 each, but Binga said he wanted to see the association put together a budget before he turned over the money. A budget was made, but Binga never paid them any money. Binga, however, told the bank cashier he was making the loan and he wanted two cashier's checks equaling a total of $10,000. This money, too, eventually went to Binga.[32]

Prosecutors presented evidence of a fourth Binga deal of June 20, 1929, involving Henry M. Shackelford, a seventy-five-year-old former caterer from New Jersey. Shackelford came to Chicago in 1929 and worked for Binga as a floor walker in the bank, an elevator operator at the Binga Arcade, and a handyman. He was paid about twenty dollars a week.[33]

Shackelford bought a six-flat at 5138–5140 South Michigan Avenue from Binga for $34,000. He dealt mostly with Harry Scott, who was Binga's "chauffeur and confidential man, as far as I know," Shackelford said.[34] Shackelford couldn't pay the full purchase price, so he put down $16,000 in cash and gave "a mortgage or trust deed to secure the balance."[35] But somehow there was also a note for $7,500, which allegedly had Shackelford's endorsement. After Binga's bank closed, the receiver also found a loan check dated June 20, 1929, for $7,500 with Shackelford's endorsement. But on the stand, Shackelford said he never received $7,500, never signed an endorsement, and in fact didn't know anything about it: "I have been informed I signed a note for $7,500. I know nothing about it at all," he testified.[36] Cantey testified that this too went to Binga.[37]

Shackelford may have elicited a laugh or two when he also testified that he never received any money from the banker except for this: "The biggest piece of money I ever received from Mr. Binga was a five cent piece to go across the street and buy a newspaper."[38]

Two hand trucks stuffed with bank documents, ledgers, and stacks of papers had been wheeled into the courtroom for the prosecution's case. Cantey's testimony connected the dots for the prosecution's case, explaining how these various transactions ultimately went to Binga in various forms. And while Thompson questioned Cantey for hours that turned into days, spanning from Tuesday to Thursday (May 23–25), he was gentle with his star witness.

That wouldn't be the case with Cashen's cross-examination, which was described by the *Chicago Defender* as "most merciless." For her part, Cantey was "quick witted, alert and clever."[39]

INEZ CANTEY WAS THE OTHER HALF OF THE EQUATION INVOLVING ALL THESE signed notes and loan checks. Her testimony showed where the money went. And invariably she said it went to "Mr. Binga."

"I took this document (deposit slip) with the loan check and deposited it to Mr. Binga's credit, this check,"[40] Cantey said in reference to the $6,500 in the Holloman/Pyramid transaction.

And then on the Worthington note:

"From whom did you get the cash?" Thompson asked.

"Must have got it from the bank teller but I don't see his stamp on it," Cantey testified.

"How much did you get?" Thompson asked.

"$8,000," Cantey replied.

"What did you do with the $8,000 after you obtained it from the paying teller?" Thompson asked.

"Put it in Mr. Binga's vault," Cantey said, explaining that the "vault" was Binga's "safety deposit box." [41]

She also testified that she had seen the note with Shackelford's signature and at Binga's direction exchanged it for $7,500.[42] Cantey said the same thing about the loan check of the Burial Association, which she exchanged for $10,000. She testified that Binga told her to take $17,500 in cash to cover a $17,000 check from his personal account for the purchase of the old Kenwood National Bank building at 4636 South Park Avenue, which was intended to house Binga's planned new bank, the South Park National Bank. He told her to put the remaining $500 to his credit for commissions. The bank's books, according to Cantey's testimony, show an item of $17,000 carried as an "exchange for clearing"[43] (checks held over when there aren't sufficient funds to cover the check amount). Cantey said she signed the $17,000 check for Binga, and at his direction.

And what did she do with the check after she picked it up?

"I put it in the file of the Kenwood National Bank Building," she said.

And then what happened to it?

"I destroyed it," she replied,[44] to her recollection around December 1930 (which was five months after the bank closed).

Cantey's testimony lasted two full days, during which Binga sat motionless as he calmly watched his former confidential secretary testify in minute detail as to what went on behind his bank's doors.[45] The *Defender* described her testimony as "emphatic" and said that "on numerous occasions she seemed eager."[46]

As Binga watched his former trusted assistant testify, the *Defender* reported, he "appeared to have some of the old Binga fight in him," in contrast to his first trial in 1932, during which "he sat slouched in his seat and looked dejected." This time, "he doesn't smile nor does he frown. . . . Not once during the time Miss Canty [*sic*] was testifying on one or two occasions on which she made statements that were decidedly damaging, did he appear affected."[47]

Cashen's cross-examination of Cantey provided more theater than damage to her testimony, but he managed to raise questions about her memory on key issues, such as her testimony about whether she remembered cashing the Worthington transaction.

It quickly became contentious. At one point, Cantey said she thought Cashen was trying to confuse her.[48] At another point, Cashen insisted that the court inspect a piece of paper Cantey took out of her pocketbook while on the stand—it turned out to be blank.

Cashen drilled Cantey over questions of self-interest. On cross-examination, he got her to acknowledge that in April or June of 1930, Binga paid off $5,000 of her $20,000 mortgage on an apartment building she owned at 5924 South Park Avenue, next door to the Bingas.[49]

Cashen also raised the question of whether her attorney Clarence Darrow had made any deal with the state for leniency in exchange for her testimony.

"Miss Cantey, do you expect any leniency for your testimony here?" Cashen asked.

"Not me," she replied.

"Not any?"

"No sir."[50]

Amid objections from prosecutors that were overruled, Cashen asked if Cantey knew of any deal that had been cut for her. "I do not know," she said. She also testified that she signed a waiver of immunity before testifying before the grand jury.[51]

Later, while Cashen was still cross-examining her, the prosecutor, Thompson, shadowed him while trying to look at documents he held. Cashen wheeled around and told the court, "It gives me the creeps, he follows me like I don't know what."[52]

Cashen also sarcastically referred to the prosecutor's young second chair, Marshall V. Kearney, then in his first year as an assistant Cook County state's attorney, as the "junior assistant" or "another county heard from" when Kearney raised objections.[53] Kearney would go on to a distinguished seventy-three-year career with such cases as his 1934 conviction of Roger "The Terrible" Touhy and Basil "The Owl" Banghart for the kidnapping of Jake Factor, a onetime Prohibition-era gangster[54] (although the abduction eventually turned out to be a hoax).

The prosecutors returned the sarcasm. Thompson once refused to get a state exhibit, saying, "We won't be errand boys for him [Cashen]."[55] And Kearney complained about Cashen's relentless objections.[56]

Indeed, Cashen raised a blinding flurry of more than eighty objections during the Cantey testimony alone—more than half of them sustained. He also interrupted the questioning more than forty times, and tempers and patience wore thin. The acrimony would continue during Cashen's presentation of the defense and the state's cross-examination. Eventually, Binga couldn't take it anymore.

25

"You Killed My Wife"

AFTER EIGHT DAYS AND TWELVE WITNESSES, ON WEDNESDAY, MAY 31, 1933, the state rested its case. It was now time for Jesse Binga's defense. It took less than two days.

While there was certainly tension in the sixth-floor courtroom of the Cook County Criminal Courts building, at least for the attorneys and Binga, the state's testimony was fairly pedestrian for the rough-and-tumble environment of "26th and Cal." That changed when Binga was cross-examined, but not until the end of the defense. First there was the business of character witnesses.

Character witnesses are usually just window dressing for the defense. They talk about the reputation of the defendant, but their testimony isn't probative; that is, they don't prove or disprove the elements of the crimes charged. The most they do is say what a swell guy the defendant is and that he's truthful and honest. Binga's lawyer John Cashen presented a dozen character witnesses for Binga, and they were an impressive mix: two Roman Catholic priests, a Protestant minister, two politically powerful lawyers, the owner of a currency exchange, a jeweler, a doctor, an architect, an oil company manager, a manufacturer, and the business manager of the Chicago Real Estate Board.

The first to testify was Father Joseph F. Eckert, the German priest and longtime friend of Jesse Binga, who was now the pastor at St. Anselm Catholic Church. Father Eckert wore his clerical collar and a determined look as he approached the witness stand. His testimony, like that of all the character witnesses, was short and to the point.

CASHEN: "Do you know the defendant, Jesse Binga?"

ECKERT: "Yes, I do."

CASHEN: "How long have you known him, Father?"

ECKERT: "Since September, 1921."

CASHEN: "Since September, 1921 up to April, 1931, have you had occasion to see Jesse Binga?"

ECKERT: "Very often."

CASHEN: "Father, do you know people that know Jesse Binga?"

ECKERT: "Yes sir."

CASHEN: "Do you know the defendant Jesse Binga's general reputation in the city of Chicago for honesty and integrity?"

ECKERT: "He always was considered honest."

[*After an objection*] CASHEN: "Just answer, Father, yes or no."

ECKERT: "Yes."

CASHEN: "Is that reputation good or bad?"

ECKERT: "Good."[1]

Each following witness was pretty much the same. Father F. B. Cannell, who met Binga in 1903, said Binga always had a good reputation. Rev. Bryce U. Taylor, who lived a block south of Binga, said the same. Edward J. Frankford, a jeweler who once had a store next to Binga's bank and had an account there, also said Binga had a reputation for honesty.[2] And on it went.

Cashen presented a range of character witnesses, from business executives to civic leaders. H. H. Haylett worked with Binga on the Greater South Side Chamber of Commerce. Thomas D. Nash, a former third ward alderman and politically powerful Democrat who was then attorney for Cook County treasurer Joseph P. McDonough and who in 1934 would become the treasurer himself, also testified to Binga's good reputation, as did another lawyer, Thomas H. Cannon, who once served as a member of the State Board of Pardons and Paroles and who like Binga was a member of the Catholic Order of Foresters. Cannon said he had known Binga for more than twenty-five years. All of these witnesses said Binga's reputation was straight and true. The witnesses had known Binga for as few as four years to as many as thirty years. All said the same thing: Binga's reputation was solid.[3]

Prosecutor Donald L. Thompson didn't cross-examine any of Binga's character witnesses, except for Michael Montague, Chicago manager of the Anthony Wells Oil Corporation, 215 West Randolph Street, and that was with just one question asking if Montague had done a number of real estate transactions with Binga. Cashen's objection to that question was sustained, even as the witness said he would like to answer. When there is little to gain in cross-examining character witnesses, particularly those with an array of good credentials like this group, a lawyer will do well to leave it alone. Thompson left it alone.[4]

One thing was crystal clear from this testimony: if Binga were guilty of the crimes charged, it would be greatly out of character for him. Binga was proud of his reputation, his signature *B* on his bank's passbooks, and his self-made success. He wasn't used to being challenged publicly, which might explain what happened next.

ON THURSDAY, JUNE 1, SHORTLY BEFORE NOON, JESSE BINGA WALKED SLOWLY to the witness stand. He had a slight stoop and seemed tired and uncomfortable, maybe a bit agitated. For a man who generally looked younger than his age, at this moment he looked every bit of his sixty-eight years.[5] Binga would be the last witness for his defense and the only one to directly contradict the facts of the prosecution's case. His freedom would largely hinge on his testimony.

On direct examination, Cashen's questions were predictably soft and at first biographical. Binga testified to his birth in Detroit, his years as a barber and a Pullman porter, his travels to the west and his arrival in Chicago before the 1893 world's fair. Binga never mentioned his years in St. Paul, Minnesota, with his first wife and only child. He just said he left Detroit when he was twenty-two and "stopped by Chicago and then I went West. . . . Out to California and through the northwest."[6]

Cashen then walked Binga through the embezzlement charges. On each one, Binga gave consistent blanket denials.

Did he ever "steal or embezzle any money, any negotiable instruments, any property of any kind, from the Binga State Bank, or from any one connected with the Binga State Bank?" Cashen asked.

"I did not," Binga said.[7]

He gave the same emphatic answer to each charge: the $8,000 note signed by his longtime tenant and friend Charles Worthington; the $6,500 note with the Pyramid Life Insurance Company later replaced by Fountain Thurman's note; the two $5,000 notes signed by John H. Minor, Maurice Anderson, Robert A. Armstrong, and Cyril L. Duprey for the Commonwealth Burial Association; and the $7,500 note signed by his onetime elevator operator Henry Shackelford.

Each time he was asked if he "converted" any of that money from these transactions to his own use, and each time Binga said the same thing: "I did not."[8] Binga also testified that he never had anyone sign a negotiable instrument in blank, nor did he direct his assistant Inez Cantey to have someone do so.[9]

Cashen's questions directed Binga through each element of the charges, and Binga refuted each one. Binga said he never had anyone sign a blank piece of paper, and in the Worthington transaction, he simply asked Worthington to sign an $8,000 note. Worthington knew what he was signing, Binga said, and Binga himself put up security for the note in the form of a second mortgage of $9,000 on his row of buildings from 4712 to 4746 South State Street. That was the block known as the "Binga Block," for which Binga said he paid $240,000 or $250,000 fifteen or sixteen years earlier.[10] The Binga Block was part of his legendary State Street holdings.

The Pyramid Life Insurance transaction involving $6,500 was a loan of securities to that insurance company, and a couple of months before the bank closed, he had Fountain Thurman sign a note for the same amount, Binga testified, although his testimony didn't explain why. According to Binga's testimony, the loaned securities were two $3,000 mortgages from Charlotte Smith, the bank's switchboard operator, and a $500 bond. Binga said Smith held title to the mortgaged property—two buildings each with two flats at 5014 and 5026 Federal Street—on the bank's behalf. And when the bank closed, she quitclaimed her interest in that property to the bank, Binga said.[11]

As for the $10,000 deal with the Commonwealth Burial Association, Binga testified that the four signers were paid the $10,000 on June 20, 1929. Binga said he received none of it.[12]

Throughout his testimony, Binga said his dealings were honest and true. They were, however, unorthodox. It was certainly strange to have the switchboard operator hold bank property in her name. And there was no explanation for why he asked his old friends Thurman and Worthington to sign notes for no clear purpose. And the $7,500 Shackelford loan check was not explained except for Binga's denial of receiving any cash from it.

Binga also tried to clarify his dealings involving his new proposed bank. He testified that he went to Washington, D.C., twice to meet with the comptroller of currency and was given permission to seek subscriptions for capital stock for the proposed South Park National Bank.[13] He further acknowledged that he was a trustee for that bank and was the custodian for the money received, although he said Cantey was in possession of the funds.

CHAPTER 25

While he said he had "explicit confidence in her," Binga said he never directed "Miss Cantey" to draw a $17,000 check on his personal account for payment to the Kenwood National Bank, as part of the proposed South Park National Bank deal. And he was never told that his bank was carrying that check for forty-five days as an overdraft. He said if there was an overdraft, he would have discovered it right away because he received a report of such problems every morning.[14]

As to an issue of foreclosure of the first mortgage on the Kenwood National Bank building, he said a $45,000 payment was made to the Kenwood National Bank for the purchase of the bank building that was to become the South Park National Bank. He said the bank's receiver was trying to collect it, but he had it in his assets in the bank and it had never been released. He also said $37,000 was paid to the Kenwood National Bank.[15] The two payments were never fully explained.

Binga testified that he couldn't fully explain the financing of this deal because he had no documents, books, papers, or records of any transactions involved with the trial because "they took all of my papers, the State's Attorney and everything." Binga said, "I went there [to the bank] about a year after—the week before the bank closed, and they insulted us, they refused to let us have anything or look at my papers."[16]

Finally, Binga explained that he turned over virtually all his assets to the bank in hopes of saving it. He said he surrendered his six hundred shares of bank stock eight or ten days before the bank closed. That stock cost him "$72,000 or $120 a share," he said. And six days after the bank closed, Binga said, he turned over his $600,000 worth of real estate to "Charlie Jackson to reorganize the bank." Binga said he did so for the benefit of depositors, "people who had been doing business with me for twenty years, and the rent from that [real estate] was from eight to ten thousand dollars a month."[17]

In short, he said, he did everything he could to save his bank.

AND THEN PROSECUTOR THOMPSON BEGAN HIS CROSS-EXAMINATION. IT didn't take long for tensions to rise.

When Thompson was circling around the question of the Fountain Thurman note for $6,500, Binga became evasive:

THOMPSON: "What did you do with the note after Fountain Thurman signed it?"
BINGA: "I never had the note in my hand."
THOMPSON: "You knew Fountain Thurman signed it, didn't you?"

BINGA: "I asked Thurman to sign it."

THOMPSON: "For what purpose?"

BINGA: "For to make the loan."

THOMPSON: "What loan?"

BINGA: "The loan that was on the note."

THOMPSON: "What was the loan that was on the note?"

BINGA: "$6,500."

THOMPSON: "To whom was the loan made?"

BINGA: "You get me excited so I can [*sic*] answer, really. You get me so I can't answer."

THOMPSON: "I do not want to get you excited."

BINGA: "You come at me and I have so much trouble, it kind of takes the nerve out of me. I will be frank, I can't."

THOMPSON [*voice rising*]: "Now take it easy."

BINGA: "I can't take it easy if you holler at me like that."

THOMPSON PAUSED AND THEN RETURNED TO THE THURMAN NOTE, WHICH Binga said he never had in his hand. "It was handled exclusively by Miss Cantey," Binga said. Binga said he asked Cantey to have Thurman sign the note, and he also asked Thurman to sign the note. Thompson resumed his questioning.

THOMPSON: "What else did you tell him?"

BINGA: "I don't remember anything else."

THOMPSON: "Why, you would not just ask a man to sign a note and not tell him what you wanted to do with it, would you?"

BINGA: "That depends."

THOMPSON [*loudly*]: "All right. What did it depend upon in this case? . . . I will tell you what you did with it."

BINGA [*shaking*]: "Really, I will tell you, to be frank, you have the nerve on me. I have had so much trouble, you killed my wife, you have taken my property. You can't do any more."[18]

Binga threw his arms up, came off the witness chair, and walked away, as the *Chicago Defender* reported, "wailing."[19] He went over to the counsel table and sat down next to his lawyer.

"They are persecuting me," Binga cried, according to the *Defender* account. "They have killed my wife, now they are trying to kill me. I've lost all I owned, and now they are persecuting me. Stop this thing or I'll go mad."[20]

Some men and women hurried out the door as the courtroom filled with noise and murmurs of questions about what had just happened. Bailiffs rushed to Binga, and people twisted in their seats to get a better look. One bailiff rapped for order and Judge Fardy said, "Just a minute," as he surveyed the courtroom, excused the jurors, and adjourned court, telling everyone to be back in five minutes.[21]

Binga's lawyer Cashen later lamented the situation, saying Binga's outburst was the act of a man with a "broken spirit," while prosecutors called it a theatrical ploy to get the sympathy of the jurors.[22]

When order was restored and the trial resumed, Binga came back to the stand and said, "I apologize, your Honor, and the jury, I am sorry."[23] As Thompson continued his cross-examination, Binga often responded with "I do not remember" or a flat-out denial.

When asked about the bank's bookkeeping, Binga said that he was not familiar with the details of the bank's clerical work. That sort of thing, he said, was done by others.[24] Binga said he had complete confidence in Cantey and didn't hover over her to monitor her work.[25]

He said some of the money in question went into the account of "Jesse Binga, rents, that was the bank account and real estate account. The real estate as I explained to you, was both for the bank's property and my property."[26] His account was apparently comingled with bank property, according to his testimony.

Binga denied any wrongdoing, such as the criminal charge involving his longtime tenant Charles Worthington and $8,000. He repeated under cross-examination that he never told Worthington to sign a blank piece of paper and he never told Worthington that he wanted to get the signatures of "a number of tenants" for a deal he wanted to do.

"Oh I could not have told him that," Binga said. "That would be a lie."[27]

Regarding the check for $17,000 drawn on his account and signed with his name by Cantey, he said he never told her to do so.

"That is a bold lie told by Miss Cantey," Binga said.[28]

BY THE AFTERNOON THAT THURSDAY, JUNE 1, THE PROSECUTION WAS MAKING its closing argument. Cashen made his summary on Friday, June 2, and the case was given to the jury by midafternoon that day. And then Binga waited.

Shortly past midnight, after nearly ten hours of deliberation, the jury informed the judge that it had reached a verdict.[29]

26

Waiting and Hoping

CLOSE TO 1:00 A.M. SATURDAY, JUNE 3, 1933, THE JURY FILED BACK INTO JUDGE James F. Fardy's courtroom, along with some sleepy-eyed reporters and a few people in the gallery. A weary and exhausted Jesse Binga took his place at the defense table to hear his fate. When the verdict of "guilty" was read, Binga remained still, and his face showed no hint of emotion.[1]

The jury foreman, a thirty-nine-year-old white West Sider, whom the 1930 census listed as a food industry salesman, likely delivered the verdict to the court. Although Binga had been accused of embezzling $32,000, the signed jury verdict found him "guilty of larceny as charged in the indictment; and we further find from the evidence the value of the property so stolen to be twenty-two thousand ($22,000) and no 00/100 dollars."[2] The verdict amount—different from that alleged—was not explained, but perhaps the jury cleared Binga of the $10,000 transaction with the Commonwealth Burial Association and deducted that amount from the verdict.

Now, three years after the state closed his bank, Jesse Binga was a convicted felon. He also seemed very alone. A story in Baltimore's weekly *Afro-American* newspaper said, "After the jury found him guilty he was without friends. Only a handful of colored people attended the trial. Those who had in the years gone by accepted the hospitality of the banker and his wife could not be found. Even his nephew, [Henry] Binga Dismond, now a physician in New York, who Binga helped through the University of Chicago, was not there."[3]

The *Chicago Tribune*, which had been largely straightforward in its coverage, ran the story about Binga's guilty finding on page 6, and the *Chicago*

Daily News put it on page 3, perhaps because of the lateness of the verdict. But much of their coverage was placed inside the paper. The popular black newspaper the *Pittsburgh Courier* put the story on page 1, although a week later—presumably because of deadlines for the weekly paper.[4]

Binga had been under indictment for thirty months, and the case was continued more than forty times.[5] On November 3, 1933, Binga was sentenced to one to ten years in prison.[6] Earlier that day, all charges against his codefendants—Inez Cantey, Harry Scott, Thomas R. Webb, and DeWitt Curtis—were dropped because of their cooperation with the prosecution.[7]

Binga's appeal would take two more years, going all the way up to the Illinois Supreme Court. Binga was free on bond during this time, and his public demeanor was unwaveringly optimistic. When the Illinois Supreme Court agreed to review his case in August 1934, Binga appeared before the court's clerk and reportedly "signed his $15,000 bond and walked smilingly out."[8]

Binga told a *Chicago Defender* reporter, "I know I am right and am therefore confident everything will come out all right."[9]

Still, the waiting and the hoping clearly took a toll.

MANY PEOPLE IN THE BLACK BELT SEETHED OVER THE VERDICT. WHY BINGA? Why was a black bank one of the first to fall? It was a repeat of an old theme. As many saw it, when a black man gets ahead, he's the first to be taken down. It was a suspicion born of experience.

As the black press pointed out, the jury was white, the judge was white, and the attorneys for both sides were white. The *Pittsburgh Courier* said, with an Associated Negro Press story, that Binga was "fighting the white man's law with tears and anger."[10]

"When they put him in jail, it almost caused a revolution," said the legendary black radio pioneer Richard Stamz, who came to Chicago in 1919 at the age of thirteen.[11]

Indeed, Binga meant more to the everyday man and woman in the Black Belt than he did to the black elite. To the cooks, porters, waiters, and cab drivers, he was a race hero by example. He was what their children could aspire to be. He was why Timuel Black's father, like many other parents in the Black Belt, took his child to see the bank.

"He was the biggest name," said Stamz. "He was a national name."[12]

Indeed, Jesse Binga's rise and fall became "a kind of parable of the success and failure of Black Capitalism."[13] Binga and his iconic *B* were a symbol of black capitalism. He was known as the man who stood his ground before and after the race riots of 1919 and kept his head high.

And he succeeded like few others. While he wasn't necessarily beloved, his accomplishments were revered.

"They talked about him like he was a god," said Dempsey Travis in an interview in 1998. "Binga was *the* man." Travis was a Chicago business-man and author who once had an office across the street from the Binga Arcade. He said his father and uncle both lost money in the Binga State Bank, but they never lost respect and affection for Binga. "He was *the* man," Travis repeated.[14]

Travis, who described his upbringing as "upper lower class," said when he once considered buying land to develop in Chatham Park, he thought, "Why not buy the whole block, you know. Binga was whispering in my ears, he was kicking me in the butt and I said why not. Yeah, he was a real inspiration, no question about that."[15]

Binga's fall was a psychic blow to the Black Belt. It was as though its financial dreams had been swept away. "His failure means more than the failure of Jesse Binga," a business writer for the *Pittsburgh Courier* asserted. It meant "a backward step of 25 years for Negroes in the financial field in Chicago." And still, "his downfall meant more than this"—it meant the fall of an empire that could have bolstered black enterprise for years to come. Now, the *Courier* writer lamented, "Negroes in this city will have to start all over again."[16]

Thousands of people would sign petitions on Binga's behalf. Many observers were convinced that the legal process was flawed and discrim-inatory, among them a major white banker, John A. Carroll, onetime president of the Chicago and Cook County Bankers Association. While he said Binga's Bank "was not representative of the best banks" in the Clearing House Association, he said it was "a good bank" and had been admitted to the association without much question. So why, he asked, wasn't Binga helped, in 1930? When the bank closed, Carroll said, "a lying statement was given to the press which asserted that the Binga bank was not a member of the Clearing House Association."[17] Binga's bank had been a member for years.

As a member of the Clearing House Association, Binga should have had its protection—after all, that was part of its purpose. And while Mel-vin Traylor, president of the First National Bank of Chicago, dismissed the importance of the Binga Bank, Carroll said, "I told him that if he could have seen the thousands of colored people assembled around those closed banks on the Saturday night following the closing of the Binga bank without prospect of their Sunday dinners to come, he would under-stand how much it meant."[18]

And, Carroll added, Binga had a certified check for $200,000, with which he offered to keep his bank open, but state auditor Oscar Nelson refused it, saying that Binga needed more than twice that.

The closing of the Binga State Bank started a domino effect that "shook the confidence of the public," Carroll said, "and depositors in outlying banks all over the city began to check out to loop banks."[19]

All six banks in the Black Belt closed during the Great Depression; two of them, Binga's and Anthony Overton's, were black owned. Overton still had his cosmetics company, and *Chicago Defender* editor and Binga backer Robert Abbott still had his newspaper, but even the gambling game policy—an important source of cash infusion in the Black Belt—was being taken over by whites by the end of the 1930s.[20]

Carroll issued a warning. He said that Binga should have had the Clearing House Association's protection, and that in turn could have helped many other banks. "A little fire is quickly trodden out, which being suffered, rivers cannot quench," he said. "And you will find that the fire which started at 35th and State Streets [Binga's bank] will reach your own doorstops soon."[21]

Chicago's bank-closing ordeal during the Depression would turn out to be among the worst in the nation. And Binga's conviction felt as though a last gasp of hope had expired in the Black Belt.

SHORTLY BEFORE THE ILLINOIS SUPREME COURT MADE A FINAL DECISION IN the Binga case, Jesse Binga was a guest speaker at a Chicago meeting of the national black fraternity Alpha Phi Alpha, of which he was an honorary member. James D. Powell, who would later become an advertising executive and partner in a firm with offices in the Binga Arcade building, was sitting in the audience.

Powell was impressed by Binga, and his Arcade building. "It was beautiful," he said. "We didn't have much like that south of the Loop. Everything was the best." Binga "was a giant," Powell said. "No question about it. His work was shown by the buildings he left."[22]

But on the day of that Alpha Phi Alpha meeting, Binga was a man alone.

"It was a speech pleading for mercy," Powell said. "It was a very pitiful plea." Powell said Binga "wanted all the brothers to have faith in him. I was shocked. . . . I felt bad at this situation. No one said a word after the speech."[23]

The *Chicago Defender* later reported that Binga "was loud in praise of the activities of the fraternity."[24] Nonetheless, Powell said, when Binga finished his speech, there was no applause, just silence.[25]

CHAPTER 26

ON FEBRUARY 21, 1935, THE ILLINOIS SUPREME COURT AFFIRMED THE LOWER court's ruling of Binga's guilt. On April 5, the Illinois Supreme Court denied a rehearing of the case.[26] Eleven days later, Jesse Binga would be on his way to one of the most dangerous prisons in the country.

Although part of its ruling was technical, the Illinois Supreme Court found that "while there was testimony of the good reputation of the defendant prior to the charge laid in the indictment, we cannot say that the evidence did not show his guilt beyond all reasonable doubt. The jury had before it the records of the bank and the testimony of all the witnesses. We have reviewed that testimony and are convinced that it fully supports the verdict."[27]

The court also held that Binga would be guilty even if the bank's board of directors subsequently approved his actions, casting off another argument of Binga's attorney. The original judgment was affirmed.

JESSE BINGA WASN'T THE ONLY BANKER TARGETED DURING THE GREAT DEPRESsion, but he was one of the first. On June 29, 1929, there were 1,314 state banks in Illinois. More than half of them were shuttered during the next four years.[28] During that time, 144 of Chicago's 193 state banks failed, were suspended, or went into voluntary liquidation—the highest state bank failure rate of any urban area in the United States during the Depression.[29] The public was outraged and scared, and politicians responded. In the spring of 1931, Cook County State's Attorney John A. Swanson began targeting failed banks.[30] By November, he had indicted fifty-seven bankers, including Binga.[31]

All along Binga argued that he had done nothing wrong and done everything he could to save the bank. Binga said he surrendered almost all his assets to the bank for the benefit of his depositors. Binga estimated he gave at least $578,000 worth of property, but that figure was disputed by Oscar DePriest, the trustee in bankruptcy and Binga's onetime friend.[32] Binga did, however, seem to turn over almost all his assets, although his bankruptcy case indicated he might have tried to manipulate some real estate titles to protect himself. Nonetheless, depositors did recover some of their losses—twelve cents on the dollar.

Binga himself was basically broke, according to bankruptcy documents. He couldn't even make bail when he was first arrested and was only released when strangers put up his bond.[33] He was declared bankrupt in 1930, and his property was eventually turned over to DePriest as trustee. Binga, however, insisted his property was being mismanaged. He claimed he turned over some $600,000 worth of real estate, which should be bringing in some $8,000 to $10,000 a month. Binga said despite this high monthly income, DePriest only showed $3,000 was collected, half of which went to creditors.[34]

"Mr. Binga's statements are vague, untrue and apparently deliberately misleading," read a statement provided by DePriest's lawyers, William L. Dawson and Irvin C. Mollison, to the *Chicago Defender*. They said that "all of the property owned by Jesse Binga was depreciated, obsolescent buildings, which are now beyond repair and which entail large and excessive maintenance costs."[35]

DePriest's lawyers claimed that Binga couldn't even pay the $40,000 bills for coal to heat the buildings, let alone keep them up. They added that there was only a "small grain of truth" in Binga's $600,000 figure because every piece of real estate in his bankruptcy schedule, with the exception of a few vacant lots, had mortgages almost equal to the value of the properties, which they claimed were inflated by Binga to get "excessive loans."[36] The Depression added further price deflation to those values, and Binga had not paid property taxes for several years.

"Mr. Binga was obviously insolvent several years prior to December 1930 when he was adjudicated a bankrupt," according to the lawyers' statement.[37]

The bankruptcy would drag on during Binga's imprisonment.

CERTAINLY, THE BINGA STATE BANK WAS JUST ONE OF THOUSANDS TO CLOSE during the Great Depression of the 1930s. And it appears that Jesse Binga's actions that led to his conviction were largely designed to save or expand his banking operations, which would include protecting his depositors. He lost his fortune and remained defiant about his integrity and honesty.

The evidence against Binga, however, was compelling. Several friends and longtime acquaintances testified against him, as did several former employees, including his most trusted confidant, Inez Cantey. Only one witness contradicted the damning evidence against him, and that witness was Binga himself. The Illinois Supreme Court was convinced there was enough evidence for a conviction. After that, his legal options were gone. He was going to prison.

Binga would maintain his innocence until the day he died.

27

The Giant with a Hundred Eyes

AS HIS PRISON TRANSPORT TURNED ONTO A STRAIGHT FLAT ROAD, JESSE BINGA felt nauseated and weak, and his thinking was foggy. His new home ahead rose above the farm fields like a looming fortress on the prairie some forty miles southwest of Chicago, near the blue-collar city of Joliet. The last years had been a long ordeal for Binga. His posture was stooped, his mind was frail, and more than a few people, including his attorney, thought Binga had suffered something akin to a nervous breakdown.[1] Now, at the age of seventy, he faced one to ten years in one of the toughest prisons in America.

As they came up to the little redbrick house at the main gate, greenery peeked out from the landscaped parkway. On first blush, visitors might mistake this roadway for part of an expansive park, at least until they saw the thirty-two-foot-high gray walls topped with watchtowers manned by armed guards. This was Stateville Correctional Center, a maximum-security prison holding some 3,200 men, including murderers, rapists, street toughs, and stickup men—some of the most dangerous in the country. As they approached the tiny house at the main gate, there were several ominous roadside signs: warnings to motorists against picking up hitchhikers.[2]

As Binga was processed, he made his way through a series of thick metal doors, some made of steel bars, and as each closed, it was accompanied by the finality of a clang and lock. And then Binga heard the noise. He was surrounded by it: the constant shouts of inmates mixed with the chatter of a thousand chirping canaries and the yipping of dozens of dogs—some of the numerous pets of inmates.[3] Binga was in the center of a nightmarish din.

Inside the walls of Stateville, Binga saw the outlines of five huge circular buildings. One of them was the mess hall, and the other four were towering round cell blocks, or roundhouses, each four tiers tall, called panopticons.[4] Based on an eighteenth-century prison design, each roundhouse faced a rotunda centered with a guardhouse that rose as high as the surrounding roundhouse so that only a few guards were needed to monitor hundreds of inmates. Picture a bicycle wheel, where the rim is the roundhouse facing in, and the axle is the guardhouse. The name "panopticon" is rooted in Greek mythology. Panoptes was a giant with a hundred eyes; the name Panoptes is Greek for "all seeing."

Into this highly watched world came Jesse Binga. He had lost his wife, his fortune, his job, and his stature, and now this proud and private banker saw his privacy disappear. His life would now be monitored every minute of every day. Of course, Binga knew this moment was coming, when his appeals were denied and his 1933 sentence upheld, but the reality had to be more jarring than he imagined, particularly for a man used to giving orders instead of taking them.

The indoctrination began earlier, on April 16, 1935, at the Diagnostic Depot in the nearby Illinois State Penitentiary in Joliet, a medieval-looking prison with an entrance that resembled a castle, with bulky limestone walls rising into turrets.

There Binga was ordered to empty his pockets and put his bills, coins, and personal belongings into a bag with his name stenciled on the side. Standard procedure called for him to be ordered to strip and submit to a naked search, with his arms, torso, legs, and crotch patted and poked.[5]

Next he was instructed about his mail: he could list as many as six people who would be allowed to visit or exchange letters with him.[6] Binga's file jacket listed only one "correspondent"—"Grand Niece—Mrs. [Anna] McKinley Dent," who was living with her family in Binga's house at 5922 South Park Avenue.[7]

Binga's prison mug shot (fig. 19) shows a front view with a straight-ahead no-nonsense look despite his reported "emotional instability" and "intellectual deterioration."[8] In it he has black-and-gray-flecked hair and two dark moles, one below his right eye and another on the center of his right cheek. Below the adjacent profile view is his assigned prisoner number, 1306F. Binga's weight was marked at 177 pounds, and his height measured a half inch shy of five feet, ten inches. Binga was also listed as having a large burn scar on his right wrist[9]—perhaps from his days of fixing radiators and boilers, or maybe the scar was actually from the 1878 stabbing in Detroit or the 1933 basement explosion.

CHAPTER 27

Fig. 19. *Jesse Binga's mug shot, taken at the Illinois State Penitentiary in Joliet, April 1935.* ILLINOIS STATE ARCHIVES.

In the front view mug shot, Binga is wearing a bowler hat and a thick, elegant overcoat. He would have been ordered to surrender his clothing and wear a prison-issue blue hickory shirt, blue denim trousers, white socks, shoes, and a cap.[10] All his new clothing would be stenciled with his new identity—his prisoner number.[11] Standard procedure would have called for him to be ordered to a bathroom where all body hair was removed, including pubic hair, and then he would have showered before dressing in his prison clothing.[12]

The next few days would normally have been used for physical and mental examinations, but Binga's health was so shaky that his psychometric test was delayed and he was promptly assigned to sick bay. His physical examination revealed he also had bilateral inguinal hernias and hemorrhoids. At the time of admission, "he showed a marked impairment of memory, emotional instability, intellectual deterioration," and "faulty judgment as a result of senility."[13]

Although his memory was foggy and his judgment faulty, the psychometric test taken one month after his initial processing showed that Binga had not lost one of his strongest traits: his intellect. At age seventy, he still was found to be of "high average intelligence."[14]

Later, a blood test revealed another problem. On May 18, 1935, Binga was given a Wassermann test. The result was "four plus"—a high positive for syphilis.[15]

INMATES WITH SYPHILIS OR VENEREAL DISEASE WERE BARRED FROM PRISON jobs involving food handling, and treatment was routinely prescribed on the initial processing at the Diagnostic Depot in Joliet before assignment to a prison.[16] Stateville inmates with sexually transmitted diseases were segregated from the general population in a single division called the "shot line," where they were given medical treatments. Their clothes were laundered separately, they worked separately, and they ate separately. They were confined to a specific area in the dining hall, and they could only use utensils specifically designated for the shot line.[17]

It's unclear how long Binga was in sick bay, but he was "taken off the shot line by the doctor on account of his age and physical condition," according to a prison physician in a 1936 parole hearing report. Binga's health was then characterized as "poor."[18]

Although the Wassermann test is mentioned several times in Binga's prison records, the actual word "syphilis" comes up only once. In fact, the test isn't always specific to syphilis; it can indicate other diseases such as malaria or tuberculosis, but none of those are mentioned anywhere in Binga's prison record. Wassermann tests can also yield false positives, even when the person doesn't have syphilis.

In a December 3, 1937, Parole Board hearing, a physician's report from November 13, 1937, said Binga's health was "poor," and his Wassermann was "four plus on April 20, 1935, and again on May 17, 1936, and makes no mention of his present condition so far as syphilis is concerned."[19]

Binga's prison files, however, don't reveal any obvious physical symptoms related to syphilis or treatments for syphilis. Certainly a sexually transmitted disease would seem out of character for the aging banker and devout Roman Catholic, but his prison documents repeat the findings several times.

Perhaps syphilis caused his dementia, although his condition seemed to inexplicably improve with time. Treatments for syphilis had been available since 1910, and penicillin became effective in the 1940s.

Binga's syphilis diagnosis—if in fact it was a true diagnosis, and that remains questionable—is still an unexplained detail of a man who once told the parole board he was always against "that red light stuff."[20]

BINGA SEEMED MUCH HIMSELF DURING A PRISON VISIT WITH JOURNALIST P. L. Prattis in September 1935—at least at first.

CHAPTER 27

Binga told Prattis, who was once city editor of the *Chicago Defender*, that he began each day in prison with an hour of prayer. The reporter, who met with Binga along with "McKinlay" Dent, the husband of Binga's niece, said there didn't seem to be any Jim Crow in the prison visitors' dining area, where whites and blacks sat side by side. He also found the warden to be as friendly "as a long lost brother," and he said they weren't relegated to the service elevator as visitors. He learned that Binga also bunked with white inmates. During that 1935 visit, Binga said his health was "reasonably good," and that "the prison officials exercise due regard for it."[21]

How did Binga mix with the other inmates in the prison population?

Prattis wrote, " 'Well,' he [Binga] answered with a wan sort of smile, 'you know, in here you are known by the associates you DON'T keep. I spend most of my time with a couple of white men whom I used to know as businessmen in Chicago. They are my room mates."[22]

Binga remained defiant, Prattis reported: " 'I cannot be broken,' he boasted and promised. 'I stood stoutly against the hoodlums who bombed my home fourteen years ago. I stood up then because I thought I was serving my people. I call upon the same strength now.' "[23]

Binga's health, however, remained poor most of the time he was in Stateville, according to prison records, but around May 1937, he was well enough to be placed in Cell House C and assigned light work in the chapel.[24] Binga assisted the priest with Communion wafers and vestments used for Mass on Sundays and helped prepare the chapel for movies on Saturdays. In the chapel he could take comfort in his faith and also, perhaps, stay out of the way of the more threatening elements of the prison population.

Visits from Father Joseph Eckert and Sisters of the Blessed Sacrament buoyed Binga's spirits, but it was difficult for them to see him in prison.

"A more pitiful sight one could not behold than to visit this poor aged man in prison," the sisters wrote. "His stay did good work for God, though, as the Franciscan Father in charge each time we visited the Jail voiced his praises. His firm faith and beautiful spirit of prayer upheld him spiritually and caused him to be a marvelous example of faith and piety to those around him."[25]

When Dent and Prattis visited in 1935, Binga may have talked tough, but when he asked Prattis what he thought his chances were for release, Prattis said he averted his eyes. "How could I help but encourage him," Prattis wrote, "this old man whose light is so nearly extinguished? Have you ever tried to keep a match burning?"[26]

FORTUNATELY FOR BINGA, STATEVILLE GOT A NEW WARDEN SIX MONTHS AFTER
he arrived, shortly after his visit from Prattis. Joseph E. Ragen, the son
of a Clinton County sheriff and a Navy veteran of World War I, was a
reformer. He transferred from the head post at a prison in Menard with
orders to clean up the twin prisons of Joliet and Stateville.[27] It was a big
job. When Binga arrived, the prison had seen years of corruption, and it
provided a so-called country club atmosphere for felons, some of whom
ran an open-air market of shacks nicknamed "Maxwell Street" that offered
gambling, moonshine, and marijuana—the latter two distilled and grown
on the prison grounds.[28] Some prison guards were drunk on the job; some
others, who got their jobs only through political clout, were lackadaisical.
Many inmates and guards ignored the required uniforms and wore civil-
ian clothes.[29] Food—some stolen from the kitchen—was stacked in cells,
and some inmates used curtains to cover their cell doors and windows.
And the prisoners' many dogs, cats, and canaries were not only used as
pets; they also provided a small business as they were bred and then sold
on the outside.[30] These pets created a stomach-churning stink that wafted
through the prison, particularly on hot summer days.

Ragen changed all this. He got rid of the pets and enforced many of
the forgotten and ignored rules, such as wearing uniforms. He cleaned
up the littered prison yard and tore down the shacks of "Maxwell Street."
Using transfers, enforcing rules, and searching cells—250 trucks of con-
traband was hauled away—he systematically dismantled the some dozen
gangs at Stateville, including three main ones: an Italian gang, an Irish
gang, and the "Powerhouse Outfit," an amalgam of felons of all stripes.[31]
These gangs constantly jousted among themselves and shook down unaf-
filiated inmates, a practice that too was soon curtailed by Ragen. His
arrival was a blessing for inmates like Binga, who was not in a gang and
was unsteady on his feet and vulnerable because of his age. Binga, however, helped protect himself by keeping a low profile, first in sick bay and
then in the chapel.

Stateville's population was unique and dangerous. Including its sister prison in Joliet, there were 5,600 inmates, of which more than one in
six were killers—a microcosmic city of 737 murderers and thousands of
assorted felons. There were several thousand robbers, thirty kidnappers,
249 men convicted of manslaughter, more than 600 burglars, thirty extor-
tionists, and one horse thief.[32]

Binga's category of embezzlement was a distinctly smaller group of
thirty-six inmates. There were also eight inmates serving time for writing

bad checks, sixty-two for forgery, and three for making false statements to bank examiners.[33]

For his part, Binga was a model prisoner. After his arrival in April 1935, he quickly rose from the automatic starting point of *C* on the prison merit system to an *A* rating by mid-October.[34] That advancement was as fast as it could happen under prison rules, and with an *A* rating, Binga earned an additional credit of ten days of time served every month.[35]

His days were filled with numbing routine and structure. Single file to the shower, strip, and then with a guard's command enter the shower, at another command exit the shower, dry off, march out. No talking, no standing on clothes, no shoes on benches.[36]

Rarely was a prisoner allowed to walk alone through the prison, and when in line there was to be no crowding, no pushing, no shoving, no walking with hands in pockets.[37] No coverings were allowed on lights in the cell, the windowsill was not to be used as a shelf, only approved books were permitted, and prisoners were told not to close their cell door too hard or open it too quickly. And, prisoners were required to "keep your cell walls, bars, windows, bed, wash basin, toilet, stool, floor and furniture in the cleanest condition possible."[38]

The living of everyday life was prescribed in excruciating detail. Prisoners could have only "approved" visits, and those visitors could only come for one hour every two weeks. In the dining room, certain signals had to be used for passing the bread, salt, or condiments. A prisoner could only talk in a "low tone with the man on either side of you," he couldn't leave "edibles" on his plate, and when a bell rang to signal the end of the meal, all talking had to stop.[39]

How and when a prisoner could walk, talk, stand, sit, or sleep were all subject to rules. Breaking these rules could drop him on the merit system and cost him time.

Jesse Binga never had an infraction.

FROM THE MOMENT JESSE BINGA WALKED INTO PRISON, THERE HAD BEEN A campaign to get him out. Friends, ministers, and big names in Chicago business including utilities mogul Sam Insull and a Peabody Coal executive joined the chorus.

From the beginning, Binga's trial lawyer John F. Cashen Jr. had argued that Binga could never properly prepare his defense. "While Mr. Binga was under severe nervous strain, something happened to Mr. Binga which mentally made him incapable of either remembering or able to explain the many transactions of the bank," he wrote in a July 8, 1935, letter to the chairman of the Board of Pardons and Paroles.[40]

Cashen wrote that Binga's mental condition didn't rise to the level of an insanity defense; in fact, Binga was focused on trying to save his bank by turning over all his property for the benefit of depositors, to no avail. But the bank's permanent closing, he said, presented Binga with an unfathomable failure that "broke him physically and mentally."[41]

Over the course of this campaign, Binga was supported by the cardinal, two bishops, and a number of Protestant ministers, and, of course, Father Eckert and the Sisters of the Blessed Sacrament.[42] On July 7, 1935, the sisters sent a Western Union telegram to the parole board that read: "MAY I CALL TO YOUR ATTENTION THAT THOUSANDS OF THE NEGRO PEOPLE OF CHICAGO HAVE SIGNED PETITIONS FOR CLEMENCY AND ARE ANXIOUSLY AWAITING THE RETURN OF MR. BINGA TO SOCIETY."[43] Another telegram of support was sent by the Minsters of the Interdenominational Union of Chicago.

On July 9, 1935, a group of seven "friends" appeared before the Illinois Parole Board, including the well-connected Rev. A. J. Carey Jr., pastor of the Woodlawn Church, and noted social worker Ada S. McKinley.[44] Interestingly, none of these friends were former directors of the Binga State Bank. And old friend and *Chicago Defender* editor Robert S. Abbott, who sued Binga over the bank failure, didn't seem to be part of the efforts to free him, although his paper reported on the efforts to do so.

Indeed, Binga was supported by hundreds of petition signers and others he never met or knew. Binga was something more than just a felon trying to get out, as Reverend Carey explained to the parole board: Binga was "the symbol of the south side . . . a symbol of achievement." Reverend Carey testified that Binga, like many bankers, was merely caught in a massive economic depression. He continued, "There is a darned large percentage of people of our race group have not had much of an opportunity in life. When one man does rise above the average that man becomes an inspiration to the group. . . . He was a symbol of achievement, a thing we took pride in and from a moral standpoint done much to improve the town or community. Because he means a great deal to us, we do not want him to die in prison."[45]

Despite this formidable crusade, by late October 1935, Governor Henry Horner, who once presided over Jesse Binga's incompetency case brought by Eudora Binga, denied the prisoner's application for executive clemency.[46] Binga remained in Stateville.

But at his first parole hearing in 1936, Binga would be able to speak for himself—bolstered by some notable supporters.

ON MARCH 31, 1936, CLARENCE DARROW ARRIVED AT STATEVILLE CORRECTIONAL
Center along with a priest and two nuns. He wasn't there to visit old clients
such as the notorious murderer Nathan Leopold Jr., who was doing time
there.[47] No, Darrow had come to Stateville to help Jesse Binga in his appearance before a subcommittee of the State Parole Board. It would be Darrow's
last official appearance on behalf of a client before his death two years later.

Darrow was a lifelong advocate for civil rights. Although he had represented Binga's former trusted employee Inez Cantey when she testified
against Binga, Darrow had known Binga for about thirty years, and he
told the parole board that Binga "is a man of fine character" and that
Binga lost his fortune by trying to keep his bank open.[48]

The priest who accompanied Darrow was Father Eckert, and the nuns
were Sisters of the Blessed Sacrament.[49] Father Eckert and the sisters, who
often visited Binga and brought him food and gifts, presented a petition
"signed by 10,000 colored people."[50]

"I never gambled," Binga said to the parole board. "I was always against
that red light stuff. I worked hard against it, for I was really interested in
the uplift. . . . If you let me out, eighty percent of the people in Chicago
are for me today, and would come to me. . . . I did no wrong. . . . In the
winter time, I never put out colored people who could not pay their rent.
I tided them over. I never pushed anybody for rent."[51]

Binga's comments were wide ranging, from his innocence to giving up
all his wealth to try to save the bank, and then his testimony turned reflec-
tive and rambling, as if he had revealed too much of himself: "Don't think
I am saying too much I, I, I. I do not want to be impressing you like that.
I have always refrained from expressing myself for what I did. It was me
and my God. My poor mother made me take baskets of food to poor people who could not pay rent, when I was a boy . . . I am not following the
subject as I should be."[52]

Binga was supported by an array of people that included a future saint, a
former parole board member, and some of the wealthiest men in Chicago.

The Reverend Mother Katharine Drexel, who founded the Sisters of
the Blessed Sacrament and who would be canonized as Saint Katharine
Drexel in 2000, was keenly interested in the push to have Binga released
and encouraged Mother M. Benedict of St. Anselm Catholic Church to
"do all she could to aid in Mr. Binga's release." Mother Benedict contacted
"men of prominence, both colored and white," to sign on to the effort.[53]

Thomas Cannon, a former head of the Illinois Parole Board and an
officer of the Catholic Order of Foresters—of which Binga was a member—
praised Binga for his thirty years of work "among his own race of people"

and offered to be Binga's sponsor.[54] A report by the Division of Pardons and Paroles predicted that if Binga were freed, the "probability of no violation" was 86 percent.[55]

There were letters presented at the parole hearing from Sam Insull, the Chicago Park District, the National Association of Colored Women, the president of the Peabody Coal Company, the Chicago Real Estate Board, and numerous other people and organizations "from all walks of life in behalf of this man." There were even letters of support from several businesses that together lost close to $45,000 in deposits when Binga's bank closed.[56]

There was also a letter from Binga's trial court judge, James F. Fardy, who said, "I have no feeling in the matter," and "any action taken by your honorable board will be agreeable to the court." The judge's letter said he would not object to whatever decision was made.[57]

Darrow gave a brief talk and said that despite Judge Fardy's letter—which Darrow didn't think was strong enough—he had talked to the judge himself, and Fardy had given Darrow permission to tell the board that the judge was in favor of the parole of Jesse Binga.[58]

Despite all this support, parole was denied. Binga would have to wait more than a year and a half to be heard again.

IN A DECEMBER 3, 1937, PAROLE HEARING, WHEN BINGA WAS ASKED IF HE HAD anything to add to what he said at the previous hearing, he said, "Well, I don't know. Only an eloquent prayer to my God is all. I tried to abide by what has been done. I have always lived a life open and above-board."[59]

His testimony was short and to the point, unlike previous interviews. Binga said he could "easily, easily" earn enough money to support himself if released. And when asked if there was anything further he had to add, he said, "Eloquent silence is my motto, and I thank you very much."[60]

On December 9, 1937, the subject of the Wassermann test for syphilis came up at an executive session of the parole board, and the case was continued "to find out whether or not this man is non-infectious at this time."[61]

Apparently it was determined that Binga was not infectious because in another executive session on January 20, 1938, the board said that, pending a report on where Binga would live and work and the identity of his sponsor, he "should be released at this time."[62]

Binga was going home.

28

"The Footsteps of God"

ON SATURDAY, FEBRUARY 26, 1938, JESSE BINGA STEPPED OUT OF STATEVILLE Correctional Center into the crisp winter air with temperatures in the mid-30°s. Binga could see his breath. After nearly three years in prison Jesse Binga was a free man.[1]

When he arrived at his old house in Chicago, a newspaper photo shows him walking up the steps with his overcoat open and a faint trace of a smile on his face. He is immaculately dressed in his usual suit, shined shoes, thick overcoat, and gray fedora.[2] He looked like he was merely coming home from another day of work at the bank as opposed to a stint in a state penitentiary.

He was first greeted with a big hug from little Carrie Dent, daughter of McKinley Dent and Anna Dent, Binga's grandniece. The Dents took care of Binga's house at 5922 South Park Avenue while Binga was at Stateville. The Dents lived in Binga's house and often visited him in prison, where little Carrie would play among the small boulders laid out in the prison garden.[3] When Binga came home, the *Chicago Defender* reported, Carrie "kissed him in childish glee," and "tears trickled down his face."[4]

Binga's sponsor was his old friend Father Joseph Eckert, who was still pastor at St. Anselm Catholic Church. Binga had to have a job to be paroled, so Father Eckert gave him a position as the janitor for the church at Sixty-First Street and Michigan Avenue. Binga had once donated money for a stained glass window for the church and money for its construction, and now he would clean and maintain it. Binga told the *Chicago Daily News* that he would devote the rest of his life to "religious work among his people."[5]

His pay at St. Anselm was about $10 a week, for an annual salary in 1938 of $435,[6] a far cry from the more than $8,000 to $10,000 per month he had grossed from his real estate holdings in his days of riding high.[7] He tried unsuccessfully to resurrect his real estate business, but according to *Black Metropolis*, Binga eventually secured "a less menial job."[8]

"Look at me, how could I do physical work?" Binga asked the *Chicago Daily News* reporter. "I am 73. How could I even take up shoe shining again? But I'll do mental work, I'll convince my people of the comforts of religion."[9]

Binga reiterated a belief in his innocence that never diminished.

"I am not responsible for the depression which swept away over 100 banks in the Chicago area," Binga said to the *Defender* reporter. "I'm a poor man today because I did everything in my power to sustain my long-standing record of honesty and reliability. . . . [I] was a builder not a destroyer."[10]

BINGA SOON SETTLED INTO A QUIET ROUTINE OF WORK AND WORSHIP. EVERY day at 6:00 A.M., Binga walked from his house to St. Anselm, where he dusted the altar and collected hymnals until 2:00 P.M. He also helped the parish by keeping the books straight. And he served as an honorary usher at the church, and he "may be considered a pillar of our St. Vincent DePaul Society," according to a parish report in May 1946.[11]

Binga delighted in helping during Mass (fig. 20) and fixing breakfast for the schoolchildren on Sundays after their first Communion and on holidays, much as he did with Eudora back in the day.

The Sisters of the Blessed Sacrament held a special place in Binga's heart even before they faithfully visited him in prison and campaigned for his release. The sisters were in charge of educating the children in the parish school, and Binga was also devoted to the school, which he had supported years ago.

Every Sunday, and almost every night, he had dinner at the convent with the sisters "until he was not able to walk anymore. He always said the Sisters were his best friends," they reported. They, in turn, considered him a devoted supporter and one of their greatest benefactors.[12]

By Easter of 1939, the sisters were still commenting on how overjoyed they were to have Jesse Binga back during services. Referring to an 8:30 A.M. service on Holy Thursday, they wrote, "It was an added joy for the Sisters of St. Anselm's who had prayed so much for the release of good Mr. Binga, to see him carrying the canopy again and allowed to enter upon his former priveleges [*sic*]."[13]

Fig. 20. *Jesse Binga* (third from right) *going to Mass with other parishioners at St. Anselm Catholic Church, 6045 South Michigan Avenue, some time after his release from prison.* COURTESY OF MICHAEL O'REILLY AND THE ST. ANSELM ARCHIVES.

"The only thing I have left now is my home at 5924 [*sic*] South Park Avenue," Binga told a reporter shortly after his release from prison. "I'll live there alone. My wife died just before I was sent away. I'll manage to pay the taxes as best I can and meanwhile I'll go among my own people and tell them that the only right way to live is in the footsteps of God."[14]

Two months later he was standing in line in Renters' Court with a crowd of others who, like himself, were fighting evictions. Binga still lived in his house on South Park Avenue, but a court had already ruled that the house actually belonged to the receiver for his long-shuttered bank.[15] Even a Christmas fund-raising benefit wouldn't be enough to save his home.[16] Eventually he would move in with a nephew. In court he was just delaying the inevitable; it was yet another indignity for the gray-haired banker.

Still, he always had the church; it was Binga's refuge.

ALTHOUGH JESSE BINGA WAS OUT OF PRISON, HE WAS STILL SHADOWED BY HIS past. His bankruptcy case would not be finally settled until 1941, and his name was still stained with a criminal conviction, so Father Eckert and others launched efforts to fix that. They sought a full pardon.

Father Eckert enlisted the efforts of Chicago attorney G. L. Griffin, who filed the application and made Binga's arguments before the Pardon Board in 1940.[17] Griffin, like Binga, was a devoted Catholic, which probably helped Eckert recruit him. Griffin was a graduate of DePaul University, and his full-time job was attorney for the Chicago Transit Authority and the Chicago Surface Lines.[18]

Griffin's filing was a bit premature since Binga's parole wouldn't be over until February 1941. Griffin explained the urgency to the board by saying that Binga was now seventy-five years old and suffering from "severe heart trouble." To starkly emphasize his point, he said, "If a messenger were to come into this room at this time [and say] that he [Binga] were dead I would not be surprised."[19]

Griffin reiterated all the old arguments: Binga gave up all his assets to save the bank, he was merely a victim of the Depression, and he had an "exemplary" record in prison. He finished by saying, "If this [pardon] is not done at this time one of the great Negro leaders of Chicago will be allowed to pass to his eternity with a stigma over him."[20]

A letter from Binga's trial court judge, James F. Fardy, was submitted in support of a pardon for Binga. The judge, who called Binga a "victim of the financial panic that was then in existence,"[21] said he believed that "the ends of justice will be best served by returning this man, who is now in the evening of life, his full liberty and restoration of Civil rights."[22]

But it was not to be, not this time. The Parole Board refused to recommend a full and complete pardon.[23]

By November 1940, Binga was feeling good enough to make a comeback, and he was granted permission to go back into the real estate business.[24] Soon he had a broker's license.

His parole agent said Binga's "physical and mental health is excellent for a man of his age. He has made no violation of his agreement with the parole Board and has always been cheerful and happy on my visits."[25] The parole agent recommended a full discharge.

On February 21, 1941, Binga successfully completed his parole and was discharged.[26]

ON A CHILLY WEDNESDAY, MARCH 12, 1941, JESSE BINGA WALKED INTO THE warmth of his old bank building at 3452 South State Street, where he joined a crowd of spectators who were there to watch an auction.

When Binga was released from prison, he was broke, at least according to most official records. The long list of properties he had turned over to bankruptcy were underwater, with heavy mortgages and few or no payments made to keep current.

The remaining assets of the Binga State Bank were for sale; Binga had acquired many of these parcels during his some thirty years as a real estate broker and banker. The list of properties filled an eight-page folder and included apartment buildings, residences like a ten-room mansion at Thirty-Seventh Street and Michigan Avenue, stores, and the bank building itself.[27]

Binga came merely to watch. He didn't bid because he had nothing to bid with. Some $769,597 worth of assets went up for sale, but the final gavel brought in a total of only $82,760.[28] All of it went to expenses and creditors.

The stately Greek temple of a bank that was once the pride of the Black Belt was sold for a paltry $5,525. The auction prices were so low that a lawyer for the depositors vowed to fight the sales.[29]

Binga seemed upbeat at first, telling a reporter, "I'm starting over. This isn't the end for me. I've opened a real estate office at 3100 South Parkway and I'll come back . . . strong."[30]

As Binga watched the auction, he showed little emotion, until one particular house went up for sale—then his eyes welled up and his mouth tightened. The house was at 3324 South Vernon Avenue, the same house where he and Eudora were married.[31]

THE LOBBYING FOR A PARDON CONTINUED, AND TWO DAYS AFTER HIS SEVENTY-sixth birthday, Jesse Binga reportedly was given a full pardon from Republican governor Dwight H. Green.[32] (Binga's attorney told reporters the pardon was granted on April 12, 1941,[33] but State of Illinois records could not confirm a pardon.)

Binga, however, never made a comeback. After his reported pardon, he was still living on $10 a week from his work at St. Anselm. But it's unclear whether he was able to continue to do much work after 1941.

By 1946, Binga was taking all his dinners at the convent at 6024 South Indiana Avenue.[34] His good friend and tireless supporter Father Eckert had been reassigned in 1940, having been appointed provincial of the southern province of the Society of the Divine Word and pastor of St. Rose of Lima Catholic Church in the Gulf Coast city of Bay St. Louis, Mississippi, near Biloxi.[35]

Now in his eighties, Binga lived his life largely with the church. The sisters arranged birthday parties for him at the convent, where old friends and some former coworkers were invited and tributes were made. Binga also stayed active with church management. He served as a St. Anselm trustee, and Cardinal Samuel Stritch appointed him to various church committees.[36]

When he wasn't at the church, Binga often spent time with his cousin's son and old employee Ripley Binga Mead Sr. Starting work for Binga in 1907, Mead once drove bundles of cash from the Binga Bank to the First National Bank downtown in a green Model T truck accompanied by a passenger with a sawed-off double-barreled shotgun.[37]

In the 1940s Mead had a real estate office at Sixty-Sixth Street and Langley Avenue, where Jesse would often go to sit and visit. Ripley's wife, Jessie Cole Mead, also once worked for Binga and enjoyed sitting with him. Ripley's son, Ripley Binga Mead Jr., remembered Jesse Binga most from when he saw him there around 1947 and 1948. Binga would walk from St. Anselm to the Mead's family's real estate office, and after a couple of hours, Ripley Binga Mead Sr. would drive him back to the church.

"He was well dressed, neat, clean," the younger Mead said years later. He "always wore a tie, never seemed to feel sorry for himself, never reminisced."[38]

"He'd walk out there every day," Mead recalled on another occasion. "He'd come and just sit in the office at the front window."[39]

"Just sit (by) the window and talk," Mead continued. "He was doin' the best he can, he was a hard worker. He'd never brag or anything." But, Mead said, one thing was clear: Binga still had a presence and an aura of a man who was once somebody; you knew "he'd been there."[40]

29

"Old Age and Sorrow"

AT ABOUT 6:00 P.M. ON FRIDAY, JUNE 9, 1950,[1] JESSE BINGA CLIMBED THE stairs heading to his bedroom at 3636 South Prairie Avenue, where he lived with his nephew Albert Roberts. More than halfway up, he jerked to a stop, frozen in his steps by a "slight stroke."[2] He lost his balance, lurched forward, and fell over the banister, fracturing his left arm and suffering a nasty gash on the top of his head.[3]

As he was rushed to St. Luke's Presbyterian Hospital, he remained conscious, and friends who later came to visit said he "displayed his characteristic ruggedness."[4] Four days later, however, on Tuesday afternoon, June 13, Binga died. He was eighty-five.

Cause of death was listed as "Chronic Myocarditis," an inflammation of the heart.[5] The sisters from St. Anselm Catholic Church said that throughout his life, "Mr. Binga never lost his spirit," but at the time of his death, he was "feeble and worn out by old age and sorrow."[6]

Obituaries listed three nephews and a niece as survivors: Roberts, Ripley Mead (Sr.), attorney Will Robinson, and Mrs. Jessie Barnes. Binga's son, Bethune Binga, was not mentioned.[7]

Jesse Binga died penniless, and it took some time and effort to notify Bethune of his father's death, Bethune's daughter Dorothy Binga Taylor recalled years later. A friend of one of Jesse's relatives knew a detective who "located my father through the police," Taylor said. Her father and her grandfather Jesse "didn't correspond," she said.[8]

A funeral mass was held at St. Anselm on Tuesday, June 20. The Knights of Columbus were well represented, and Binga's pallbearers were members of the Catholic Order of Foresters, which Binga had joined forty years ago in his days at St. Monica Church.[9]

"He donated so much money to the churches, it was a large funeral," Taylor remembered years later, having attended the service, as did her sister, Inez Johnson. The burial was on one of those June days where the wind made it feel chillier than the actual temperature of the high sixties, and more than a few people wished they'd worn a coat to the cemetery. "The priest put him in the grave with the highest remarks you could ever hear of," Taylor said.[10]

Binga was buried next to his wife Eudora in Oak Woods Cemetery, the oldest cemetery in Chicago, dating back to 1854. Located at 1035 East Sixty-Seventh Street, Oak Woods is the final resting place of countless famous Chicagoans, white and black, including white lawyer and civil rights proponent Clarence Darrow, black social activist Ida B. Wells, white physicist Enrico Fermi, black four-time Olympic gold medalist Jesse Owens, white Chicago mayor William Hale "Big Bill" Thompson, and, from many years later, the city's first black mayor, Harold Washington. Oddly enough, Oak Woods also is the gravesite for the remains of 4,275 Confederate soldiers who died in Chicago's Camp Douglas, a Civil War prisoner-of-war camp.

Binga is buried beneath a tall, thick granite monument (fig. 21). It's topped with a cross draped in the robe of Jesus. On one side it's inscribed BINGA−RAY and ornamented with a giant overlapping scrolled *B* and *R*; the *B* somewhat resembles the script *B* of Binga Bank fame. The other side (not shown in the figure) is marked JOHNSON, with a scrolled *J*. It was paid for by Jesse's wife Eudora and Binga's brother-in-law, John "Mushmouth" V. Johnson, which is why there is a granite vase on each side of the marker with the letter *J*. Mushmouth is buried here, with his name facing the roadside. His name appears on the monument along with that of his mother, Ellen; his father, John; his two sisters, Louisa Ray (and her husband, Clement) and Eudora Binga; and an Albert Johnson.

One name that doesn't appear in the chiseled stone on the monument is that of Jesse Binga (fig. 22). As of this writing, his grave remains unmarked.

Fig. 21. *The Binga family memorial in Oak Woods Cemetery.*

Fig. 22. *Binga's grave in Oak Woods Cemetery, Chicago; his name was never added to the family headstone.*

ACKNOWLEDGMENTS

IT WOULD BE IMPOSSIBLE TO HAVE DONE THIS BOOK WITHOUT THE SUPPORT and encouragement of a great many people, most of all Dawn Hayner, my wife. Dawn is not only a smart, careful, and perceptive reader, she also makes everything possible, and that includes the Binga book.

To find facts, anecdotes, and details for any story, you need a lot of help, and I had plenty. I'd like to thank a host of Binga family members, librarians, scholars, and contemporaries of Jesse Binga who were kind enough to help me in many facets of Binga's life. Three key supporters for this project were Michael Flug, retired senior archivist at the Harsh Archival Processing Project at the Chicago Public Library's Vivian G. Harsh Research Collection; and historians and authors Ellen Skerrett and Suellen Hoy. I am grateful for their endless help, enthusiasm and wisdom. All three were crucial advisers and guides for the Binga project. They also all possess that most essential quality needed for this work: a relentless curiosity.

Two other people who were believers in the Binga project and gave me encouragement through their constant support and skillful advice were Jill Lisette Petty, my kind and insightful editor at Northwestern University Press, and Todd Musburger, an incredible agent but more so a person of high integrity and discernment. I also want to give a special thanks to Lori Meek Schuldt, whose copyediting was smart, perceptive, and thorough. And, of course, I want to thank Northwestern University Press.

Key to my research were several Binga family members who helped in large and small ways, including Ripley Binga Mead Jr., whose parents worked at Binga's bank; Carolyn Louise Dent Johnson, who for several years lived in Binga's house and welcomed Binga home in 1938; Thomasina Binga, who got me started at the beginning; and Binga granddaughters Dorothy Binga Taylor and Inez Johnson. And I'd also like to thank Timuel D. Black Jr., Truman K. Gibson Jr., Dempsey J. Travis, Bertha Simms Baker, Junius Gaten, George Fowler, Ann Roseman, Dorothy O'Keefe, James D. Powell, and Richard Stamz for their interviews and firsthand accounts.

I am grateful to Chip Canty, a relative of Binga's top aide, Inez Cantey. Chip provided me with some of Inez Cantey's correspondence and gave tips to further research that provided details of the working relationship of Cantey and Binga. And I'd like to thank Mae Whitlock Gentry for her guidance through Edwin Harleston's letters and for her kind permission to use photos of his two paintings that were displayed in a 1927 Art Institute exhibit.

I cannot thank enough two veteran journalists, Rich Cahan and Dave McKinney, for all their research help and guidance. Both are total pros. And I would like to thank the *Chicago Sun-Times* for its early support and help—I first learned of Jesse Binga while doing a *Sun-Times* story on some of the oldest Chicago families. I'd also like to thank Detroit journalist Ken Coleman for his guidance. The scholarship and works of Christopher Robert Reed were also extremely helpful in understanding the World's Columbian Exposition of 1893 and the early years of Chicago's Black Belt.

I offer a special thanks to countless research librarians at various universities and city libraries for their kindness, patience, and skill in helping me find obscure newspaper and magazine articles, documents, and letters concerning Binga and his time. I've always found research librarians in general to be a special group of professionals who find a certain joy in helping to carefully guide authors, reporters, and the purely curious through the endless doorways to the past.

Many institutions were of particular help in researching the Binga story or finding historic photos, including the Chicago Public Library's Vivian G. Harsh Research Collection—specifically assistant curator Beverly Cook, and curator Robert Miller; the Chicago Public Library; the Chicago History Museum; the Department of Special Collections and University Archives, W. E. B. Du Bois Library, University of Massachusetts–Amherst; the Edwin A. Harleston and Edwina Harleston Whitlock family papers at the Stuart A. Rose Manuscript, Archives, and Rare Book Library, Emory University; the Ryerson and Burnham Libraries at the Art Institute of Chicago; the Burton Historical Collection, the Detroit Public Library; Chicago's Newberry Library, particularly for its collection of Pullman employment records; and the Illinois State Archives and David Joens, its director.

I'd also like to thank a few people I've never met who were instrumental in guiding me through the life and times of Jesse Binga. Sociologist Charles S. Johnson was a key researcher and guiding author for the Chicago Commission on Race Relations' report *The Negro in Chicago: A Study of Race Relations and a Race Riot*, published by the University of Chicago

Press (1922). It is a penetrating and thorough look at the Chicago race riots of 1919 and an incredible piece of scholarship and meticulous reporting that has become a model for others. It is a classic. I also thank St. Clair Drake and Horace R. Cayton, authors of the seminal study *Black Metropolis, A Study of Negro Life in a Northern City*, also published by the University of Chicago (1945); and Abram L. Harris, author of *The Negro as Capitalist: A Study of Banking and Business among American Negroes*, published by the American Academy of Political and Social Science (1936).

I want to thank the numerous early twentieth-century reporters who recorded many of the moments in time that have helped flush out the everyday public and private life of Jesse Binga and others, particularly those journalists who worked at the *Chicago Defender* and the *Broad Ax*. I also thank the journalist and author Roi Ottley, for his wonderful mid-twentieth-century work, including his book *The Lonely Warrior: The Life and Times of Robert S. Abbott, Founder of the "Chicago Defender" Newspaper* (1955).

NOTES

Chapter 1

1. Anecdotes in this chapter come from Timuel D. Black Jr., telephone interviews by the author, November 12, 1998, and April 9, 1999.

2. Timuel, the grandson of slaves, grew up to work with Martin Luther King Jr. in the civil rights movement and later helped Harold Washington Jr. become Chicago's first black mayor in 1983. As a member of the U.S. Army during World War II, Black took note of how German prisoners of war were allowed to eat with white American soldiers while black American soldiers were not. And he was profoundly moved by a visit to Buchenwald, where he could "see and feel and hear the cries" of the concentration camp prisoners at its liberation in 1945. It reminded him of the harsh plight of his enslaved grandparents. See Michael Drapa, "A Lifetime Championing Civil Rights," University of Chicago (website), October 20, 2014, https://www.uchicago.edu/features/a_lifetime _championing_civil_rights/. An earlier lesson, however, came in that trip with his father to the Binga Bank.

Chapter 2

1. "Binga Bombed for Fifth Time in Six Months," *Chicago Tribune*, June 18, 1920; Chicago Commission on Race Relations (CCRR), *The Negro in Chicago: A Study of Race Relations and a Race Riot* (Chicago: University of Chicago Press, 1923), 126.

2. "Mr. and Mrs. Jesse Binga Will Not Move From Their Comfortable Home, 5922 South Park Ave, Notwithstanding the Fact, That it has Been Bombed Fire Times, Costing Them Many Thousands of Dollars to Repair or Put It In Order Again," *Broad Ax*, July 3, 1920, 1.

3. "Building Up Somebody's Civilization, Why Not Yours?" *Chicago Defender*, October 28, 1922, 4.

4. "Mrs. Binga, Wife of Ex-Banker, Is Buried," *Chicago Defender*, April 1, 1933, 1.

5. CCRR, *Negro in Chicago*, 122; "Flats Blown Up; Explosion Kills Child," *Chicago Daily Tribune*, February 28, 1919, 1.

6. The bombings included the following:

1. March 20, 1919, bombing of real estate office at 4724 State Street: CCRR, *Negro in Chicago*, 123; William M. Tuttle Jr., *Race Riot: Chicago in the Red Summer of 1919* (New York: Atheneum, 1970), 176.

2. November 12, 1919, bombing of real estate office: CCRR, *Negro in Chicago*, 125.

3. December 3, 1919, bombing of house at 5922 South Park Avenue: CCRR, *Negro in Chicago*, 125; "Bomb at Home of Colored Real Estate Dealer," *Chicago Tribune*, December 4, 1919, 19.

4. December 27, 1919, bombing of house: CCRR, *Negro in Chicago*, 125.

5. February 6, 1920, bombing of house: "Fourth Bomb for Negro's Home in White Section," *Chicago Tribune*, February 7, 1920.

6. June 18, 1920, bombing of Binga's house: "Binga Bombed for Fifth Time in Six Months"; CCRR, *Negro in Chicago*, 126.

7. November 23, 1920, bombing of house: CCRR, *Negro in Chicago*, 126.

8. August 25, 1921, bombing of house: "Binga's Guard Tries Gun Play After Bombing," *Chicago Tribune*, August 26, 1921.

9. August or September 1921 bombing of house: "Bomb Rips Front Porch from Jesse Binga's Dwelling: Dynamite Home of Jesse Binga Seventh Time Banker Says He Will Let House Stand as Monument to Law and Disorder," *Chicago Defender*, September 3, 1921, 3; "Bombing Binga," *Chicago Defender*, September 3, 1921, 16. The September 3 *Defender* stories may be a reiteration of the August bombing (both reports say it was on a Thursday night), and the *Tribune* and *Defender* both call this the seventh bombing of Binga's home.

7. "Hunt for DePriest Bombers," *Chicago Defender*, April 9, 1921, 1; Tuttle, *Race Riot* 175.

Chapter 3

1. The anecdote in this first section of the chapter is based on and quoting from "Wonders by Women," *St. Paul Daily Globe*, February 10, 1889, 12.

2. James O'Donnell Bennett, "Binga's Secret for Success," *Chicago Tribune*, May 8, 1927, 1.

3. "Binga: Commune in Mali," City Population, accessed April 27, 2019, https://www.citypopulation.de/php/mali-admin.php?adm2id=6203; "Monte Binga," Google, accessed April 27, 2019; "Binga, Congo," Google, accessed April 27, 2019; on Binga village in Zimbabwe, see Wikipedia, s.v. "Binga village," last modified May 31, 2018, https://en.wikipedia.org/wiki/Binga_village.

4. Carol E. Mull, *The Underground Railroad in Michigan* (Jefferson, N.C.: McFarland, 1952), 32–34; Philip J. Schwarz, *Migrants against Slavery: Virginians and the Nation* (Charlottesville: University Press of Virginia, 2001), 169; Wilbur H. Siebert, *The Underground Railroad: From Slavery to Freedom* (New York: Macmillan, 1898; facsimile repr., Palala Press, 2015), 76.

5. Bennett, "Binga's Secret for Success," 1.

6. U.S. Census for following years: 1850, Seventh Census, Schedule 1, 27th District, City of Detroit, County of Wayne, Michigan, p. 121, William Binga (spelled Binger) family, Dwelling No. 1443, Family No. 1737, enumerated September 21, 1850; 1870, Ninth Census, Schedule 1, First Precinct, Sixth Ward, City of Detroit, County of Wayne, Michigan, p. 52, William Binga Family, Dwelling No. 379, Family No. 411, enumerated June 14, 1870; 1880, Tenth Census, Schedule 1, City of Detroit, Wayne County, Michigan, p. 24, William Binga Family, House No. 657, Beaubien Street, Dwelling No. 209, Family No. 244, enumerated

June 5, 1880, all accessed via Ancestry.com. Also on file at U.S. National Archives and Records, 7358 South Pulaski Road, Chicago.

7. U.S. Census, 1910, Thirteenth Census, Third Ward, Chicago, Sheet No. 10A, Jesse Binga Dwelling, East 36th Place, Family No. 205, enumerated April 23, 1910, accessed via Ancestry.com.

8. Binga said his mother was white. Case Report of Mental Health Officer, Illinois State Penitentiary, July 6, 1935, signed by Edward H. Schaller, M.D., Psychiatrist.

9. Junius B. Wood, "One Chicago Bank Is Entirely Colored," *Chicago Daily News*, December 14, 1916, 5.

10. David M. Katzman, *Before the Ghetto: Black Detroit in the Nineteenth Century* (Urbana: University of Illinois Press, 1973), 91–92.

11. "Wonders by Women," 12.

12. Certificate of Death, Michigan, Department of State—Division of Vital Statistics, Certificate and Record of Death, December 24, 1897, p. 642.

13. David M. Katzman, *Before the Ghetto*, 44.

14. Katzman, *Before the Ghetto*, 44–47; Scott Martelle, *Detroit (A Biography)* (Chicago: Chicago Review Press, 2012), 50–51.

15. Bagg quoted in Katzman, *Before the Ghetto*, 35.

16. Katzman, *Before the Ghetto*, 59.

17. Werner Sollors, ed., *Interracialism: Black-White Intermarriage in American History, Literature and Law* (Oxford: Oxford University Press, 2000), 38.

18. Bennett, "Binga's Secret for Success."

19. 1870 census, William Binga Family.

20. Katzman, *Before the Ghetto*, 61, 1880 census, William Binga Family.

21. 1880 census, William Binga Family.

22. Bennett, "Binga's Secret for Success," 1; Inez V. Cantey, "Jesse Binga: The Story of a Life," *The Crisis*, December 1927, 329.

23. 1850, 1870, and 1880 census for William Binga Family.

24. "Saying and Doings," *Detroit Free Press*, September 29, 1878, 1.

25. Katzman, *Before the Ghetto*, 97.

26. Katzman, *Before the Ghetto*, 14–15; Martelle, *Detroit (A Biography)*, 39–40.

27. Katzman, *Before the Ghetto*, 3, including the following anecdote of the celebration.

28. Copy of photo in author's possession.

29. Katzman, *Before the Ghetto*, 76.

30. Bennett, "Binga's Secret for Success."

31. Cantey, ""Jesse Binga: Story of a Life,"329, 352.

32. Bennett, "Binga's Secret for Success."

33. "Wonders by Women," 12. There is no Binga daughter listed in the census with the name Amy or Amelia; Amy might have been another relative.

34. Advertisement listed under "Miscellaneous," *St. Paul Daily Globe*, March 4, 1888, 16.

35. "Time, Tide and Tonics: The Patent Medicine Almanac," U.S. National Library of Medicine, National Institutes of Health, last updated April 27, 2012, https://www.nlm.nih.gov/hmd/almanac/index.html.

36. "Wonders by Women," 12.

37. *Merriam Webster's Collegiate Dictionary*, deluxe ed. (Springfield, Mass.: Merriam-Webster, 1998), s.v. "balm of Gilead."

38. "National Assessment of Adult Literacy—120 Years of Literacy," National Center for Education Statistics, U.S. Department of Education, accessed March 3, 2019, https://nces.ed.gov/naal/lit_history.asp.

39. Cantey, ""Jesse Binga: Story of a Life," 329; J. Clay Smith Jr., *Emancipation: The Making of the Black Lawyer, 1844–1944* (Philadelphia: University of Pennsylvania Press, 1993), 64; "Yearly Index of Law School Graduates: Class of 1877," University of Michigan Law School, accessed March 3, 2019, http://www.law.umich.edu/historyandtraditions/students/Pages/GraduateListByYear.aspx.

40. Case Report of the Mental Health Officer, Illinois State Penitentiary, Joliet, Illinois, March 7, 1936. In Binga's prison file at the Illinois State Archives, Springfield, Ill.

Chapter 4

1. This was what Binga himself said when asked later when he came to Chicago: "In 1892, just about the time of the World's Fair." Binga testimony in trial transcript of *The People of the State of Illinois v. Jesse Binga*, Supreme Court of Illinois Case 22692, May 19–June 3, 1933, Microfilm Roll No. 30-4111, Illinois State Archives, Springfield (hereafter cited as Binga Trial Transcript). Preparations for the World's Columbian Exhibition were under way in 1892, and the fair opened May 1, 1893.

2. Binga's height estimated by a younger relative: Ripley Binga Mead Jr., interview by the author, February 1998, at Mead's real estate office, 322 East Seventy-Fourth Street, Chicago. Average heights for Binga's time are found in Richard H. Steckel, "A History of Standard of Living in the United States," EH.net, Economic History Association, accessed March 4, 2019, http://eh.net/encyclopedia/a-history-of-the-standard-of-living-in-the-united-states/.

3. Binga's physical description is based on photos and portraits taken at various times in Binga's life.

4. Cantey, "Jesse Binga: Story of a Life," 329.

5. Abram L. Harris, *The Negro as Capitalist: A Study of Banking and Business among American Negroes* (Philadelphia: American Academy of Political and Social Science, 1936), 9–12.

6. Harris, *Negro as Capitalist*, 5.

7. Harold F. Gosnell, *Negro Politicians: The Rise of Negro Politics in Chicago* (1935; repr., Chicago: Phoenix Books, University of Chicago Press, 1966), 81.

8. Christopher Robert Reed, *Black Chicago's First Century*, vol. 1, *1833–1900* (Columbia: University of Missouri Press, 2005), 69.

9. St. Clair Drake and Horace R. Cayton, *Black Metropolis: A Study of Negro Life in a Northern City* (1945; repr., Chicago: University of Chicago Press, 1993), 433–34.

10. Drake and Cayton, *Black Metropolis*, 433–34.

11. Drake and Cayton, *Black Metropolis*, 433.

12. Pullman Company Employee and Labor Relations, *Discharge and Release Records*, vol. B, *1888–1890*, Newberry Library, Chicago.

13. Perry R. Duis, *Challenging Chicago: Coping with Everyday Life, 1837–1920* (Urbana: University of Illinois Press, 1998), 27, 32, 49.

14. The story of Binga's travels and work history for these years is based on the accounts in Cantey, "Jesse Binga: Story of a Life," 329, 350, 352; James O'Donnell Bennett, "Plans, Work, Binga's Secret for Success," *Chicago Tribune*, May 8, 1927, 1; Pullman Company Employee and Labor Relations, *Discharge and Release Records*, vol. A, *1880–1887*; vol. B, *1888–1890*; vol. C, *1890–1895*; vol. D, *1895–1901*, Newberry Library, Chicago (hereafter cited as Pullman Records); Frances J. Binga v. Jesse C. Binga Divorce file, Certificate of Evidence, filed September 26, 1901, in Archives of the Clerk of the Circuit Court of Cook County, Chicago (hereafter cited as Binga Divorce file).

15. Binga v. Binga, Circuit Court of Cook County Gen. No. 218433 Term No. 8293, court transcript, September 21, 1901, in Binga Divorce File.

16. Cantey, "Jesse Binga: Story of a Life," 329.

17. Pullman Records, vol. B; Binga Divorce file; court transcript testimony of Frances Binga.

18. Cantey, "Jesse Binga: Story of a Life," 329.

19. Cantey, "Jesse Binga: Story of a Life," 329.

20. Cantey, "Jesse Binga: Story of a Life," 329.

21. Cantey, "Jesse Binga: Story of a Life," 329; Pullman Records, vol. C.

22. Mead, interview, February 1998.

23. Cantey, "Jesse Binga: Story of a Life," 329.

24. Emmett Dedmon, *Fabulous Chicago* (New York: Random House, 1953), 124.

25. Dedmon, *Fabulous Chicago*,125; City of Chicago, *Landmark Designation Report*, April 7, 2005; James R. Grossman, Ann Durkin Keating, and Janice L. Reiff, eds., *The Encyclopedia of Chicago* (Chicago: University of Chicago Press, 2004); Ishbel Ross, *Silhouettes in Diamonds: The Life of Mrs. Potter Palmer* (New York: Harper and Bros., 1960), 28–32.

26. Harris, *Negro as Capitalist*, 154.

27. Arna Bontemps and Jack Conroy, *Anyplace but Here* (1945; repr., Columbia: University of Missouri Press, 1966), 12.

28. Ann Durkin Keating, *Rising Up from Indian Country: The Battle of Fort Dearborn and the Birth of Chicago* (Chicago: University of Chicago Press, 2012), 29.

29. Keating, *Rising Up from Indian Country*, 30. Bontemps and Conroy, *Anyplace but Here*, 15.

30. Bontemps and Conroy, *Anyplace but Here*, 15.

31. Keating, *Rising Up From Indian Country*, 29.

32. Bontemps and Conroy, *Anyplace but Here*, 14.

33. Bontemps and Conroy, *Anyplace but Here*, 16–20.

34. Bontemps and Conroy, *Anyplace but Here*, 1.

35. A. T. Andreas, *History of Chicago: Earliest Period to the Present Time*, vol. 1, *Ending with the Year 1857* (Chicago: A. T. Andreas, 1884), 604.

36. Thomas Lee Philpott, *The Slum and the Ghetto: Neighborhood Deterioration and the Middle-Class Reform, Chicago 1880–1930* (New York: Oxford University Press, 1978), 117.

37. Drake and Cayton, *Black Metropolis*, 50; Andreas, *History of Chicago*, 604.

38. Drake and Cayton, *Black Metropolis*, 38.

39. Drake and Cayton, *Black Metropolis*, 36.

40. Drake and Cayton, *Black Metropolis*, 50–51.

41. John H. Jordan, *Black Americans 17th Century to 21st Century: Black Struggles and Successes* (self-pub., Trafford, 2013), 8.

42. Drake and Cayton, *Black Metropolis*, 39.

43. Don Hayner, "The Meads and Bingas," *Chicago Sun-Times*, 150th Anniversary booklet, March 1, 1987.

44. Hayner, "Meads and Bingas."

45. Hayner, "Meads and Bingas."

46. Mead, interview, February 1998.

47. Grossman, Keating, and Reiff, *Encyclopedia of Chicago*, 280.

48. Susan E. Hirsch and Robert I. Goler, *A City Comes of Age: Chicago in the 1890s* (Chicago: Chicago Historical Society, 1990), 47–48.

49. Cantey, "Jesse Binga: Story of a Life," 329.

50. Philip S. Foner and Ronald L. Lewis, eds., *The Black Worker*, vol. 4 (Philadelphia: Temple University Press, 1979), 73; Larry Tye, *Rising from the Rails: Pullman Porters and the Making of the Black Middle Class* (New York: Henry Holt, 2004), 45, 88.

51. Tye, *Rising from the Rails*, 46.

52. Tye, *Rising from the Rails*, 31–32.

53. Tye, *Rising from the Rails*, 61.

54. *Pullman Palace Car Regulations for Conductors and Porters* (1885), Newberry Library, Chicago.

55. Bennett, "Plans, Work, Binga's Secret for Success,"1.

Chapter 5

1. Truman K. Gibson Jr., interviewed in January–February 1998, said Binga "knew figures and knew what he wanted to do." See also "Fun Facts about the World's Columbian Exposition," Field Museum (Chicago), accessed April 13, 2019, https://www.fieldmuseum.org/fun-facts-about-worlds-columbian -exposition; Julie K. Rose, "A History of the Fair," August 1, 1996, http://xroads .virginia.edu/~ma96/wce/history.html; U.S. Census Bureau, "POP Culture: 1890," last revised July 18, 2017, https://www.census.gov/history/www /through_the_decades/fast_facts/1890_fast_facts.html; "Chicago, United States 1893 World's Columbian Exposition," America's Best History, accessed April 13, 2019, https://americasbesthistory.com/wfchicago1893.html.

2. Patrick Meehan, "Ferris Wheel in the 1893 Chicago World's Fair," Hyde Park Historical Society (website), accessed March 9, 2019, http://www.hydepark history.org/2015/04/27/ferris-wheel-in-the-1893-chicago-worlds-fair/.

3. John F. Wasik, *The Merchant of Power: Sam Insull, Thomas Edison and the Creation of the Modern Metropolis* (New York: Palgrave Macmillan, 2006), 69–70.

4. Wasik, *Merchant of Power*, 70.

5. Dempsey J. Travis, "Chicago Jazz Trails, 1893–1950," *Black Music Research Journal* 10, no. 1 (Spring 1990): 82, https://www.jstor.org/stable/779537?read -now=1&seq=1#page_scan_tab_contents.

6. Robert W. Rydell, "Editor's Introduction: 'Contend, Contend!'" in *The Reason Why the Colored American Is Not in the World's Columbian Exposition*, by Ida B. Wells, Frederick Douglass, Irvine Garland Penn, and Ferdinand L. Barnett, xi– xlviii (Urbana: University of Illinois Press, 1999), xxx–xxxii.

7. See Rydell, "Editor's Introduction," xxx–xxxii; Frederick Douglass, introduction to Wells et al., *Reason Why*, 7–16.

8. Rydell, "Editor's Introduction," xxvi–xxvii.

9. Rydell, "Editor's Introduction," xxvii.

10. Rydell, "Editor's Introduction," xxix.

11. Rydell, "Editor's Introduction, xiii.

12. Ida B. Wells, "Class Legislation," in Wells et al., *Reason Why*, 42.

13. I. Garland Penn, "The Progress of The Afro-American Since Emancipation," in Wells et al., *Reason Why*, 44–64.

14. F. L. Barnett, "The Reason Why," in Wells et al., *Reason Why*, 73–74.

15. Douglass, introduction, 13.

16. Rydell, "Editor's Introduction, xxx.

17. Plessy v. Ferguson, 163 U.S. 537 (1896); Brown v. Board of Education, 347 U.S. 483 (1954).

18. Rydell, "Editor's Introduction," xvi.

19. Christopher Robert Reed, *"All the World Is Here!" The Black Presence at White City* (Bloomington: Indiana University Press, 2000), 58.

20. Reed, *"All the World Is Here!"* 75–76.

21. Rose, "History of the Fair."

22. Rydell, "Editor's Introduction," xi–xlvii.

23. Rydell, "Editor's Introduction," xvii–xviii.

24. Rydell, "Editor's Introduction," xxxi.

25. Rydell, "Editor's Introduction," xxxi; illustrated map in author's possession.

26. Rydell, "Editor's Introduction," xxxii.

27. Rydell, "Editor's Introduction," xxxiii.

28. Donald Preston, *The Scholar and the Scalpel: The Life Story of Ulysses Grant Dailey* (Chicago: Afro-Am Publishing, 1966), 10–11.

29. Roi Ottley, *The Lonely Warrior: The Life and Times of Robert S. Abbott, Founder of the "Chicago Defender" Newspaper* (Chicago: Henry Regnery, 1955), 7.

30. David Colbert, ed., *Eyewitness to America: 500 Years of American History in the Words of Those Who Saw It Happen* (New York: Vintage Books, 1998), 332–33.

Chapter 6

1. Duis, *Challenging Chicago*, 278.

2. Duis, *Challenging Chicago*, 275, 399n2.

3. Dewey R. Jones, "Chicago Claims Supremacy," *Opportunity*, March 1929, 92.

4. Drake and Cayton, *Black Metropolis*, 433–34.

5. Duis, *Challenging Chicago*, 117.

6. Duis, *Challenging Chicago*, 116.

7. Binga Trial Transcript, Jesse Binga testimony, 822.

8. "Central Station, Chicago Terminal. Also known as Illinois Central Depot," Digital Research Library of Illinois History Journal, March 7, 2017, https://drloihjournal.blogspot.com/2017/03/central-station-chicago-terminal-also.html; "Central Station," Chicagology, accessed April 14, 2019, http://chicagology.com/goldenage/goldenage021/.

9. Duis, *Challenging Chicago*, 277.

10. Duis, *Challenging Chicago*, 276.

11. Anthony J. Binga Sr., "Jesse Binga, Founder and President of Binga State Bank" (address delivered to Afro-American Historical and Genealogical Society National Archives, Washington, D.C., September 11, 1981), 4.

12. "Black History Month: A Medical Perspective; Hospitals," Duke University Medical Center and Archives, last updated March 1, 2019, https://guides .mclibrary.duke.edu/blackhistorymonth/hospitals.

13. "Big Business Swells Hospital Fund," *Chicago Defender*, January 18, 1930; James O'Donnell Bennett, "Offer $414,500 in 20 Minutes to Help Negroes," *Chicago Tribune*, January 17, 1930, 15.

14. Albert Barnett, "Provident Hospital—A Saga of Service to Suffering Mankind," *Chicago Defender*, October 9, 1954, 4.

15. Grossman, Keating, and Reiff, *Encyclopedia of Chicago*, 655.

16. Barnett, "Provident Hospital," 4.

17. Ernest Ludlow Bogart and John Mabry Mathews, "The Panic of 1893 and the Banks," in *The Centennial History of Illinois*, vol. 5, *The Modern Commonwealth, 1893–1918*, ed. Clarence Walworth Alvord (Springfield: Illinois Centennial Commission, 1920), 394.

18. Charles Hoffman, *The Depression of the Nineties: An Economic History* (Westport, Conn.: Greenwood, 1970), 56–58, 63.

19. Bogart and Mathews, "Panic of 1893 and Banks," 402.

20. Melvin I. Urofski, "Pullman Strike," in *Encyclopaedia Britanica*, last updated November 29, 2018, https://www.britannica.com/event/Pullman-Strike.

21. Victoria Brown, "Advocate for Democracy: Jane Addams and the Pullman Strike," in *The Pullman Strike and the Crisis of the 1890s: Essays on Labor and Politics*, ed. Richard Shneirov, Shelton Stromquist, and Nick Salvatore (Urbana: University of Illinois Press, 1999), 137.

22. Tye, *Rising From The Rails*, 70–71.

23. Frank Young, "Binga Put Personal Pride before Depositors' Savings; Wrecked Bank," *Afro-American*, June 17, 1933, 21.

24. Charles Hoffman, *Depression of the Nineties*, 107.

25. Grossman, Keating, and Reiff, *Encyclopedia of Chicago*, 511.

26. Grossman, Keating, and Reiff, *Encyclopedia of Chicago*, 511.

27. Philpott, *Slum and Ghetto*, 24.

28. "In the Matter of the Application of Jesse Binga for Pardon," signed by Jesse Binga and his attorney John Cashen and stamped as received June 28, 1935, unnumbered p. 4, Jesse Binga prison file, Illinois State Archives, Springfield, Ill. (hereafter cited as Pardon Application).

29. Pullman Records, vol. C (1890–1895) and vol. D 1895–1901. However, Binga's first wife claimed that Binga also was working as a Pullman porter in Boston in 1901; see Binga Divorce file.

30. Chicago City Directory lists Binga at 3738 Armour Avenue in 1897. See also U.S. Census, 1900, Twelfth Census, Schedule 1, Chicago, Cook County, Ill., for the 3700 block of South Armour Avenue, enumerated June 12, 1900, accessed via Ancestry.com.

31. U.S. Census, 1900, for 3700 block of South Armour Avenue.

32. James R. Grossman, *Land of Hope: Chicago Black Southerners and the Great Migration* (Chicago: University of Chicago Press, 1989), 127; Allan H. Spear,

Black Chicago: The Making of a Negro Ghetto, 1890–1920 (Chicago: University of Chicago Press, 1967), 14–15.

33. Spear, *Black Chicago*, 15.

34. Hemesath, *From Slave to Priest* 217–19.

35. The biographical information on Father Tolton relies heavily on Hemesath, *From Slave to Priest*, 218–19. Death toll from "Sun God Is Pitiless," *Chicago Daily News*, July 10, 1897, 1.

36. Hemesath, *From Slave to Priest*, 208.

37. Cyprian Davis, *The History of Black Catholics in the United States* (New York: Crossroad, 1995), 152.

38. The 4 percent represents the three hundred to six hundred parishioners in a city with a population of fifteen thousand blacks.

39. A. Binga Sr., "Jesse Binga, Founder," 4.

40. Davis, *History of Black Catholics*, 30.

41. Davis, *History of Black Catholics*, 36–37.

42. "St. Monica Court Catholic Order of Foresters," *Broad Ax*, January 6, 1912.

43. Suellen Hoy, *Good Hearts: Catholic Sisters in Chicago's Past* (Urbana: University of Illinois Press, 2006), 7.

44. Hoy, *Good Hearts*, 88.

45. Hoy, *Good Hearts*, 88.

46. Hoy, *Good Hearts*, 89, 95.

47. Dorothy A. Drain, "Catholic Capsules," *Chicago Defender*, August 5, 1972, 27.

48. *Chicago Citizen*, April 30, 1892; Hemesath, *From Slave to Priest*, 200, 202.

49. Hemesath, *From Slave to Priest*, 202, 233.

50. Hemesath, *From Slave to Priest*, 45, 192, 197, 212; "Priest Born a Slave," *Daily Inter Ocean* (Chicago), July 19, 1897.

51. As described in Hemesath, *From Slave to Priest*, 213.

52. Father Tolton to Rev. Mother Catherine, June 5, 1891, Archives of the Sisters of the Blessed Sacrament, Bensalem, Pa., now in the Catholic Historical Research Center of the Archdiocese of Philadelphia (hereafter cited as Sisters of the Blessed Sacrament Archives).

53. "Sun God Is Pitiless." Davis, *History of Black Catholics*, 162; Hemesath, *From Slave to Priest*, 216.

Chapter 7

1. Richard C. Lindberg and Carol Jean Carlson, *Chicago: Yesterday and Today* (Chicago: West Side Publishing, 2009), 41; Edmund M. Burke and Thomas J. O'Gorman, *Chicago City Hall 100* (Chicago: Horto Press, 2009), 66.

2. Michigan Marriage Records, 1867–1952, Record number 1315, 1885 Leelanau-Wexford, Wayne County, p. 352.

3. Dorothy Binga Taylor, telephone interview by the author, January 1, 1999. She recalled, "When I was a little girl, I found in a trunk correspondence from my grandfather asking for her (Frances's) hand in marriage."

4. Copy of family photo in author's possession.

5. Census 1881—Recensement, of Canada for Josiah Scott family, Schedule 1, District Kent, Chatham, Ontario, Division 2, p. 154, accessed via Ancestry.com.

6. Certificate of Live Birth, State of Michigan, Department of Community Health, no. 121-7-49.

7. Taylor, interview.

8. Taylor, interview; Cantey, "Jesse Binga: Story of a Life," 329.

9. Binga Trial Transcript, 821.

10. Katzman, *Before the Ghetto*, 116.

11. City Directory of St. Paul, 1887–1888, shows a Jesse G. Binga, as a "col'd barber" living at 501 Bradley.

12. Pullman Records, vol. A.

13. "A Sister's Devotion," *Detroit Free Press*, July 23, 1896, 10.

14. "Sister's Devotion."

15. "The Double Murder, The Trial of John H. Thomas for Killing His Wife and Step-daughter," *Detroit Free Press*, May 19, 1875, 1.

16. "Sister's Devotion."

17. "Sister's Devotion."

18. "The Other Side of It," *Detroit Free Press*, July 24, 1896, 7.

19. "Other Side of It."

20. "Exit Thomas, The End of Hastings Street Tragedy," *Detroit Free Press*, May 23, 1875, 1.

21. "Exit Thomas."

22. Katzman, *Before the Ghetto*, 116.

23. "Wonders by Women."

24. This account comes from pleadings filed by Frances J. Binga as complainant, Bill for Divorce, Frances J. Binga v. Jesse C. Binga, Gen. No. 218433, Term No. 8293, Cook County Chancery Court, June 5, 1901, in Binga Divorce file.

25. David S. Tanenhaus, "Justice for the Child: The Beginning of the Juvenile Court in Chicago," *Chicago History* 27, no. 3 (Winter 1998–1999): 14–15.

26. Certificate of Evidence filed September 26, 1901, which includes court testimony of September 21, in Binga Divorce file.

27. Cook County Marriage Index, 1871–1920 (text only), marriage of Frances Scott (Binga) to J. Oscar Davis, October 21, 1901, Chicago, Cook County, Ill., accessed via Ancestry.com.

Chapter 8

1. The first seven paragraphs of this chapter are largely based on the article "Woe on Vernon Avenue," *Daily Inter Ocean* (Chicago), August 19, 1900, 1.

2. Philpott, *Slum and Ghetto*, 150; "Woe on Vernon Avenue," 1.

3. "Woe on Vernon Avenue," 1.

4. "Woe on Vernon Avenue," 1.

5. "Woe on Vernon Avenue," 1.

6. Grossman, Keating, and Reiff, *Encyclopedia of Chicago*, 80.

7. Philpott, *Slum and Ghetto*, 150.

8. Richard R. Wright Jr., "The Economic Conditions of Negroes in the North," in *Southern Workman*, vol. 37, (Hampton, Va.: Hampton Institute Press, 1909), 608.

9. Wright, "Economic Conditions of Negroes," 608.

10. John V. Johnson bought 3324 Vernon from Franny E. Pridmore on June 1, 1901, by warranty deed filed June 8, 1901, according to records of the Cook County Recorder of Deeds.

11. Drake and Cayton, *Black Metropolis*, table 1, p. 8.

12. "Exterior and Interior Views of Jesse Binga's Bank," *Broad Ax*, December 25, 1909, 1.

13. Anthony J. Binga, Sr., "The Jesse Binga I Knew" (typescript, December 1979), 2–3, private collection; A. Binga Sr., "Jesse Binga, Founder."

14. Binga Trial Transcript, Binga testimony, 822.

15. Bennett, "Binga's Secret for Success," 1; "Exterior and Interior Views of Binga's Bank."

16. Bennett, "Binga's Secret for Success," 1; "Exterior and Interior Views of Binga's Bank."

17. Bennett, "Binga's Secret for Success," 1.

18. Mead, interview, February 1998.

19. Bennett, "Binga's Secret for Success," 1.

20. Quotation from Ripley Binga Mead Sr., who began working for Binga in 1907, in Dempsey J. Travis, *An Autobiography of Black Chicago* (Chicago: Urban Research Institute, 1981), 258.

21. "Jesse C. Binga the Real Estate Wizard," *Chicago Defender*, November 5, 1910, 1.

22. A. Binga Sr., "Jesse Binga I Knew," 3.

23. Dempsey Travis, interview by the author at Travis's office on East Eighty-Seventh Street in Chicago, March 8, 1998; Dempsey Travis, telephone interview by the author, April 1998. In these interviews, he based this information on his own interview of a director of Binga's bank.

24. "Exterior and Interior Views of Binga's Bank."

25. Philpott, *Slum and Ghetto*, 150–51; "Rents to Go Higher This Year, Is Belief of Tenants' League," *Chicago Defender*, April 12, 1924, 3.

26. Philpott, *Slum and Ghetto*, 150–51.

27. Philpott, *Slum and Ghetto*, 150–51.

28. Travis, *Autobiography of Black Chicago*, 258.

29. Amanda I. Seligman, *Block by Block: Neighborhoods and Public Policy on Chicago's West Side* (Chicago: University of Chicago Press, 2005), 178.

30. Fair Housing Act, Pub. L. 90-284, 82 Stat. 73 (1968).

31. Philpott, *Slum and Ghetto*, 150–51.

32. "Race Rioting in Chicago," *Broad Ax*, May 27, 1905, 1.

33. "Race Rioting in Chicago."

34. "Race Rioting in Chicago."

35. "Afro-Americans Are Meeting with Success in the Real Estate Business in Chicago," *Broad Ax*, November 23, 1907, 1.

36. "Afro-Americans Meeting with Success in Real Estate."

37. Philpott, *Slum and Ghetto*, 150–51.

38. "Afro-Americans Meeting with Success in Real Estate."

39. "Jesse Binga Has No Partners in the Real Estate Business," *Broad Ax*, January 11, 1908. This appeared as a news item; it did not appear to be a paid advertisement.

40. Bennett, "Binga's Secret for Success."

41. Lucius C. Harper, "Dustin Off the News: Binga Represented a Business Era That Was Crude, Rough, Uncultured," *Chicago Defender*, June 24, 1950, 7.

42. Mead, interview, February 1998; Ripley Binga Mead Jr., interview by the author, June 4, 1998, at his real estate office, 322 East Seventy-Fourth Street, Chicago; "Jesse Binga Celebrated his Forty-Seventh Birthday Anniversary, *Broad Ax*, April 13, 1912, 1.

43. "Afro-Americans Meeting with Success in Real Estate,"1.

44. "Binga the Real Estate Wizard," 1.

45. "Block of Stores and Flats Leased for Thirty Years," *Broad Ax*, October 29, 1910.

Chapter 9

1. "Exterior and Interior Views of Binga's Bank," 2.

2. Curt Eriksmoen, "Black Editor got started in Fargo," *Bismarck Tribune*, February 26, 2012, https://bismarcktribune.com/news/columnists/curt-eriksmoen/black-editor-got-started-in-fargo/article_f25b89ca-5f20-11e1-8f48-0019bb2963f4.html; Elaine Thatcher, "Julius Taylor and the Broad Ax," Utah Humanities, 2008, https://www.utahhumanities.org/stories/items/show/162.

3. Ottley, *Lonely Warrior*, 6, 13, 23–24.

4. Jesse Binga Real Estate and Loans advertisement in *Broad Ax*, August 29, 1908.

5. In a column listing, *Broad Ax*, August 7, 1909; "Block of Stores and Flats Leased for Thirty Years."

6. Mead, interview, February 1998.

7. Bogart and Mathews, "Panic of 1893 and Banks," 416n49.

8. Bogart and Mathews, "Panic of 1893 and Banks," 417.

9. Bogart and Mathews, "Panic of 1893 and Banks," 418.

10. Bogart and Mathews, "Panic of 1893 and Banks," 418; Lizabeth Cohen, *Making a New Deal: Industrial Workers in Chicago, 1919–1939* (New York: Cambridge University Press, 1990, 2008), 79.

11. Cantey, "Jesse Binga: Story of a Life," 350.

12. The description of the bank's signs and offerings of the bank come from pictures accompanying "Exterior and Interior Views of Binga's Bank."

13. The giant letter *B* can been seen clearly in a photo accompanying an article by Roberty W. Bagnall, "Lex Talionis: A Story," *The Crisis* 23, no. 6 (April 1922): 255.

14. Harper, "Dustin Off the News."

15. Harris, *Negro as Capitalist*, 28, 31.

16. Douglass quoted in Harris, *Negro as Capitalist*, 26.

17. Harris, *Negro as Capitalist*, 27–35, 42.

18. Harris, *Negro as Capitalist*, 46.

19. Harris, *Negro as Capitalist*, 46.

20. Harris, *Negro as Capitalist*, 46–47.

21. Roi Ottley, "Trace Negro Burial Societies, Rituals to Pre-Civil War Roots," *Chicago Sunday Tribune*, September 18, 1955, 11.

22. Ottley, "Trace Negro Burial Societies."

23. Harris, *Negro as Capitalist*, 46.

24. Harris, *Negro as Capitalist*, 47.

25. Muriel Miller Branch, "Miller, Maggie L.," in *American National Biography*, July 2004, https://doi.org/10.1093/anb/9780198606697.article.1002267.

26. Harris, *Negro as Capitalist*, 47.

27. "The Lincoln Savings Bank," *Chicago Defender*, June 13, 1914, 1.

28. "Exterior and Interior Views of Binga's Bank," 2, 3.

29. "Jesse Binga: Banker—Begin the New Year with Us," *Chicago Defender*, Dec. 23, 1911, 8.

30. "Lincoln Savings Bank."

31. Cantey, "Jesse Binga: Story of a Life," 350.

Chapter 10

1. The "Certain Sayings of Jesse Binga" come from Bennett, "Plans, Work, Binga's Secret for Success."

2. *Stenographic Verbatim Report*, Parole Board, Illinois State Penitentiary, Docket No. 61, Prison No. 1306-F, Jesse Binga, April 1, 1936, p. 5, in Binga prison file, Illinois State Archives, Springfield, Ill.

3. "One Day in the Life of a Banker," *Chicago Defender*, February 24, 1912, 1.

4. Information for the description in this paragraph comes from Herman Clayton, "The Game Policy," Illinois Writers Project (IWP) "Negro in Illinois" papers, Harsh, box 35, folder 13, pp. 1–2, Vivian G. Harsh Research Collection, Woodson Regional Library of the Chicago Public Library (hereafter cited as IWP papers), https://www.chipublib.org/fa-illinois-writers-project-2/; Andrew G. Paschal, "Policy: Negroes' Number Game," IWP papers, Harsh, box 35, folder 23, p. 2. On Barnum, see also Melissa Houston, "P. T. Barnum's Lottery," Connecticut History.org, September 30, 2013, https://connecticuthistory.org/p-t-barnums-lottery/.

5. Information for the description in this paragraph comes from Clayton, "Game Policy."

6. Herman Clayton, "Local Policy Barons," IWP papers, Harsh, box 35, folder 17, pp. 3–4.

7. Clayton, "Local Policy Barons," p. 3; Mathilde Bunton, "'Policy' Negro Business," IWP papers, Harsh, box 35, folder 11, p. 13.

8. Paschal, "Policy: Negroes' Number Game," p. 5.

9. Gosnell, *Negro Politicians*, 126.

10. Duis, *Challenging Chicago*, 8.

11. Nathan Thompson, *Kings: The True Story of Chicago's Policy Kings and Numbers Racketeers; An Informal History* (Chicago: Bronzeville Press, 2002), 20; Gosnell, *Negro Politicians*, 126.

12. Gosnell, *Negro Politicians*, 126.

13. See photo in "Mushmouth Johnson's Emporium Saloon," Chicago Crime Scenes Project, February 20, 2009, http://chicagocrimescenes.blogspot.com/2009/02/mushmouth-johnsons-emporium-saloon.html.

14. Gosnell, *Negro Politicians*, 126.

15. Drake and Cayton, *Black Metropolis*, 485.

16. Funeral bill from October 14, 1907, in Inventory in the Matter of the Estate of John V. Johnson, deceased, Probate Court of Cook County, Estate file

of John V. Johnson, Archives of the Clerk of the Circuit Court of Cook County, Daley Center, Chicago (hereafter cited as Johnson Estate file).

17. Thompson, *Kings*, 21.

18. Robert M. Lombardo, *The Black Mafia: African-American Organized Crime in Chicago; 1890–1960*, Crime Law and Social Change 38 (Dordrecht, Neth.: Kluwer Academic Publishers, 2002), 33–65, at 37.

19. Mathilde Bunton, "The Negro in Business: 'Policy Sam,'" IWP papers, Harsh, box 35, folder 18, 1–8.

20. Gosnell, *Negro Politicians*, 126–27.

21. Gosnell, *Negro Politicians*, 126–27.

22. Gosnell, *Negro Politicians*, 126.

23. Drake and Cayton, *Black Metropolis*, 486.

24. "Mushmouth Seen in Plot to Kill," *Chicago Daily Tribune*, November 13, 1903, 4.

25. Karen Abbott, *Sin in the Second City Madams, Ministers, Playboys and the Battle for America's Soul* (New York: Random House, 2008), 225–26.

26. Gosnell, *Negro Politicians*, 127.

27. Kevin J. Mumford, *Interzones: Black/White Districts in Chicago and New York in the Early Twentieth Century* (New York: Columbia University Press, 1997), 22.

28. Grossman, Keating, and Reiff, *Encyclopedia of Chicago*, 563, 855.

29. Mumford, *Interzones*, 23.

30. Mumford, *Interzones*, 27.

31. CCRR, *Negro in Chicago*, map on facing page to 342.

32. Mumford, *Interzones*, 27.

33. Mumford, *Interzones*, 38.

34. Gosnell, *Negro Politicians*, 127.

35. Gosnell, *Negro Politicians*, 127.

36. Funeral bill, Johnson Estate file.

37. "Chips," *Broad Ax*, September 20, 1902, 1.

38. Spear, *Black Chicago*, 76.

39. The account given in this and the following four paragraphs are based on Fenton Johnson, "The Story of Cecelia Johnson," June 18, 1942, IWP papers, Harsh, box 11 folder 10, pp. 1–8.

40. "Negress Leads Co-Ed Society Three Years," *Chicago Record-Herald*, July 22, 1907, 1.

41. F. Johnson, "Story of Cecelia Johnson."

42. "Negress Leads Co-Ed Society" Other newspaper stories are mentioned in F. Johnson, "Story of Cecelia Johnson." And there were follow-up stories in the *Chicago Record Herald*—such as "Did Not Pose as White Girl," *Chicago Record Herald*, July 24, 1907—and elsewhere; see, for example, "Color Line Rends U. of C. Sorority," *Chicago Tribune*, July 22, 1907, 1; "Girl Is Cousin of 'Mushmouth'; Mother in St. Louis," *Inter Ocean*, July 24, 1907, 1.

43. "Negress Leads Co-Ed Society."

44. Background information in this section on "passing" comes from Arna Bontemps and Jack Conroy, "The Invisible Migration," in Bontemps and Conroy, *Anyplace but Here*, 122–34.

45. Mead, interview, June 4, 1998.

46. Advertisement in *Chicago Defender*, July 29, 1911.

47. Ottley, *Lonely Warrior*, 13.

48. Ottley, *Lonely Warrior*, 68–69.

49. Drake and Cayton, *Black Metropolis*, 168–69.

50. Bontemps and Conroy, "Invisible Migration,"132.

51. Bontemps and Conroy, "Invisible Migration," 132.

52. Bontemps and Conroy, "Invisible Migration," 132.

53. "Negress Leads Co-Ed Society," 1.

54. "Did Not Pose as White Girl."

55. F. Johnson, "Story of Cecelia Johnson," 7.

56. Affidavit dated June 30, 1908, in Johnson Estate file.

57. According to Fenton Johnson; see F. Johnson, "Story of Cecelia Johnson."

58. F. Johnson, "Story of Cecelia Johnson," 6; "John Johnson," *Broad Ax*, September 21, 1907.

59. F. Johnson, "Story of Cecelia Johnson," 6.

60. "John Johnson."

61. City of New York Department of Health, Certificate and Record of Death No. 18767, September 12, 1907.

62. Thompson, *Kings*, 22–23.

63. "John Johnson."

64. Funeral bill, in Johnson Estate file.

65. Final Account, in Johnson Estate file.

66. Final Account, in Johnson Estate file; "John Johnson"; and Gosnell, *Negro Politicians*, 126.

67. Marriage certificate from State of Illinois Cook County, issued on February 19, 1912, and signed on February 2, 1912, by Rev. E. T. Martin.

Chapter 11

1. "The Johnson-Binga Wedding the Most Elaborate and the Most Fashionable," *Broad Ax*, February 24, 1912, 1; "Binga-Johnson Wedding the Most Brilliant Ever Held in Chicago," *Chicago Defender*, February 24, 1912, 1.

2. Quoted in Gerri Major and Doris E. Saunders, *Gerri Major's Black Society* (Chicago: Johnson Publishing, 1976), 305.

3. *Stenographic Verbatim Report*, Parole Board, Illinois State Penitentiary, Docket No. 61, Prison No. 1306-F, Jesse Binga, April 1, 1936, p. 4, Binga Prison file, Illinois State Archives, Springfield, Ill.

4. Eudora quitclaimed Mushmouth's property to him on September 6, 1906 (see Johnson Estate file). John Johnson died on September 12, 1907, with four survivors: his mother, Ellen Johnson; two sisters, Eudora Johnson and Louise Ray, and a brother, Elijah Johnson. Louisa was executrix and Eudora was sole legatee for the estate. Ellen inherited a portion of the estate but died before the estate was settled. Louisa and Elijah each sold and assigned a one-fifth portion of the estate to Eudora. After sales and assignments were completed, Eudora received three-fifths and Louise two-fifths of the estate, according to the final accounting and inventory of the estate of John V. Johnson filed January 2, 1912, in Cook County Probate Court (see Johnson Estate file).

5. Drake and Cayton, *Black Metropolis*, 548.

6. "Johnson-Binga Wedding Most Elaborate."

7. "Johnson-Binga Wedding Most Elaborate."

8. "Binga-Johnson Wedding Most Brilliant."

9. "Binga-Johnson Wedding Most Brilliant."

10. "Binga-Johnson Wedding Most Brilliant."

11. "Men of the Month: A Young Dentist," *The Crisis* 15, no. 5 (March 1918): 229; Carl Stephens, ed., *The Alumni Record of the University of Illinois, Chicago Departments Colleges of Medicine and Dentistry School of Pharmacy* (Dixon, Ill.: Rogers Printing, 1921), 304.

12. "Vance Anderson Has Invented and Patented a Safety Street Car Fender," *Broad Ax,* July 11, 1914.

13. "Binga-Johnson Wedding Most Brilliant."

14. The 1900 census shows Tinley living with a mother-in-law named Morrison (Eudora's mother's maiden name) and living in the same house at 5830 Wabash Avenue as Eudora and renting from John Johnson. U.S. Census, 1900, Twelfth Census, Schedule 1–Population, Ward 34, Hyde Park Township, Chicago, Cook County, Ill., District 1080, Sheet No. 3 B, John Johnson Family at 5830 Wabash, Family No. 54, enumerated June 4, 1900, accessed via Ancestry.com.

15. Marriage license from the State of Illinois County of Cook, issued February 19, 1912, and signed February 20, 1912, by Reverend E. T. Martin, copy obtained from Cook County Clerk. The information on the courting of several years is from "Mr. Binga's Box Party," *Broad Ax,* January 1, 1910.

16. "Binga-Johnson Wedding Most Brilliant."

17. "Wife of Jesse Binga Dies; Trial Postponed," *Pittsburgh Courier,* April 1, 1933, 1.

18. Fifth Census of Canada, 1911, Chatham, Ontario, Bethune Binza [misspelling of Binga] family, Dwelling No. 65, Family No. 65, enumerated June 5, 1911, accessed via Ancestry.com.

19. "Johnson-Binga Wedding Most Elaborate."

20. "Johnson-Binga Wedding Most Elaborate."

21. "Binga-Johnson Wedding Most Brilliant."

22. Doris L. Rich, *Queen Bess, Daredevil Aviator* (Washington, D.C.: Smithsonian Institution Press, 1993), 20, 22, 30.

23. Rich, *Queen Bess,* 22, 30, 81, 110.

24. Major and Saunders, *Black Society,* 306.

25. Major and Saunders, *Black Society,* 304.

26. "Chicago Is Automobile Center of World," *Chicago Defender,* November 16, 1912, 7.

27. ". . . And About Chicago," *Chicago Defender,* May 22, 1915, 5.

28. Gibson, interviews, January and February 1998.

29. "The First Negro Colonel: John R. Marshall of Chicago to Enjoy that Distinction," *New York Times,* June 22, 1898.

30. "Harsh, Vivian Gordon 1890–1960," in *Contemporary Black Biography,* Encyclopedia.com, accessed April 15, 2019, https://www.encyclopedia.com/education/news-wires-white-papers-and-books/harsh-vivian-gordon-1890-1960.

31. CCRR, *Negro in Chicago*, 59.

32. Ottley, *Lonely Warrior*, 216.

33. "Exterior and Interior Views of Binga's Bank," 2.

34. W. E. B. Du Bois, "Postscript," *The Crisis* 37 (December 1930): 425.

35. Ottley, *Lonely Warrior*, 85.

36. Frederic H. H. Robb, ed., *The Negro in Chicago 1779–1929*, vol. 2 (Chicago: Washington Intercollegiate Club of Chicago and International Student Alliance, 1929), 281.

37. Spear, *Black Chicago*, 66.

38. "That Jim Crow School," *Chicago Defender*, March 29, 1913, 4.

39. Spear, *Black Chicago*, 67–69, quotation at 67.

40. Spear, *Black Chicago*, 69.

41. "Chips."

42. Spear, *Black Chicago*, 82.

43. Spear, *Black Chicago*, 82–83.

44. "Booker T. Washington Bitterly Denounced as a Traitor to His Race," *Broad Ax*, March 2, 1912, 1.

45. "Lynchings: By Year and Race," provided by Archives at Tuskegee Institute, Famous Trials by Professor Douglas O. Lynder (website), accessed April 15, 2019, https://www.famous-trials.com/sheriffshipp/1084-lynchingsyear.

46. "State Street Carnival Opens Tonight," *Chicago Defender*, August 17, 1912.

47. "Miss Hattie Holliday Crowned Queen of State Street Carnival," *Chicago Defender*, August 31, 1912.

48. Davarian L. Baldwin, *Chicago's New Negroes: Modernity, the Great Migration and Black Urban Life* (Chapel Hill: University of North Carolina Press, 2007), 115.

49. Baldwin, *Chicago's New Negroes*, 114.

50. Baldwin, *Chicago's New Negroes*, 115.

51. "Miss Hattie Holliday Crowned."

Chapter 12

1. Ben Hecht, *A Child of the Century* (New York: Simon and Schuster, 1954), 127–29.

2. Geoffrey C. Ward, *Unforgivable Blackness: The Rise and Fall of Jack Johnson* (New York: Vintage Books, 2006), 289.

3. Drake and Cayton, *Black Metropolis*, 433–34.

4. "Martha Winchester, Pioneer Resident, Is Laid to Rest," *Chicago Defender*, January 9, 1937, 22.

5. William Howland Kenney, *Chicago Jazz: A Cultural History, 1904–1930* (New York: Oxford University Press, 1993), 15.

6. Kenney, *Chicago Jazz*, 15.

7. Carl Sandburg, *The Chicago Race Riots: July 1919* (New York: Harcourt, Brace and Howe, 1919), 49.

8. Joel Greenberg, *A Natural History of the Chicago Region* (Chicago: University of Chicago Press, 2002), 245.

9. Olivia Mahoney, *Images of America: Douglas/Grand Boulevard, A Chicago Neighborhood* (Chicago: Arcadia Publishing, 2001), 9. Chicago Fact Book Consortium, *Local Community Fact Book Chicago Metropolitan Area, Based on the 1970 and 1980 Censuses* (Chicago: Chicago Review Press, 1984), 96–99.

10. Chicago Fact Book Consortium, *Local Community Fact Book Chicago*, 96–99.

11. Chicago Fact Book Consortium, *Local Community Fact Book Chicago*,96–99.

12. Mahoney, *Images of America*, 7.

13. Drake and Cayton, *Black Metropolis*, 53, 175,176.

14. Drake and Cayton, *Black Metropolis*, 12.

15. Travis, interviews, March 8, 1998, and April 1998.

16. "Held Up at the Door of His Bank," *Buffalo Enquirer*, July 15, 1910, 9; "Thief Saved from Lynchers by Police," *St. Louis Star and Times*, July 15, 1910, 3.

17. Gosnell, *Negro Politicians*, 127–28. Motts is described as a protégé to Johnson not only in Gosnell, *Negro Politicians*, but also in Charles Russell Branham, "The Transformation of Black Political Leadership in Chicago, 1864–1942" (Ph.D. diss., University of Chicago, 1981).

18. "Mrs. Jackson Passes after Long Illness, Body Returned East for Burial," *Chicago Defender*, November 3, 1988, 4.

19. Thompson, *Kings*, 51.

20. *Stenographic Verbatim Report*, April 1, 1936, p. 5.

21. Kenney, *Chicago Jazz*, 8.

22. John Litweiler, "A Swingin' Town: Chicago and Jazz Go Way Back," *Chicago Tribune*, August 31, 1988. The attribution is from Richard Want, a music professor the University of Illinois–Chicago.

23. Map of Chicago South Side Jazz, c. 1915–c. 1930, Chicago Jazz Archive, University of Chicago Library.

24. Kenney, *Chicago Jazz*, 14.

25. CCRR, *Negro in Chicago*, 323–324.

26. Mumford, *Interzones*, 30.

27. Quoted in CCRR, *Negro in Chicago*, 323–24.

28. Quoted in CCRR, *Negro in Chicago*, 323–24.

29. "Robert T. Motts, Owner and Manager of the Pekin Theater," *Broad Ax*, July 5, 1911, 1.

30. Thompson, *Kings*, 32.

31. "Robert T. Motts, Owner and Manager of Pekin Theater."

32. Kenney, *Chicago Jazz*, 7.

33. Robin F. Bachin, *Building the South Side: Urban Space and Civic Culture in Chicago 1890–1919* (Chicago, London: University of Chicago Press, 2004), 276.

34. "One Day in the Life of a Banker."

35. "Mrs. Binga Purchases New Electric," *Chicago Defender*, April 20, 1918.

36. CCRR, *Negro in Chicago*, map on facing page to 342.

37. Interview with Grace Garnett [by J. Bougere, July 30, 1941], on her role in the origin of the "kitchenette apartments," IWP papers, Harsh, box 37, folder 25.

38. Much of the biographical information in this section on Robert Abbott comes from Ottley, *Lonely Warrior*.

39. Ottley, *Lonely Warrior*, 83.

40. Ottley, *Lonely Warrior*, 84.

41. Ottley, *Lonely Warrior*, 88.

42. Ottley, *Lonely Warrior*, 86.

43. Ottley, *Lonely Warrior*, 87.

44. Ottley, *Lonely Warrior*, 85.

45. Ottley, *Lonely Warrior*, 87–88.

46. Ottley, *Lonely Warrior*, 87–88.

47. Ottley, *Lonely Warrior*, 90.

48. Ottley, *Lonely Warrior*, 90.

49. "Binga-Johnson Wedding Most Brilliant."

50. "Mr. Jesse Binga, Banker, Almost Loses Eyesight," *Chicago Defender*, September 23, 1911, 1.

51. "Suicide Due to Snubs," *Chicago Record-Herald*, September 13, 1912.

52. "Suicide Due to Snubs."

53. "Mrs. Johnson Tries Suicide," *New York Times*, September 12, 1912; Lucius Harper, "Dustin Off the News: Jack Johnson Was the Most Colorful Ring Character," *Chicago Defender*, June 22, 1946, 1; Charles J. Johnson, "The Short, Sad Story of Café de Champion—Jack Johnson's Mixed-Race Nightclub on Chicago's South Side," *Chicago Tribune*, May 25, 2018.

Chapter 13

1. Real estate records of the Cook County Recorder of Deeds list date of deed transfers, the parties involved, the age of the house, and the square footage; Cook County Recorder of Deeds, 118 N. Clark Street, Chicago (hereafter cited as Cook County real estate records). See also U.S. Census, 1910, Thirteenth Census, Track 17, Seventh Ward, Chicago, Cook County, Ill., for family of Patrick Grimes, 5922 South Park Avenue, Dwelling No. 27, Family No. 113, enumerated April 18–19, 1910, accessed via Ancestry.com.

2. James T. Farrell to Ellen Skerrett, April 8, 1977. Skerett, a Chicago author and historian, gave the author a copy and permission to use this letter.

3. Farrell to Skerrett.

4. Binga Trial Transcript, Cantey testimony, 402.

5. Cook County real estate records.

6. "Mr. and Mrs. Binga Will Not Move."

7. ""Mr. and Mrs. Binga Will Not Move."

8. "Mrs. Binga Purchases New Electric."

9. Information about Binga's neighbors comes from U.S. Census, 1920, Fourteenth Census, Sixth Ward, Chicago, Cook County, Ill., Jesse Binga Family, 5922 South Park Ave., Dwelling No. 10, enumerated January 5, 1920, accessed via Ancestry.com.

10. Carolyn Louise Dent-Johnson, telephone interview by the author, December 14, 1998.

11. Bertha Simms Baker, telephone interview by the author, December 15, 1998. Baker was a friend of Carolyn Louise Dent-Johnson.

12. Baker interview; Dent-Johnson interview.

13. Dent-Johnson interview.

14. Bennett, "Plans, Work, Binga's Secret for Success."

15. H. Binga Dismond was Jesse Binga's first cousin twice removed.

16. A. Binga Sr., "Jesse Binga I Knew." Binga's father, William, was brother to Anthony Binga Jr.'s father, and Dismond was frequently referred to as a foster

or adopted son of Jesse. Anthony Binga Jr. was Dismond's guardian, according to this paper, p. 6.

17. George Vass, "Reaching the Pinnacle in Athletics," *Chicago Sun-Times*, February 19,1982, 11.

18. "Binga Dismond Wins Suburban Quarter," *New York Times*, February 23, 1916.

19. Major and Saunders, *Black Society*, 326.

20. Alan E. Oestreich, "H. Binga Dismond, MD—Pioneer Harlem Physician and Much More," *Journal of the National Medical Association* 93, no. 12 (December 2001): 497–501, at 499–500.

21. Oestreich, "Dismond—Pioneer Harlem Physician," 499–500.

22. Taylor interview, January 1, 1999.

23. Dorothy Binga Taylor, telephone interview by the author, February 3, 1999.

24. Sixth Census of Canada, 1921, Population B, Ward 4, Chatham, Ontario, Kent, District 93, Subdistrict 75, Family of Bethune Binga, in household of Renalie Scott, House No. 10, 113 King St., E, enumerated June 1, 1921, accessed via Ancestry.com; Taylor, interview, January 1, 1999.

25. Inez Johnson, telephone interview with the author, February 5, 1999.

26. Taylor, interview, February 3, 1999; "Pvt. Jesse C. Binga," Find a Grave, February 18, 2015, https://www.findagrave.com/memorial/142779566; Jesse C. Binga obituary, *Vancouver Sun*, April 25, 2012, http://vancouversunandprovince .remembering.ca/obituary/jesse-binga-2003-1065859003.

27. Taylor, interview, January 1, 1999.

28. CCRR, *Negro in Chicago*, 53.

Chapter 14

1. CCRR, *Negro in Chicago*, 289–90.

2. CCRR, *Negro in Chicago*, 286.

3. CCRR, *Negro in Chicago*, 289–90.

4. Adam Cohen and Elizabeth Taylor, *American Pharaoh, Mayor Richard J. Daley: His Battle for Chicago and the Nation* (Boston: Little, Brown, 2000), 28.

5. CCRR, *Negro in Chicago*, 288–89.

6. CCRR, *The Negro in Chicago*, 286.

7. CCRR, *The Negro in Chicago*, 293.

8. "Explosion of a Bomb Does Heavy Damage," *Chicago Defender*, July 7, 1917, 1.

9. Tuttle, *Race Riot*, 175.

10. Philpott, *Slum and Ghetto*, 147–48.

11. Travis, *Autobiography of Black Chicago*, 258.

12. Tuttle, *Race Riot*, 102.

13. Philpott, *Slum and Ghetto*, 161.

14. "Move Out Posters Flood Hyde Park," *Chicago Defender*, November 29, 1919, 1.

15. Quoted in CCRR, *Negro in Chicago*, 122.

16. CCRR, *Negro in Chicago*, 195.

17. Spear, *Black Chicago*, 206.

18. Tuttle, *Race Riot*, 5.

19. "Men of the Month: Young Dentist"; Stephens, *Alumni Record of Dentistry School*, 304.

20. Robert Mark Silverman, *Doing Business in Minority Markets, Black and Korean Entrepreneurs in Chicago's Ethnic Beauty Aids Industry* (New York: Garland, 2000), 46–50.

21. Certificate of Death, State of Illinois, State Board of Health, Bureau of Vital Statistics, November 17, 1917, copy obtained from State Board of Health. According to Cook County, Illinois, Marriages Index, accessed via Ancestry .com, Theodore R. Mozee married Cecelia Johnson on May 21, 1912.

22. Don Hayner and Tom McNamee, *Metro Chicago Almanac: Fascinating Facts and Offbeat Offerings about the Windy City* (Chicago: Chicago Sun-Times and Bonus Books, 1993), 75.

23. "Flats Blown Up."

24. "Flats Blown Up."

25. "Bomb Throwers Still Operate Unmolested," *Chicago Defender*, April 12, 1919.

26. Tuttle, *Race Riot*, 176.

27. Tuttle, *Race Riot*, 176.

28. "Two Bombs Smash Homes of Negroes," *Chicago Daily Tribune*, March 20, 1919, 1.

29. Tuttle, *Race Riot*, 176; CCRR, *Negro in Chicago*, 534.

30. "Two Bombs Smash Homes of Negroes."

31. CCRR, *Negro in Chicago*, 533.

Chapter 15

1. The anecdote in this opening section of the chapter is taken entirely from Carl Sandburg, *The Chicago Race Riots: July 1919* (New York: Harcourt Brace and Howe, 1919), 12–13.

2. The *Certain Sayings* quotations come from the previously cited 1927 *Chicago Tribune* story by Bennett, "Plans, Work, Binga's Secret for Success." The date of the pamphlet comes from John N. Ingham and Lynne B. Feldman, *African-American Business Leaders: A Biographical Dictionary* (Westport, CT: Greenwood Press, 1994), 77.

3. Bennett, "Plans, Work, Binga's Secret for Success."

4. Quoted in Bennett, "Plans, Work, Binga's Secret for Success."

5. "Mr. and Mrs. Jesse Binga Delightfully Entertained in Honor of Mr. and Mrs. James Cole of Detroit Michigan, *Broad Ax*, December 27,1919, 1; "Mr. and Mrs. Binga on Christmas Evenening Gave Their Eighth Annual Twilight Party at the St. Elizabeth New Assembly Hall, Forty-First Street and South Michigan Avenue, *Broad Ax*, January 1, 1927, 1; "The Twilight Party Given by Mr. and Mrs. Jesse Binga, At the Vincennes Hotel, Saturday Evening—Christmas—Was the Most Brilliant Social Function, So Far Held, By the Wealthy, Property Holding Colored People, Residing In Chicago," *Broad Ax*, January 1, 1921, 1; "Chicago Society En Masse at Binga Xmas Matinee," *Chicago Defender*, January 3, 1925.

6. "Mrs. Binga, Wife of Ex-Banker is Buried," *Chicago Defender*, April 1, 1933, 1.

7. "Police 'Pinch' Neighbors at 'Negro's House,'" *Chicago Daily Tribune*, May 3, 1915, 7.

8. Candace Staten, "Anthony Overton (1865–1946)," Blackpast, June 3, 2014, https://www.blackpast.org/african-american-history/overton-anthony-1865-1946/.

9. Dickerson quoted in Travis, *Autobiography of Black Chicago*, 209.

10. Dickerson quoted in Robert J. Blakely with Marcus Shepard, *Earl B. Dickerson: A Voice for Freedom and Equality* (Evanston, Ill.: Northwestern University Press, 2006), 169.

11. Travis interview, March 8, 1998.

12. Ottley, *Lonely Warrior*, 160. Copied from L. Harper, "Northern Drive to Start," *Chicago Defender*, February 10, 1917, in IWP papers, Harsh, box 33, folder 2.

13. "Negro Bank for Chicago," *New York Age*, September 24, 1908, 1.

14. CCRR, *Negro in Chicago*, 602.

15. CCRR, *Negro in Chicago*, 79.

16. Spear, *Black Chicago*, 159.

17. CCRR, *Negro in Chicago*, 602–3.

18. "Top of the world" quotation from CCRR, *Negro in Chicago*, 602–3.

19. "Bursting Shells Rain 'Round Lieut. Dismond," *Chicago Defender*, August 24, 1918.

20. Oestreich, "Dismond—Pioneer Harlem Physician," 498.

21. CCRR, *Negro in Chicago*, 301.

22. CCRR, *Negro in Chicago*, 177.

23. CCRR, *Negro in Chicago*, 231.

24. Tuttle, *Race Riot*, 208.

25. Philpott, *Slum and Ghetto*, 163.

26. Tuttle, *Race Riot*, 172.

27. "Ignore the Defender's Warning—Get Roiled Up," *Chicago Defender*, April 21, 1917.

28. "Ignore Defender's Warning."

29. *Tribune* quotation from Philpott, *Slum and Ghetto*, 159.

30. Philpott, *Slum and Ghetto*, 163.

31. CCRR, *Negro in Chicago*, 200–201.

32. Spear, *Black Chicago*, 25.

33. Spear, *Black Chicago*, 24.

34. Spear, *Black Chicago*, 26, 11–27; CCRR, *Negro in Chicago*, 184.

35. CCRR, *Negro in Chicago*, 200–201.

36. Binga quoted in Sandburg, *Chicago Race Riots*, 49.

37. CCRR, *Negro in Chicago*, 201.

38. Wood, "One Chicago Bank Is Entirely Colored."

39. Tuttle, *Race Riot*, 249.

40. "Binga State Bank Stockholders Meet," *Chicago Defender*, April 24, 1920.

41. Philpott, *Slum and Ghetto*, 165.

42. Black, interview, November 12, 1998, in which he described how his parents were met by family members at the Illinois Central's Twelfth Street rail station.

43. "The Line of Inequality among Negroes Is Almost Imperceptible," *Broad Ax*, December 25, 1909, 1.

44. CCRR, *Negro in Chicago*, 342.

45. CCRR, *Negro in Chicago*, 342.

Chapter 16

1. Tuttle, *Race Riot*, 37; CCRR, *Negro in Chicago*, 22, 655–67. The CCRR study gave incident summaries that provided the story lines of the victims recounted in this chapter.

2. CCRR, *Negro in Chicago*, 666.

3. Tuttle, *Race Riot*, 5. The primary narrative of the beginning of the riot comes from Tuttle, *Race Riot*, 1–10; and CCRR, *Negro in Chicago*, 4–7.

4. Mead, interview, February 1998.

5. Harris quoted in Tuttle, *Race Riot*, 6.

6. CCRR, *Negro in Chicago*, 4.

7. CCRR, *Negro in Chicago*, 1, 4.

8. Tuttle, *Race Riot*, 8; CCRR, *Negro in Chicago*, 5.

9. CCRR, *Negro in Chicago*, 5–6.

10. CCRR, *Negro in Chicago*, 27.

11. CCRR, *Negro in Chicago*, 26.

12. CCRR, *Negro in Chicago*, 29.

13. "Concerning all of these stories it may be stated that the coroner had no cases of deaths of women and children brought before him." CCRR, *Negro in Chicago*, 1; see also "Rumors," in CCRR, *Negro in Chicago*, 25–40. *Defender* quotations in CCRR, *Negro in Chicago*, 31.

14. "Black Soldiers in American Wars: Chicago's 'Fighting 8th' and the 370th Regiment," *Black History Heroes* (blog), accessed April 16, 2019, http://www .blackhistoryheroes.com/2010/02/black-soldiers-in-american-wars-eighth .html.

15. CCRR, *Negro in Chicago*, 663–64; Tuttle, *Race Riot*, 40.

16. CCRR, *Negro in Chicago*, 658.

17. Tuttle, *Race Riot*, 54.

18. CCRR, *The Negro in Chicago*, 667.

19. Tuttle, *Race Riot*, 57.

20. CCRR, *Negro in Chicago*, 1.

21. "For Action on Race Riot, Radical Propaganda among Negroes Growing and Increase of Mob Violence Set Out in Senate Brief for Federal Inquiry," *New York Times*, October 5, 1919, 10.

22. Tuttle, *Race Riot*, 14.

23. Tuttle, *Race Riot*, 22.

24. Tuttle, *Race Riot*, 254.

25. CCRR, *Negro in Chicago*, 1.

26. CCRR, *Negro in Chicago*, 665–67.

27. CCRR, *Negro in Chicago*, 134.

Chapter 17

1. "Bomb at Home of Colored Real Estate Dealer," 19.

2. Christopher Robert Reed, *The Rise of Chicago's Black Metropolis, 1920–1929* (Urbana: University of Illinois Press, 2011), 43.

3. "Mr. and Mrs. Binga Delightfully Entertained."

4. "The Bingas Entertain," *Chicago Defender*, January 3, 1920.

5. "Mr. and Mrs. Binga Delightfully Entertained."

6. "Chas. Jackson Made Vice President of Binga State Bank," *Chicago Defender*, January 31, 1920, All Around the Town section.

7. "U. G. Dailey, 75, Is Dead; Noted Negro Doctor," *Chicago Tribune*, April 23, 1961.

8. "Burdened Souls Seeking Freedom," IWP papers, Harsh, box 149, folder 4, p. 2.

9. Hammett Washington-Smith, *Dictionary of Literary Biography*, vol. 50, *Afro-American Writers Before the Harlem Renaissance; Fenton Johnson (1888–1958)* (Farmington Hills, Mich.: Gale, 1986), 202. Fenton eventually resigned in 1917 over a business dispute about how the magazine was being run, and it folded in 1918.

10. "Mr. and Mrs. Binga Delightfully Entertained."

11. "Mr. and Mrs. Binga Delightfully Entertained."

12. "Binga Bombed for Third Time," *Chicago Tribune*, December 28, 1919. A Linotype was a typesetting machine used in newspaper production and commercial printing.

13. CCRR, *Negro in Chicago*, 125.

14. Philpott, *Slum and Ghetto*, 151.

15. "Bomb Rips Front Porch."

16. "Bomb Rips Front Porch."

17. "Fourth Bomb for Negro's Home."

18. CCRR, *Negro in Chicago*, 125–26.

19. CCRR, *Negro in Chicago*, 126.

20. CCRR, *Negro in Chicago*, 126. He had offered that award before: "Jesse Binga, the Banker, Offers a Reward of One Thousand Dollars for the Arrest and Conviction of the Party or Parties Who Bombed His Home December 22, 1919," *Broad Ax*, January 21, 1920.

21. CCRR, *Negro in Chicago*, 131.

22. CCRR, *Negro in Chicago*, 131.

23. James T. Farrell, *The Young Manhood of Studs Lonigan* (1932; repr., Urbana: University of Illinois Press, 1993), 294.

24. CCRR, *Negro in Chicago*, 131.

25. CCRR, *Negro in Chicago*, 131.

26. CCRR, *Negro in Chicago*, 126.

27. CCRR, *Negro in Chicago*, 126; "Bomb No. 6 Only Annoys Binga; Hurts Neighbors," *Chicago Tribune*, November 24, 1920.

28. "Binga's Guard Tries Gun Play."

29. "Binga's Guard Tries Gun Play."

30. "Former Policeman M'Call Denies Story in Tribune," *Chicago Defender*, September 10, 1921, 3.

31. "Binga's Guard Tries Gun Play."

32. "Binga's Guard Tries Gun Play"; "M'Call Denies Story."

33. "Binga's Guard Tries Gun Play."

34. "Bomb Rips Front Porch."

Chapter 18

1. The anecdote of the stacked cash comes from "The Opening of Binga State Bank," *Broad Ax*, January 8, 1921, 1.

2. "First Day's Deposits Binga Bank, $200,000," *Chicago Defender*, January 8, 1921, 8.

3. "Opening of Binga State Bank."

4. "Opening of Binga State Bank."

5. "Opening of Binga State Bank."

6. *Defender* quoted in Bachin, *Building the South Side*, 254.

7. "The Outlook for the Binga State Bank," *Chicago Defender*, February 14, 1920.

8. Sandburg, *Chicago Race Riots*, 49.

9. Schedule B (1), Statement of All Property of Bankrupt, in In the Matter of Jesse Binga, Bankrupt, In Bankruptcy No. 45816, In the District Court of the United States for the Northern District of Illinois, National Archives Great Lakes Region, 7358 S. Pulaski, Chicago (hereafter cited as In the Matter of Jesse Binga, Bankrupt).

10. "Opening of Binga State Bank."

11. Chuck McCutcheon and David Mark, "Politics Ain't Beanbag," *Christian Science Monitor*, November 14, 2014, https://www.csmonitor.com/USA/Politics/Politics-Voices/2014/1114/Politics-ain-t-beanbag.

12. *Stenographic Verbatium Report*, April 1, 1936, p. 5.

13. Gosnell, *Negro Politicians*, 173–74.

14. "Banker Rebels at Political Bunko," *Chicago Daily News*, March 7, 1928.

15. "Banker Rebels at Political Bunko."

16. "President Jesse Binga Brings Cheer to Catholic Children," *Broad Ax*, December 25, 1926.

17. "Mrs. Binga Buried."

18. Carolyn Louise Dent Johnson, telephone interview by the author, December 14, 1998. She lived in the Bingas' house in the 1930s.

19. "Mrs. Binga Buried."

20. "Salvation Army Puts Doughnuts on Sale Today," *Chicago Daily Tribune*, October 24, 1927, 1.

21. "Mrs. Binga Buried."

22. The description of the party invitation comes from an actual invitation now in the archives of the Vivian Harsh Collection of the Chicago Public Library.

23. "Twilight Party Given."

24. Invitation, Harsh Collection.

25. "Mrs. Binga Buried."

26. Binga Trial Transcript, Binga testimony, 826.

27. "Crowds Watch the Opening," photo in *Chicago Defender*, November 9, 1929, A10.

28. Binga Trial Transcript, Binga testimony, 826.

29. Reed, *Rise of Chicago's Black Metropolis*, 43.

30. "Editor Abbott and Wife to Tour South America," *Chicago Defender*, January 13, 1923.

31. Ottley, *Lonely Warrior*, 228–29.

32. Binga quoted in Ottley, *Lonely Warrior*, 229.

33. Ottley, *Lonely Warrior*, 227.

34. Ottley, *Lonely Warrior*, 230.

Chapter 19

1. Bennett, "Binga's Secret for Success."

2. "Congratulations Usher Binga Bank in New Home," *Chicago Defender*, October 25, 1924, 2.

3. "Congratulations Usher Binga Bank."

4. "Congratulations Usher Binga Bank."

5. "Binga State Bank to Move into New Quarters Monday," *Chicago Defender*, October 18, 1924.

6. "Binga State Bank to Move."

7. "Binga State Bank to Move."

8. "Binga State Bank," *Messenger*, January 1925, 5.

9. Bennett, "Binga's Secret for Success."

10. "Binga State Bank."

11. "Binga State Bank to Move."

12. Richard Mickey to Edwin "Teddy" Harleston, May 14, 1924, box 2, folder 2, Harleston papers.

13. "Binga State Bank to Move."

14. William J. Collins and Robert A. Margo, "Race and Home Ownership from the End of the Civil War to the Present," AEA, January 2011, 18, https://www.bu.edu/econ/files/2012/11/dp213.pdf.

15. "Mr. Jesse Binga, the Successful Banker," *Broad Ax*, October 23, 1926.

16. Bennett, "Binga's Secret for Success," 1.

17. Edwin Harleston to Elise Harleston, July 13, 1924.

18. Edwin "Teddy" Harleston to Elise Harleston, July 20, 1924, box 2, folder 3, Harleston papers.

19. Ball, *Sweet Hell Inside*, 242.

20. Edwin Harleston to Elise Harleston, July 20, 1924. See also Ball, *Sweet Hell Inside*, 242.

21. Painting nos. 28 and 29 in *The Negro in Art*, November 16–23, 1927, part of larger exhibition *Modern Paintings and Sculpture*, November 16–December 1, Art Institute of Chicago, catalog for exhibition sponsored by the Chicago Woman's Club.

22. Grossman, Keating, and Reiff, *Encyclopedia of Chicago*, 703.

23. Grossman, Keating, and Reiff, *Encyclopedia of Chicago*, 703.

24. Shelley v. Kraemer, 334 U.S. 1 (1948); Grossman, Keating, and Reiff, *Encyclopedia of Chicago*, 703.

25. Blakely, *Earl B. Dickerson*, 170.

26. "Mr. Jesse Binga, President of the Binga State Bank, Becomes Head of the Mid-South Chamber of Commerce," *Broad Ax*, August 6, 1927.

27. "Jesse Binga Joins the Illinois Bankers Association," *Broad Ax* (Salt Lake City, Utah, edition), February 1, 1913, 1.

28. Frazier quoted in Patrick Renshaw, "The Black Ghetto 1890–1940," *Journal of American Studies* 8, no. 1 (April 1974): 41–59, at 51, http://www.jstor.org/stable/27553083.

29. Drake and Cayton, *Black Metropolis*, 431.

30. "Business Men Hear Binga," *Chicago Defender*, November 17, 1923, 13. See also Andrew J. Diamond, *Chicago on the Make: Power and Inequality in a Modern City* (Oakland: University of California Press, 2017), 67.

31. "Business Men Hear Binga," 13. See also Diamond, *Chicago on the Make*, 67–68.

32. "Business Men Hear Binga," 13.

33. "Jesse Binga Faces Court in Bank Case," *Chicago Defender*, September 16, 1933, 1.

34. Reed, *Rise of Chicago's Black Metropolis*, 110.

35. Reed, *Rise of Chicago's Black Metropolis*, 112.

36. Reed, *Rise of Chicago's Black Metropolis*, 112.

37. "Seeks to Create Stronger Ties in Financial World," *Chicago Defender*, June 24, 1922, 2.

38. Reed, *Rise of Chicago's Black Metropolis*, 71.

39. Reed, *Rise of Chicago's Black Metropolis*, 72.

40. Drake and Cayton, *Black Metropolis*, 438.

41. Drake and Cayton, *Black Metropolis*, 438. Italics in original.

42. "Seeks to Create Stronger Ties in Financial World," 2.

43. "Jesse Binga Visits East," *Chicago Defender*, March 12, 1921.

44. Untitled news brief, *Broad Ax*, May 31, 1913.

45. "Jesse Binga Summering," *Chicago Defender*, July 21, 1928.

46. "Mr. Jesse Binga of the Binga State Bank Has Returned Home After a Pleasant Tour through the East," *Broad Ax*, September 2, 1922; "Vacationing at Idlewild," *Chicago Defender*, August 27, 1927.

47. "Negro Catholics Going to Chicago," *Broad Ax*, June 19, 1926.

48. "Binga Plans to Open New National Bank," *Chicago Defender*, May 4, 1929, 12.

49. "Binga Plans to Open New National Bank."

50. "Binga Plans to Open New National Bank."

51. Drake and Cayton, *Black Metropolis*, 465.

52. Drake and Cayton, *Black Metropolis*, 465.

53. "$400,000 Arcade to be Erected on South Side," *Broad Ax*, August 13, 1927.

54. "Southside Arcade Building to Be Completed Next March," *Broad Ax*, July 23, 1927, 3.

55. "$400,000 Arcade.""

56. Reed, *Rise of Chicago's Black Metropolis*, 87.

57. Reed, *Rise of Chicago's Black Metropolis*, 117.

58. Description and quotations in this paragraph are from "Jesse Binga Adds New Land Mark to City's South Side," *Chicago Defender*, February 16, 1929.

59. Vernon Jarrett, "A Conversation in a Supermarket," *Chicago Tribune*, July 20, 1979, B4.

60. Binga Trial Transcript, Charles E. Worthington testimony, 171.

61. Lynn Sweet, "Rosenwald Apartments Reopen: Who Is Chicago's Julius Rosenwald?" *Chicago Sun-Times*, October 10, 2016, https://chicago.suntimes.com /news/rosenwald-apartments-reopen-who-is-chicagos-julius-rosenwald/; Karl Zinsmeister, "What Comes Next? How Private Givers Can Rescue America in an Era of Political Frustration," Philanthropy Roundtable, November 2016, https://www.philanthropyroundtable.org/docs/default-source/guidebook -files/whatcomesnext_kz_main_essay.pdf?sfvrsn=aafa740_0.

62. Julius Rosenwald to Jesse Binga, June 21, 1929, box 17, folder 6, J. Rosenwald Papers, University of Chicago Library (hereafter cited as Rosenwald Papers).

63. Hampton-Tuskegee Endowment Fund to Julius Rosenwald, May 27, 1925, box 17, folder 6, Rosenwald Papers.

Chapter 20

1. Harris, *Negro as Capitalist*, 161.

2. *Catalogue of the Offices and Students of Atlanta University* (Atlanta: Atlanta University Press, 1910), 45; Illinois Supreme Court Abstract of People of the State of Illinois vs. Jesse Binga, October Term, 1934, 360 Ill. 18 (Ill. 1935), 195 N.E.437, https://casetext.com/case/the-people-v-binga (hereafter cited as Court Abstract), testimony of Inez Cantey, 98.

3. Information in this paragraph from W. E. Burghardt Du Bois, *Dusk of Dawn: An Essay toward an Autobiography of a Race Concept* (New York: Harcourt Brace, 1940); Anita King, comp. and ed., *Quotations in Black* (Westport, Conn.: Greenwood Press, 1981), 106; Alma Thomas, *Alma W. Thomas: A Retrospective of the Paintings* (Rohnert Park, Calif.: Pomegranate Communications, 1998), 15n1; Court Abstract, Cantey testimony, 98.

4. Court Abstract, Cantey testimony, 98.

5. Inez Cantey to Edwin Harleston, August 17, 1908, box 1, folder 3, Edwin A. Harleston and Edwina Harleston Whitlock family papers, Stuart A. Rose Manuscript, Archives and Rare Book Library, Emory University (hereafter cited as Harleston papers).

6. Court Abstract, Cantey testimony, 70.

7. Edwin Harleston to Elise Harleston, July 7, 1924, box 2, folder 3, Harleston papers.

8. See, for example, "Mrs. Binga Buried"; Mead, interview, June 4, 1998; Bennett, "Binga's Secret for Success," 1; Court Abstract, C. N. Langston testimony, 531.

9. Court Abstract, Cantey testimony, 71.

10. Court Abstract, Cantey testimony, 71.

11. Inez Cantey to Edwin "Teddy" Harleston, December 7, 1929, box 2, folder 12; Inez Cantey to Edwin Harleston, November 6, 1929, box 2, folder 12; Inez Cantey to Edwin Harleston, April 20, 1920, box 1, folder 11, all in Harleston papers.

12. Jesse Binga to W. E. B. Du Bois, December 15, 1927, W. E. B. Du Bois Papers (MS312), Special Collections and University Archives, University of Massachusetts Amherst Libraries (hereafter cited as Du Bois Papers).

13. Inez Cantey to Edwin Harleston, October 15, 1911, box 1, folder 3, Harleston papers.

14. U.S. Census, 1920, Fourteenth Census, Sixth Ward, Chicago, Cook County, Ill., Sheet No. 2A, William S. Cantey Family, 5830 Wabash Ave., Dwelling No. 15, enumerated January 7 and 16, 1920, accessed via Ancestry.com. The 1920 census shows Bessie and Marveline as rent collectors. Inez, Bessie, and Marveline are listed as employees of the bank in "Opening of Binga State Bank."

15. Fisk v. Smith, 192 Ill. App. 186 (1915).

16. Dorothy O'Keefe, telephone interview by the author, Jan.uary 25, 2000. O'Keefe was once married to Bessie's son James. C. Johnson, interview. Carolyn Johnson's mother was John Cotillier's daughter.

17. Binga to Du Bois, December 15, 1927.

18. Jesse Binga to W. E. B. Du Bois, February 11, 1927; Binga State Bank to W. E. B. Du Bois, March 5, 1927, both in Du Bois Papers.

19. "Prof. W. E. B. Du Bois, Editor of *The Crisis*," *Broad Ax*, March 5, 1927.

20. Binga to Du Bois, February 11, 1927; Binga State Bank to Du Bois.

21. "Burdened Souls Seeking Freedom," *Champion Magazine*, November 1916, IWP papers, Harsh, box 149, folder 4, p. 2, also available via Internet Archive, https://archive.org/stream/championmagazineoounse/championmagazineoounse_djvu.txt.

22. Taylor, interview, January 1, 1999.

23. Binga Trial Transcript, 449.

24. 1920 U.S. Census, William S. Cantey Family.

25. O'Keefe, interview. O'Keefe was once married to Inez Cantey's nephew James C. Cotillier.

26. O'Keefe, interview; Taylor, interview, January 1, 1999.

27. Taylor, interview, January 1, 1999.

28. Edward Ball, *The Sweet Hell Inside: The Rise of an Elite Black Family in the Segregated South* (New York: William Morrow, 2001), 241.

29. "Harleston, Edwin (1882–1931)," Johnson Collection (website), accessed March 25, 2019, http://thejohnsoncollection.org/edwin-harleston/.

30. Cantey to Harleston, August 17, 1908.

31. Inez Cantey to Edwin Harleston, February 2, 1910, box 1, folder 3, Harleston papers.

32. Cantey to Harleston, February 2, 1910.

33. Inez Cantey to Edwin Harleston, December 15, 1920, box 1, folder 11, Harleston papers.

34. Norbert L. Schuler, "Around the Negro World," *Christian Family and Our Missions* 35 (October 1940): 397; "Father Eckert Made Provincial in the South," Catholic *New World*, July 12, 1940.

35. John F. Moore, *Will America Become Catholic?* (New York: Harper and Brothers, 1931), 196–97.

36. John Evans, "Negro Catholic Converts Build Up Old Parish," *Chicago Tribune*, May 5, 1929.

37. Joseph F. Eckert, *Autobiography of Father Joseph Eckert S.V.D.* (East Troy, Wis.: Operation Recovery, Chicago Province USA, 2000), 27.

38. Joseph F. Eckert, "The Negro in Chicago," *Our Colored Missions*, January 1937, 2.

39. Harold M. Kingsley, "The Negro Goes to Church," *Opportunity: Journal of Negro Life*, March 1929, 91.

40. "Rev. J. F. Eckert in New Pastorate at St. Anselm Church," *New World*, June 17, 1932.

41. "Kulturkampf," in *Encyclopaedia Britanica*, accessed April 30, 2019, https://www.britannica.com/event/Kulturkampf.

42. "Rev. J. F. Eckert in New Pastorate."

43. Joseph Eckert, "Mission Work among the Negroes of Chicago," *Our Missions*, no. 8 (August 1925): 152.

44. Eckert, "Negro in Chicago."

45. Eckert, "Mission Work among the Negroes, 151.

46. Eckert, *Autobiography*, 36.

47. Eckert, *Autobiography*, 25.

48. Ann Roseman, telephone interview by the author, February 1998. Roseman was baptized by Father Eckert in 1928 and later followed him to St. Anselm Catholic Church.

49. Farrell, *Young Manhood of Studs Lonigan*, 294.

Chapter 21

1. "South Park National Bank Will Soon Open," *Chicago Defender*, January 18, 1930.

2. Gosnell, *Negro Politicians*, 132.

3. Gosnell, *Negro Politicians*, 133.

4. *Stenographic Verbatim Report*, April 1, 1936, p. 7.

5. "South Park National Bank Will Soon Open."

6. "South Park National Bank Will Soon Open."

7. "South Park National Bank Will Soon Open."

8. *Stenographic Verbatim Report*, Parole Board, Illinois State Penitentiary, Docket No. 109,, Prison No. 1306-F, Jesse Binga, December 3, 1937, p. 2 in Jesse Binga prison file, Illinois State Archives, Springfield, Ill.

9. "Bush Sues Jesse Binga for $55,000," *Afro-American*, October 26, 1929, 1.

10. Harris, *Negro as Capitalist*, 161.

11. Cantey to Harleston, November 6, 1929.

12. Kenney, *Chicago Jazz*, 30.

13. Robert Kuttner, "Worse Than 1929?" *The American Prospect*, https://prospect.org/article/worse-1929, accessed Aug. 1, 2019.

14. William A. Sundstrum, "Last Hired, First Fired? Unemployment and Urban Black Workers during the Great Depression," *Journal of Economic History* 52, no. 2 (June 1992): 417, http://www.jstor.org/stable/2123118?read-now=1&loggedin=true&seq=3#page_scan_tab_contents.

15. Harris, *Negro as Capitalist*, 157.

16. Harris, *Negro as Capitalist*, 159; Filing to the Secretary of State, State of Illinois, for the formation of Binga Safe Deposit Company, November 30, 1923, Illinois State Archives, Springfield, Ill.

17. Harris, *Negro as Capitalist*,163.

18. Harris, *Negro as Capitalist*, 160.
19. Harris, *Negro as Capitalist*, 158.
20. Harris, *Negro as Capitalist*, 162.
21. Jack Conroy, "Business," in *The Negro in Illinois: The WPA Papers*, ed. Brian Dolinar (Urbana: University of Illinois Press, 2013), 101.
22. "Donations to the Charity Benefit Ball," *Broad Ax*, January 22, 1910.
23. Harris, *Negro as Capitalist*, 161.
24. Forrest McDonald, *Insull* (Chicago: University of Chicago Press, 1962), 52.
25. Harris, *Negro as Capitalist*, 160.
26. Conroy, "Business."
27. Conroy, "Business."
28. Quoting from "The Great American Bank Bubble" by John A. Carroll in "The Bank Bubble," *Chicago Defender*, April 13, 1935.

Chapter 22
1. "Flames Damage St. Elizabeth's; Priests Heroes," *Chicago Tribune*, January 4, 1930, 5; Eckert, *Autobiography*, 30.
2. "Flames Damage St. Elizabeth's."
3. Eckert, *Autobiography*, 30; "Flames Damage St. Elizabeth's." Father Eckert's recollection is that firefighters carried out the younger priest; the *Tribune* article said he came out on his own and collapsed in the street.
4. "Flames Damage St. Elizabeth's; Priests Heroes."
5. Eckert, *Autobiography*, 30.
6. Eckert, *Autobiography*, 34.
7. Eckert, *Autobiography*, 29.
8. "Big Business Swells Hospital Fund," *Chicago Defender*, January 18, 1930.
9. Bennett, "Offer $414,500."
10. Bennett, "Offer $414,500."
11. Bennett, "Offer $414,500."
12. A. Binga Sr., "The Jesse Binga I Knew," 6.
13. Jesse Binga to Anthony Binga, January 30, 1930, copy in author's possession.
14. A. Binga Sr., "Jesse Binga I Knew," 6.
15. J. Binga to A. Binga.
16. Harris, *Negro as Capitalist*, 169.
17. Harris, *Negro as Capitalist*, 169.
18. Harris, *Negro as Capitalist*, 162–63.
19. Harris, *Negro as Capitalist*, 161.
20. Harris, *Negro as Capitalist*, 162; court filing, In The Matter of Jesse Binga, Bankrupt.
21. "Binga State Bank Closed Temporarily," *Chicago Defender*, August 2, 1930, 1.
22. "Segregated District Real Estate Classed as Frozen Assets," *Chicago Defender*, August 23, 1930, 1; Drake and Cayton, *Black Metropolis*, 84.
23. "Tells Inside Story of Binga Bank Crash: How Binga Bank Was Forced to Close by Men High in Banking World," *Chicago Defender*, April 6, 1935, 1.
24. "Jesse Binga Arrested," *Chicago Defender*, March 7, 1931, 6.
25. Harris, *Negro as Capitalist*, 163.

26. Editorial, *Opportunity, Journal of Negro Life*, 8, no. 9 (September 1930): 264. See also Renshaw, "Black Ghetto," 47.

27. Harris, *Negro as Capitalist*, 161.

28. *Stenographic Verbatim Report*, April 1, 1936, p. 4.

29. "Chicago's Elk Seek Arrest of Banker Binga," *Afro-American*, October 18, 1930, 4.

30. "Chicago's Elk Seek Arrest of Banker Binga.

31. The exchange between Binga and Judge Horner is based on Binga's later recollection, in *Stenographic Verbatim Report*, April 1, 1936, p. 11.

32. "Orders Mrs. Binga to Protect Banker," *Chicago Daily News*, October 9, 1930.

33. Horner quoted in John F. Cashen Jr. to Chairman of the Board of Pardons and Paroles, July 8, 1935, 1, in Jesse Binga prison file, Illinois State Archives, Springfield, Ill. Cashen was Binga's lawyer.

34. "Chicago's Elk Seek Arrest of Banker Binga."

35. W. E. B. Du Bois to Mildred Bryant Jones, August 5, 1930, Du Bois Papers.

36. "Jesse Binga, Negro Banker, Named in Bankruptcy Plea," *Chicago Tribune*, December 4, 1930, 22.

37. In The Matter of Jesse Binga, Bankrupt.

38. Inventory pp. 1–4, in In the Matter of Jesse Binga, Bankrupt.

39. Schedule A (1), in In the Matter of Jesse Binga, Bankrupt.

40. Schedule A (3), in In the Matter of Jesse Binga, Bankrupt.

41. Schedule B (5), in In the Matter of Jesse Binga, Bankrupt.

42. In the Matter of Jesse Binga, Bankrupt.

43. Schedule B (4), in In the Matter of Jesse Binga, Bankrupt, says "5924–26 South Park, valued at $35,000—of the section of recordholders who have no interest in the property mentioned but through the Bankrupt they held the properties for the Binga State Bank."

44. Petition of June 26, 1934, in In the Matter of Jesse Binga, A Bankrupt, pp. 1–2.

45. Clifford C. Mitchell, "Facts about the Binga Case," *Chicago Defender*, November 25, 1933, 1; Schedule B (1), in In The Matter of Jesse Binga, Bankrupt.

46. *Stenographic Verbatim Report*, April 1, 1936, p. 9.

47. Trustee's Final Account and Report, in In the Matter of Jesse Binga, Bankrupt, p. 2.

48. Petition, dated July 30, 1931, in In the Matter of Jesse Binga, Bankrupt, p. 1.

49. Petition, p. 3.

50. *Stenographic Verbatim Report*, April 1, 1936, p. 6.

51. *Stenographic Verbatim Report*, April 1, 1936, p. 6.

52. *Stenographic Verbatim Report*, April 1, 1936, p. 6.

53. Trustee's Final Account and Report, p.3.

Chapter 23

1. "Jesse Binga Arrested," 1.

2. "Jesse Binga Arrested," 1.

3. "Jesse Binga Arrested," 1.

4. "Jesse Binga Arrested," 1.

5. "Jesse Binga Arrested," 1.

6. "Binga Indicted; Charge $250,000 Taken at Bank," *Chicago Tribune*, May 6, 1931, 3.

7. "8 Closed Banks Ready to Pay Out $2,000,000," *Chicago Tribune*, October 23, 1931, 13.

8. "Average Deposit in Closed Banks Found to Be $118," *Chicago Tribune*, October 11, 1931, 3.

9. "Jesse Binga Arrested," 6.

10. "Jesse Binga Arrested," 6.

11. "Banker Binga Is Denied Re-Trial; Faces Prison Term," *Afro-American*, March 2, 1935, 2.

12. "Banker Binga Denied Re-Trial." For the Binga charge and DePriest counter, see Mitchell, "Facts about the Binga Case"; In The Matter of Jesse Binga, Bankrupt.

13. State of Illinois v. Jesse Binga, Indictment No. 60340, Criminal Court of Cook County, Recognizance, Real Estate Schedule signed and dated April 16, 1931.

14. "Binga Still in Jail on Soup Diet," *Chicago Defender*, March 14, 1931.

15. Recognizance bond dated April 16, 1931, for Jesse Binga in *State of Illinois v. Jesse Binga*; Pardon Application, unnumbered p. 1.

16. Pardon Application. The document was signed by Jesse Binga and his lawyer John F. Cashen. This filing also says the McNallys signed bonds in the sum of $15,000.

17. The dissolution of Binga's property wasn't completed until about ten years after he was adjudicated bankrupt.

18. U.S. Census, 1920, Jesse Binga Family, 5922 South Park Ave.

19. U.S. Census, 1930,Fifteenth Census, Fifth Ward, Block No. 67, Chicago, Cook County, Ill., Sheet No. 21 A, p. 122, Jesse Binga Family, 5922 South Parkway [note street name change], Dwelling No. 101, Family No. 359, undated, accessed via Ancestry.com.

20. Drake and Cayton, *Black Metropolis*, 403.

21. Ottley, *Lonely Warrior*, 299.

22. Preston, *Scholar and Scalpel*, 53–55; "U.G. Dailey Is Dead."

23. Eckert, *Autobiography*, 31.

24. Eckert, *Autobiography*, 34.

25. Eckert, *Autobiography*, 35.

26. Eckert, *Autobiography*, 35.

27. Eckert, *Autobiography*, 36.

28. Quotation in Jason Meisner, "26th and Cal. Courthouse Rich with History and Charm," *Chicago Tribune*, June 11, 2012.

29. "Darrow to Defend Binga Secretary," *Afro-American*, September 19, 1931, 13.

30. Inez Cantey to Elise Forrest Harleston, June 5, 1931, Harleston papers.

31. Cashen to Chairman of the Board of Pardons and Paroles.

32. "Banker Binga Sentenced to 1 to 10 Years," *Chicago Tribune*, November 4, 1933, 3.

33. Cashen to Chairman of Board of Pardons and Paroles.

34. "Banker Binga Sentenced."

35. "Mistrial in Case of Binga," *Chicago Daily News*, July 20, 1932.

Chapter 24

1. People of the State of Illinois vs. Jesse Binga, General No. 60477, verdict sheet listing all jurors and addresses, Archives of the Clerk of the Circuit Court of Cook County, in the Daley Center, Chicago. Juror descriptons came from that trial record, and background of the following jurors came from U. S. Census, 1930:

> Clarence Pitcher, jury foreman: Eighty-first Precinct, Thirtieth Ward, Block 399, Chicago, Cook County, Ill., Sheet No. 16B, 5512 Gladys, Family No. 308, enumerated April 15, 1930.
>
> Stanley Nosalik: Twenty-sixth Precinct, Thirty-eighth Ward, Block No. 386, Chicago, Cook County, Ill., Sheet No. 5 B, 2307 N. Hoyne [corrected from court file address of 7307], Family No. 94, enumerated April 6, 1930.
>
> Martin A. Pischke (spelled as signed by juror on verdict): Twelfth Precinct, Thirty-sixth Ward, Block No. 88, Chicago, Ill., Sheet 1 A, p. 170, 2153 N. Keeler, Dwelling No. 2, Family No. 2, enumerated April 2, 1930.
>
> Charles Devereux: Thirty-ninth Precinct, Thirty-eighth Ward, Block No. 466, Chicago, Cook County, Ill., Sheet 16 A, p. 54, 2916 Shakespeare, Dwelling No. 132, Family No. 340, enumerated April 12, 1930.
>
> Thomas D. Bartlett: Forty-first Ward, Block No. 111, Chicago, Cook County, Ill., Sheet No. 3 A, 5729 Cicero, Dwelling No. 6, Family No. 6, enumerated April 12, 1930.

Background for the following jurors came from U.S. Census, 1940, Sixteenth Census, Population Schedule:

> James Lynn: Forty-sixthWard, Block No. 8, Chicago, Cook County, Ill., Sheet No. 20 B, 1210 Addison St., No. of Household in Order of Visitation 477, enumerated April 8, 1940.
>
> Herbert F. Ninow: Thirty-third Ward, Block No. 5-6-7, Chicago, Cook County, Ill., Sheet No. 2 B, 3117 N. Washtenaw, No of Household in Order of Visitation 41, enumerated April 8, 1940.

All census data were accessed via Ancestry.com. See also "State Urges Life Term for Banker," *Pittsburgh Courier*, June 3, 1933, 7.

2. "Former Bank Wizard in Court on Charge of Embezzlement," *Chicago Defender*, May 27, 1933, 1.

3. "Mrs. Binga Buried."

4. "Mrs. Binga Buried."

5. "Mrs. Binga Buried."

6. "Mrs. Binga Buried."

7. "Sentence 'Jack' White to Life in Prison," *Chicago American*, January 21, 1927, My Al Capone Museum (website), posted August 2006, http://www.myalcaponemuseum.com/id123.htm.

8. "Class of 1907," Scholarly Commons, Chicago-Kent College of Law, Illinois Institute of Technology, accessed April 18, 2019, https://scholarship.kentlaw.iit

.edu/composites/11/; "Class of 1936," Scholarly Commons, Chicago-Kent College of Law, Illinois Institute of Technology, accessed April 18, 2019, https://scholarship.kentlaw.iit.edu/composites/38/.

9. "John Cashen Jr. Rites Planned for Tuesday," *Chicago Daily News*, October 4, 1965.

10. "Lenny Bruce's 4-Letter Words Defended as Social Criticism," *Chicago Sun-Times*, January 30, 1963, 16.

11. June Sawyers, "Folk Was King at Chicago's Gate of Horn," *Chicago Tribune*, March 15, 1987.

12. Binga Trial Transcript, Inez Cantey testimony, 457.

13. Binga Trial Transcript, Cantey testimony, 412.

14. Binga Trial Transcript, Worthington testimony, 160.

15. Binga Trial Transcript, Worthington testimony, 161.

16. Binga Trial Transcript, Worthington testimony, 161.

17. Binga Trial Transcript, Worthington testimony, 164.

18. Binga Trial Transcript, Worthington testimony, 171.

19. The People v. Binga 360 Ill. 18 (Ill. 1935); The People v. Binga, 195 N.E. 437 (Ill. 1935) at 438.

20. *Binga*, 360 Ill. 18; *Binga*, 195 N.E. 438.

21. Binga Trial Transcript, Worthington testimony, 180.

22. Binga Trial Transcript, Fountain Thurman testimony, 148.

23. Binga Trial Transcript, Thurman testimony, 139.

24. Binga Trial Transcript, Thurman testimony, 135.

25. Binga Trial Transcript, Thurman testimony, 140.

26. Binga Trial Transcript, Thurman testimony, 145.

27. Binga Trial Transcript, Thurman testimony, 147.

28. Court Abstract, testimony of John Holloman, 22–23.

29. *Binga*, 195 N.E. 439; Court Abstract, Cantey testimony, 72–73.

30. *Binga*, 195 N.E. 438.

31. Court Abstract, testimony of John Minor, 62.

32. Court Abstract, Minor testimony, 63–64; *Binga*, 360 Ill. 18; *Binga*, 195 N.E. 437.

33. Court Abstract, Henry Shackelford testimony, 48–50.

34. Court Abstract, Henry Shackelford testimony, 50.

35. *Binga*, 195 N.E. 439.

36. Court Abstract, Henry Shackelford testimony, 52.

37. *Binga*, 360 Ill. 18; *Binga*, 195 N.E. 437.

38. Binga Trial Transcript, Henry Shackelford testimony, 199.

39. "Binga Awaits Fate as His Lawyer Ends Plea," *Chicago Defender*, June 3, 1933, 1.

40. Binga Trial Transcript, Cantey testimony, 289.

41. Binga Trial Transcript, Cantey testimony, 302.

42. Binga Trial Transcript, Cantey testimony, 307.

43. *Binga*, 195 N.E. 439.

44. Binga Trial Transcript, Cantey testimony, 309.

45. "Binga Pleads for New Trial," *Chicago Defender*, June 10, 1933, 1.

46. "Binga Pleads for New Trial."

47. "Binga Awaits Fate," 4.

48. Binga Trial Transcript, Cantey testimony, 416.

49. Binga Trial Transcript, Cantey testimony, 405.

50. Binga Trial Transcript, Cantey testimony, 369.

51. Binga Trial Transcript, Cantey testimony, 370.

52. Binga Trial Transcript, Cantey testimony, 412.

53. Binga Trial Transcript, Cantey testimony, 458, 414.

54. "Marshall V. Kearney, 94; Practiced Law for 73 Years," *Chicago Sun-Times*, June 27, 1989.

55. Binga Trial Transcript, Cantey testimony, 438.

56. Binga Trial Transcript, Cantey testimony, 415.

Chapter 25

1. The preceding exchange between Cashen and Eckert is from Binga Trial Transcript, testimony of Joseph F. Eckert, 805–6.

2. Binga Trial Transcript, testimony of other character witnesses, 805–20.

3. Binga Trial Transcript, testimony of other character witnesses, 805–20.

4. Binga Trial Transcript, testimony of other character witnesses, 805–20.

5. "Highlights of Binga Trial" (drawing of Binga during trial), *Chicago Defender*, June 3, 1933, 12; "Binga Guilty; Asks New Trial," *Chicago Defender*, June 10, 1933; "Binga Is Frantic on Stand," *Chicago Defender*, June 3, 1933, 1; Cashen to Chairman of the Board of Pardons and Paroles, 2.

6. Binga Trial Transcript, Binga testimony, 821.

7. Binga Trial Transcript, Binga testimony, 827–28.

8. Binga Trial Transcript, Binga testimony, 828.

9. Binga Trial Transcript, Binga testimony, 829.

10. Binga Trial Transcript, Binga testimony, 845.

11. Binga Trial Transcript, Binga testimony, 835–37.

12. Binga Trial Transcript, Binga testimony, 842.

13. Binga Trial Transcript, Binga testimony, 830–33.

14. Binga Trial Transcript, Binga testimony, 831–33.

15. Binga Trial Transcript, Binga testimony, 834.

16. Binga Trial Transcript, Binga testimony, 834.

17. Binga Trial Transcript, Binga testimony, 847.

18. The preceding exchange between Thompson and Binga is from Binga Trial Transcript, Binga testimony, 849–51.

19. "Binga Frantic on Stand."

20. "Binga Frantic on Stand."

21. Binga Trial Transcript, Binga testimony, 851; "Binga Pleads for New Trial."

22. "Binga Frantic on Stand."

23. Binga Trial Transcript, Binga testimony, 851.

24. Binga Trial Transcript, Binga testimony, 853.

25. Binga Trial Transcript, Binga testimony, 857.

26. Binga Trial Transcript, Binga testimony, 863.

27. Binga Trial Transcript, Binga testimony, 864.

28. Binga Trial Transcript, Binga testimony, 871.

29. "Binga Is Found Guilty by Jury in Theft Trial," *Chicago Daily News*, June 3, 1933, 3.

Chapter 26

1. "Binga Found Guilty of Fraud; Face Prison," *Chicago Tribune*, June 3, 1933, 6. "Binga Found Guilty by Jury."

2. Jury Verdict filed June 2, 1933, the Criminal Court of Cook County, The People of the State of Illinois vs. Jesse Binga, Indictment no. 60340; 1930 U.S. Census data for jury foreman Clarence H. Pitcher.

3. Young, "Binga Put Personal Pride before Depositors' Savings."

4. "Binga Found Guity of Fraud"; "Binga Found Guilty by Jury"; "Chicago Banker Faces One to Ten Year Sentence," *Pittsburgh Courier*, June 10, 1933, 1.

5. "Binga Convicted June 2, But Case Still Pending," *Chicago Tribune*, October 25, 1933, 6.

6. "Banker Binga Sentenced."

7. Chicago Crime Commission to Illinois Parole Board, July 3, 1935, p. 2, in Jesse Binga prison file, Illinois State Archives, Springfield. The letter says one indictment of Scott and Curtis was nolle prossed on May 8, 1931, and the other indictments against Scott, Curtis, Cantey, and Webb were stricken with leave to reinstate on November 3, 1933.

8. "Binga Gets New Hearing," *Chicago Defender*, August 25, 1934, 1.

9. "Binga Gets New Hearing."

10. "Chicago Banker Faces One to Ten Year Sentence," 1, 4.

11. Richard Stamz, telephone interview by the author, ca. 2001. Stamz was ninety-five years old at the time.

12. Stamz, interview.

13. Renshaw, "Black Ghetto," 47.

14. Travis, interviews, March 8, 1998, and April 1998.

15. Travis, interviews, March 8, 1998, and April 1998.

16. William Occomy, "Business and Commerce," *Pittsburgh Courier*, June 24, 1933, 13.

17. John A. Carroll, "The Great American Bank Bubble," *Real America*, April 1935, 20; "Tells Inside Story of Binga Bank Crash," 1, 2.

18. Carroll, "Great American Bank Bubble,"20.

19. Carroll, "Great American Bank Bubble," 20.

20. Renshaw, "Black Ghetto," 51.

21. Carroll, "Great American Bank Bubble,"20.

22. James D. Powell, telephone interview by the author, July 3, 1998.

23. Powell, interview.

24. "Binga Gets New Hearing."

25. Powell, interview.

26. *Binga*, 195 N.E. 437.

27. *Binga*, 195 N.E. 440.

28. Mark Guglielmo, "Illinois Bank Failures during the Great Depression" (working paper, Center for Population Economics, University of Chicago, n.d.), 1.

29. Guglielmo, "Illinois Bank Failures," 1, 35.

30. Robert Lynn Fuller, *"Phantom of Fear": The Banking Panic of 1933* (Jefferson, N.C.: McFarland, 2012), 63.

31. Fuller, *"Phantom of Fear,"* 63.

32. Mitchell, "Facts about the Binga Case."

33. State of Illinois v. Jesse Binga; Pardon Application.

34. Mitchell, "Facts about the Binga Case."

35. Mitchell, "Facts about the Binga Case." Dawson was also Second Ward alderman and a rising political power.

36. Mitchell, "Facts about the Binga Case."

37. Mitchell, "Facts about the Binga Case."

Chapter 27

1. Cashen to Chairman of Board of Pardons and Paroles.

2. Gladys A. Erickson, *Warden Ragen of Joliet, Famous Warden of One of the World's Toughest Prisons* (New York: E. P. Dutton, 1957), 21–22.

3. Erickson, *Warden Ragen,* 41.

4. Erickson, *Warden Ragen,* 22.

5. Joseph E. Ragen and Charles Finston, *Inside the World's Toughest Prison* (Springfield, Ill.: Charles C. Thomas, 1962), 315.

6. Ragen and Finston, *Inside the World's Toughest Prison,* 315.

7. Diagnostic Depot file jacket, Binga prison file, Illinois State Archives, Springfield, Ill.; Ragen and Finston, *Inside the World's Toughest Prison,* 315.

8. Quotations from Case Report of Mental Health Officer, Illinois State Penitentiary, July 6, 1935, signed by Dr. Edward H. Schaller, Binga prison file, Illinois State Archives, Springfield, Ill.

9. Mug shot information card dated Aug. 16, 1935, Diagnostic Depot information sheet (untitled) for Jesse Binga, 1935, both in Binga prison file, Illinois State Archives, Springfield, Ill.

10. Ragen and Finston, *Inside the World's Toughest Prison,* 715.

11. Ragen and Finston, *Inside the World's Toughest Prison,* 347.

12. Ragen and Finston, *Inside the World's Toughest Prison,* 12–13.

13. Case Report of Mental Health Officer, July 6, 1935, 1.

14. Case Report of Mental Health Officer, July 6, 1935, 1.

15. Case Report of Mental Health Officer, March 7, 1936; *Stenographic Verbatim Report,* April 1, 1936, 14; *Stenographic Verbatim Report,* December 3, 1937, 5 (although his Wassermann test here is reported taken on April 20, 1935, and May 17, 1936, and both times as "four plus").

16. Ragen and Finston, *Inside the World's Toughest Prison,* 184–85.

17. Ragen and Finston, *Inside the World's Toughest Prison,* 184–85, 538.

18. *Stenographic Verbatim Report,* April 1, 1936, 15.

19. *Stenographic Verbatim Report,* December 3, 1937, 5.

20. *Stenographic Verbatim Report,* April 1, 1936, 5.

21. P. L. Prattis, "Jesse Binga, In Prison Escapes Jim Crow," *Pittsburgh Courier,* September 14, 1935, 5.

22. Prattis, "Binga Escapes Jim Crow."

23. Prattis, "Binga Escapes Jim Crow."

24. *Stenographic Verbatim Report,* December 3, 1937, 2, 5.

25. St. Anselm Catholic Church "Annals" of the Sisters of the Blessed Sacrament, recounting Binga's conviction in 1933 and then his prison years, in Sisters of the Blessed Sacrament Archives.

26. Prattis, "Binga Escapes Jim Crow," 5.

27. Erickson, *Warden Ragen of Joliet*, 25.

28. Erickson, *Warden Ragen of Joliet*, 43, 47.

29. Erickson, *Warden Ragen of Joliet*, 44.

30. Erickson, *Warden Ragen of Joliet*, 41, 44.

31. Erickson, *Warden Ragen of Joliet*, 42, 60.

32. Erickson, *Warden Ragen of Joliet*, 70.

33. Erickson, *Warden Ragen of Joliet*, 70.

34. Department of Corrections File jacket notation for Jesse Binga, in Jesse Binga prison file, Illinois State Archives, Springfield, Ill.

35. Erickson, *Warden Ragen of Joliet*, 130.

36. Ragen and Finston, *Inside the World's Toughest Prison*, 67.

37. Ragen and Finston, *Inside the World's Toughest Prison*, 66, 67.

38. Ragen and Finston, *Inside the World's Toughest Prison*, 63, 64.

39. Ragen and Finston, *Inside the World's Toughest Prison*, 71, 72, 85.

40. Cashen to Chairman of Board of Pardons and Paroles.

41. Cashen to Chairman of Board of Pardons and Paroles.

42. State of Illinois Parole Board Hearing April 1, 1936, 15.

43. Western Union telegram attched to July 9, 1935, letter to Illinois Parole Board.

44. State of Illinois Parole Board Hearing, Docket No. 7716, July 9, 1935, 4, in Jesse Binga prison file, Illinois State Archives, Springfield, Ill.

45. Parole Board Hearing, July 9, 1935, 4.

46. Chief clerk to James A. Fardy, October 26, 1935, in Jesse Binga prison file, Illinois State Archives, Springfield, Ill.

47. Darrow's eloquence helped save Leopold from execution after he and Richard Loeb were convicted in the "thrill" murder of fourteen-year-old Robert "Bobby" Franks in Chicago. Only a couple of months earlier, Loeb, who was in the nearby Illinois State Penitentiary, was murdered with a straight razor in a shower room in that smaller and older Joliet prison, "Chicago's Thrill Killers: Leopold, Loeb, and the 'Perfect Crime,'" American Hauntings, accessed April 20, 2019, https://www.americanhauntingsink.com/thrill-killers.

48. "Darrow Asks Parole of Jesse Binga from Prison at Stateville," *Chicago Tribune*, March 31, 1936, 6.

49. "Clarence Darrow Is Dead in Chicago," *New York Times*, March 14, 1938, http://www.nytimes.com/learning/general/onthisday/bday/0418.html; "Binga Freed: Takes Job in Church Vestry, Ex-Banker Freed, Enters Church Work," *Chicago Defender*, March 5, 1938, 1.

50. "Darrow Asks Parole of Binga."

51. *Stenographic Verbatim Report*, April 1, 1936, 5.

52. *Stenographic Verbatim Report*, April 1, 1936, 6.

53. From archival records of the Sisters of the Blessed Sacrament, recounting efforts to have Binga released in 1935, "Annals" of St. Anselm Catholic Church, in Sisters of the Blessed Sacrament Archives.

54. *Stenographic Verbatim Report*, April 1, 1936, 17.

55. Prediction Report of the Sociologist and Actuary, Department of Public Welfare, Division of Pardons and Paroles, April 1936, in Jesse Binga prison file, Illinois State Archives, Springfield, Ill.

56. *Stenographic Verbatim Report*, April 1, 1936, 16.

57. James F. Fardy to Division of Pardon and Paroles, March 26, 1936, in Jesse Binga prison file, Illinois State Archives, Springfield, Ill.

58. *Stenographic Verbatim Report*, April 1, 1936, 17.

59. *Stenographic Verbatim Report*, December 3, 1937, 1.

60. *Stenographic Verbatim Report*, December 3, 1937, 3.

61. *Stenographic Verbatim Report*, December 3, 1937, paragraph report from executive session listed as an addendum to report and dated December 9, 1937.

62. *Stenographic Verbatim Report*, December 3, 1937, 6, Executive Session report of January 10, 1938, added on to the report.

Chapter 28

1. Department of Public Welfare, Division of Pardons and Paroles, Illinois State Penitentiary, Stateville Division, Order for Dishcharge of Prisoner, February 21, 1941, in Jesse Binga prison file, Illinois State Archives, Springfield, Ill.; "Jesse Binga, Ex-Banker, Freed," *Chicago Defender*, March 5, 1938, 1; temperature for February 26, 1938, from Midwestern Regional Climate Center, accessed April 20, 2019, https://mrcc.illinois.edu/CLIMATE/birthday/birthday_out2 .jsp.

2. "Binga, Ex-Banker, Freed"; "Ex-Banker Gains Freedom" (photo head), *Chicago Defender*, March 5,1938, 1.

3. Family photo from Carolyn Louise Dent Johnson, private collection; C. Johnson, interview.

4. "Binga Freed," 10.

5. "Paroled Banker Binga Plans Religious Work for Negroes," *Chicago Daily News*, March 1, 1938.

6. C. M. Skyles, State Parole Agent, to Mr. T. P. Sullivan, Supt. Division of Supervision, February 1, 1941, Letter for Final Discharge, Illinois Department of Public Welfare, Chicago (hereafter cited as Final Discharge Letter).

7. *Stenographic Verbatim Report*, April 1, 1936, 2–3.

8. Drake and Cayton, *Black Metropolis*, 467.

9. "Paroled Banker Binga."

10. "Binga Freed," 10.

11. "A Tribute to Jesse Binga," *Parish Recorder*, May, 1946, 118, in Sisters of the Blessed Sacrament Archives.

12. Typed letter from 1950, alongside newspaper obituary, in Sisters of the Blessed Sacrament Archives.

13. "Holy Week, 1939. Easter Sunday," typed note, n.d. (ca. 1950), in Sisters of the Blessed Sacrament Archives.

14. "Paroled Banker Binga."

15. Wayne Whittaker, "Ex-Banker Binga in Court Again, Fighting for Home," *Chicago Daily News*, June 7, 1938.

16. "Xmas Eve Benefit to Aid Ex-Banker," *Chicago Defender*, December 17, 1938.

17. Pardon Board, Illinois State Penitentiary, Docket 8235, hearing transcript, April 10, 1940, 2 (hereafter cited as Pardon Board Hearing).

18. "G. L.Griffin, CTA Attorney, Dies at age 65," *Chicago Daily News*, August 24, 1966.

19. Pardon Board Hearing, 6.

20. Pardon Board Hearing, 7.

21. Reply of the Honorable James F. Fardy, Jude of the Superior Court of Cook County, To Notice of Hearing for Pardon, file stamped April 30, 1942; "To The Governor, Subject: Application of Jesse Binga for a Complete Pardon" (April 1940 term), signed and dated December 24, 1940. Includes denial by "Parole Board, sitting as a Pardon Board," and signed by the governor. All in Jesse Binga prison file, Illinois State Penitentiary Archives, Springfield, Ill.

22. Reply of Fardy. See also Statement of the Parole Board to Governor re: application of Jesse Binga for a Complete Pardon, April 1940 term, in Jesse Binga prison file, Illinois State Penitentiary Archives, Springfield, Ill.

23. Statement of the Parole Board.

24. Final Discharge Letter.

25. Final Discharge Letter.

26. Order for Discharge of Prisoner, February 21, 1941, Department of Public Welfare, Division of Pardons and Paroles, Illinois State Penitentiary, Stateville.

27. "Binga Bank Properties to be Sold at Auction," *Chicago Defender*, March 8, 1941, 1.

28. "Plan Action to Void Sale of Binga Bank," *Chicago Defender*, March 15, 1941, 1.

29. "Plan Action to Void Sale."

30. "Plan Action to Void Sale"; "Binga Sees Property Sold, *Chicago Herald American*, March 12, 1941.

31. "Binga Sees Property Sold." Interestingly, Martha Binga Winchester, one of Jesse Binga's sisters, who died while Jesse was still in prison, once ran an employment agency at Thirty-Second and State Streets and lived in the house at 3324 South Vernon Avenue. Her occupation was listed as "Domestic" on date of death December 16, 1936, Illinois Deaths and Stillbirths Index, 1916–1947 (text only), accessed via Ancestry.com.

32. "Green Pardons Negro Banker, An Embezzler," *Chicago Daily Tribune*, April 18, 1941, 2.

33. "Green Pardons Negro Banker."

34. Typewritten notes accompanying newspaper clippings dated April 1946, in Sisters of the Blessed Sacrament Archives.

35. "Father Eckert, 81, Dies, Was Pioneer in Convert Work," *Catholic New World*, April 2, 1965.

36. Notes and clippings, April 1946, in Sisters of the Blessed Sacrament Archives.

37. Quote from Ripley Binga Mead Sr., who began working for Binga in 1907 and that is from Dempsey J. Travis, *An Autobiography of Black Chicago* (Chicago: Urban Research Institute, 1981), 258.

38. Mead, interview, February 1998.

39. Mead, interview, June 4, 1998.

40. Mead, interview, February 1998.

Chapter 29

1. State of Illinois, "Coroner's Certificate of Death, no. 41387, Dist. 3104."

2. Hugh Gardner, "Jesse Binga, Ex-Banker, Dies," *Chicago Defender*, June 17, 1950, 1.

3. Gardner, "Jesse Binga, Ex-Banker, Dies"; "Coroner's Certififcate of Death."

4. Gardner, "Jesse Binga Dies."

5. "Coroner's Certificate of Death."

6. "Holy Week, 1939. Easter Sunday."

7. Gardner, "Jesse Binga Dies"; "Jesse Binga, 85, Famous Banker, Buried in Chicago," *Pittsburgh Courier*, June 24, 1950, 3.

8. Taylor, interview, February 3, 1999.

9. Hugh Gardner, "Jesse Binga, Former Banker, Dies Penniless at 85," *Chicago Defender*, June 24, 1950, 1.

10. Taylor, interview, January 1, 1999.

INDEX

Page numbers in **boldface** refer to illustrations.

Second to None: Chicago Stories celebrates the authenticity of a city brimming with rich narratives and untold histories. Spotlighting original, unique, and rarely explored stories, Second to None unveils a new and significant layer to Chicago's big-shouldered literary landscape.

Harvey Young, series editor